CHASING TAIL-LIGHTS to FORENSIC BALLISTICS

Memoirs of a State Police Officer, Crime Scene Investigator & Forensic Ballistics Expert

By
Charles Meyers

Copyright © 2010 by Charles Meyers

Chasing Tail Lights to Forensic Ballistics

All rights reserved. No part of this book may be reproduced or transmitted in any form or by any means, electronic, or mechanical, including photocopying, recording or by any information storage and retrieval system, without permission in writing from the publisher. No abridgement or changes to the text are authorized by the publisher.

ISBN number: 978-1-59712-471-3

DEDICATION

This is dedicated to my family; my beloved wife Nancy, my daughters, Robin, Kathy, Kim, and Kelly, my son Kurt, and the grandchildren Michael, Joseph, Thomas, Chelsea, and Lindsey. After all, the most wonderful thing about this life is family.

INVOCATION

"Were it offered to my choice, I should have no objection to a repetition of the same life from it's beginning, only asking the advantages authors have in a second edition to correct some faults of the first."

Benjamin Franklin, *Autobiography*, 1798.

Justice and Forensic Science

"How long shall we continue to blunder without the aid of unpartisan and authoritative scientific assistance in the administration of justice, no one knows, but all fair persons not conventionalized by provincial legal habits of mind ought, I should think, unite to effect some such change."
Justice Learned Hand
Park, Davis & Co. v. H. K. Mulford Co., 1911

Justice

"…and I will make Justice the measuring line…"
Isaiah 28:17

Wherever he steps, whatever he touches, whatever he leaves, even unconsciously, will serve as silent witness against him. Not just his fingerprints or his footprints, but his hair, the fibers from his clothes, the glass he breaks, the tool marks he leaves, the paint he scratches, the blood or semen he deposits or collects-All of these and more bear mute witness against him. This is evidence that does not forget. It is not confused by the confusion of the moment. It is not absent because human witnesses are. It cannot perjure itself. It cannot be totally absent. Only its interpretation can err. Only human failure to find it, study it and understand it can diminish its value.
(Harris v. United States 331 US 145, 1947)

We better know there is a fire whence we see much smoke rising than we could know it by one or two witnesses swearing to it. The witnesses may commit perjury, but the smoke cannot.
Abraham Lincoln - 1864

KEYWORD DEFINITIONS

Chasing Tail-Llghts – Police jargon describing routine road or highway patrol.

Forensic Ballistics – Term commonly used by writers and lawyers to describe Firearms and Tool Mark Identification.

Forensic Science – Scientific knowledge applied to the purposes of the law and the courts.

Firearms & Tool Mark Identification – That discipline of the Forensic Sciences directed to the examination and comparison of firearms and ammunition components, and other tools and markings they produce.

Criminalistics – The application of the instruments and methods of physical science to the detection and solution of crime.

Criminalist – A forensic scientist who by virtue of his/her education and training is considered to be acceptably competent to practice Criminalistics.

FOREWORD

It was May 2009 and my daughters and I were enjoying the last portion of our stay in Florida when I received a surprising phone call. The female voice on the other end asked, "Is this Charles Meyers speaking?" I, of course, replied "yes it is." The voice then asked, "Is this the Charles Meyers who used to be a Captain in the Michigan State Police?" I, once again replied "yes it is." The voice then advised "Please hold for your Commissioner." The next voice, Col. Munoz, told me he had a hard time tracking me down. He learned that I was awarded a Bravery medal in 1950, but never received it. I told him I never knew there was a medal due. "Well," he stated, "I have made arrangements for the North Carolina Highway Patrol to award the medal when you return to your new summer home near Lansing, North Carolina." All I could say was "wow, after 59 years…" Members of the Highway Patrol awarded the medal to me in Jefferson, North Carolina. That started me on a memory trek that covers about seventy of my eighty three years, culminating in an adult lifetime of over fifty years as a Crime Scene Investigator and Crime Laboratory Analyst in the discipline of Firearms and Tool Mark Identification or what attorneys and writers like to call "Forensic Ballistics." In the language of today, I was a forensic scientist before forensic science was cool!

Going back to 2007, I vividly recall my beautiful wife Nancy leaning over the dining room table one evening and staring with those gleaming eyes as she, out of the thin blue air, said, " Chuck, there is one thing about yourself that you have never recognized." I immediately wondered what I had done wrong or recently forgotten, and, what precipitated this unusual kind of statement from her? So, I mumbled, "What's that honey?" To my surprise she remarked, "You apparently have never realized what an amazing life you've led!" Sadly, the light of my life passed away a few months later. But her out of character remark stayed with me along with the wonderful memories of 55 years of marriage.

Then, earlier this year, an old friend and co-worker from the Michigan State Police Crime Laboratory days, Herb Olney and I were discussing an interesting case from the 60s and 70s era. Herb mentioned that he enjoyed reading a book I had written concerning forensic science cases, and asked if I intended to write another. I told him I had one roughed out, similar to the first but employing different case histories. He then remarked, "Charlie, you have had an interesting life and career, why don't you write about that?" His remarks brought Nancy's statement crashing into my consciousness. And, as I gave it all further thought, I said to myself "Nancy, you were right again."

So this is the story of an average guy, a member of the "greatest generation," who tried hard to be a good father and husband, who served his Country in war, who worked diligently at his chosen profession, who strived to be a good cop and a forensic scientist who might make a difference, who paid his taxes on time, who loved fly fishing and football, the Michigan Wolverines and Bo Schembechler, and who to this day reads a stop sign as … - --- .--. When you read this memoir you will discover why.

The memoir contains anecdotes and short stories from a couple dozen of the more interesting cases of my career. The true names of most officials and co-workers will be found herein. However, most criminal cases will not include the actual names of victims, witnesses, and criminals, in order to protect the innocent.

Charles Meyers
Lansing, NC, 2010

CONTENTS

Chapter 1 - The Early Years 1
Chapter 2 - The Mich. State Police & USS Leyte (CV-32) 19
   The Bravery Medal Incident 22
Chapter 3 - The Crime Laboratory - In the Beginning 39
   The Teen-age Sniper Case 48
   The Airman Pimp Case 52
   AFTE - The Origins 54
   The Tourmaline Murder 57
Chapter 4 - CSI - Then & Now 61
   The Trooper & the Shovel Case 64
   Charlie Marzetti 67
   The Nurse & the Nylon-66 70
   The Child & the Garbage Bag 72
   The Synagogue Murder 74
   Archie the Mummy 76
   The Serial Killer 78
Chapter 5 - The Mind Boggling Homicide 83
Chapter 6 - Late Years in Michigan 97
   The Thrill Killer 97
   The Training Division 108
Chapter 7- Delta College and Edenville 115
Chapter 8 - Florida & the Crime Lab 125
   The Island Murder 131
   The Ex-Cop Killer 134
   The Wall Sink Murders 137
   The Dirty Revolver 139
   Fats & the Hit Man 140
Chapter 9 - The Courtroom 143
   The General 144
   The Barrel Switch 147

The Plaster Cast 149
The Patent Leather Shoe 150
The Tough Judge 154
The Sleeping Judge 155
Bat Woman 156
The Outstanding Judge 156
Chapter 10 - Retirement & Consulting 159
The Dying Shark 161
The Mutilated .22 163
Larry Ziegler 164
The Prostitute Murders 167
The Kentucky Troopers Case 169
The Dentist Murder 169
The Accidental Murder 172
The CAFO 177
Fr. Tom 182
The Drunk Driver Shooting 185
Chapter 11 - Back to Teaching 193
Chapter 12 - The Later Years 205
Chapter 13 - Nancy Smith Meyers & Finis 221

Dad, Pose of the Day (circa 1926)

Grandma Mary Meyers & the Author (1944)

Mom and Dad, (circa 30s)

The Brat (circa 1928)

1

The Early Years

Born in Dayton, Ohio in 1926 but moved to Sidney, Ohio as a toddler, my early memories start there. Sidney was a pretty little town with a typical downtown square and a wonderful Catholic Church, Holy Angels. Like many families of that time, we were as poor as the proverbial church mouse. I still recall vividly the many fishing trips to Avon Lake. My love for fishing started early and never waned. On each trip to the little lake we would catch a bucket full of bluegills and sunfish. On the way home we had to drive by a huge cornfield, and I recall Dad saying "don't you think that farmer has more corn than he can use." I would take the hint and slide under the barbed wire fence, returning with five or six ears of corn. This was depression time and a plate of fried fish and corn on the cob was fantastic.

Dad had been working at Wagner Ware, one of the country's premier cast aluminum cooking ware manufacturers but now he was laid off. Through the union he was offered a chance at a job in Detroit at an auto parts manufacturer, Douglas and Lomason. Dad was a highly skilled metal polisher and made decent wages as such when work was available. We loaded our family goods in the old Essex car and made the journey up the Dixie Highway.

When we arrived we were directed to an old four family flat in the lower West side of the City. For many years, dad told the story over and over about meeting there with the owner, an old Irish man named Mr. Fillion. Immediately Dad told him that we had no money but as the old man showed us our flat, he told Dad "Don't worry about it -

pay me when you can!" Depression or not, there were at that time a lot of wonderful people in Detroit, and it was a great town.

My childhood was perhaps not remarkable for the days, with the exception, however, of my school and teachers. The school was St. Leo and the teachers were Sisters of Charity. In addition to reading, writing and arithmetic, the nuns taught me a modicum of manners and humility. They were at once beautiful and imposing in their floor length black habits and white starched collars and headliners. After all these years I can't recall many of their names, but there are two that are indelibly stamped into my mind. One was my home room teacher in the 8th grade. Her name was Sister Agnes Paula. We called her Aggie, but not to her face. She was about 6 feet tall, and weighed in at about 200 lbs. When we left school the students were required to march in step to the Church corner where we were automatically excused. If you misbehaved and Aggie spotted you, she would smack the offender in the biceps area with a doubled-up fist. Then you could carry a little knot in there home for the evening. One day she caught several of us telling smutty stories in a storage room. Unfortunately, I was the closest one to her and she spun me around, gave me a left hook in the stomach, followed by a right cross to the jaw. I stumbled across the hallway, off balance and stunned, landing in the coat closet and tearing down the roller door enroute. Aggie rolled down her habit sleeves saying, "Boys, if I ever catch you doing something like that again, someone is liable to get hurt." I recall mumbling "she'll kill us next time." It's funny though as years wear on I remember thinking that I wish I could meet her again so I could tell her how much I love her!

The other teacher I'll never forget was our principal in our Junior and Senior years (42-44). Her name was Sr. Georgianna, but for some unknown reason we called her Becky. At this time the nuns knew we would all be drafted or enlist in the service for World War II. They knew some of us might not make it back home and it affected their otherwise stern composure. We almost felt sorry for them as you could see it in their eyes. They really hated the thought of us going to war and so they lightened up on us in our senior year. One day at lunch break, the gang, including me, gathered in the office of the Principal. Becky had a small AM radio on her desk and Pete McManamon dialed in some swing music, I think it was the One O'clock Jump by Count Basie. Barney Brewer picked up Sister's waste basket, turned it upside down and started playing the drums. Meanwhile, Chuck Marceau, Tom Kuzilla, Dewey Cyr and I beat time on the desk. Suddenly, Becky walked through the doorway and everything stopped dead, until she said "well, won't one of you gentlemen offer Sister a seat?" Those were the days.

Detroit in the Thirties and early Forties was actually lots of fun and a relatively safe place. The area we lived in was on the lower west side, called Old Corktown due to many early settlers of Irish descent. Before the Sisters and mom and dad straightened me out, I hung out for a while with a neighborhood gang. We never got into real trouble although we could have on one occasion. On a Saturday, we gathered in the nearby Western Auto store and while a couple of us caused a disturbance, one of the gang stole a box of .22 cartridges. The next day, Sunday afternoon, we gathered in a vacant lot with a .22 rifle, one borrowed from a closet at one of the gang's homes. At the lot was a huge wooden water tower. a landmark in the area. We took turns shooting until the entire box of 50 cartridges was used shooting up into the tower. The people on the main street marveled at the miraculous rain coming down from a cloudless blue sky.

The police searched the neighborhood for days looking for information on the little hoodlums who damaged the tower. I know I spent every night for two weeks on my knees praying, "Dear God please don't let them catch me this time. I will never do anything that stupid again." And I kept my word to God. I knew Dad would have killed me, if I had been caught and he found out. Well, he really wouldn't kill me. That was just a kid expression.

There was one time I thought Dad would actually kill me. Our four family flat was made of stucco siding and the four car garage in the rear was the same. There were four large windows facing the back yard and the "yard" was poured concrete. It was ideal for bouncing a hard rubber ball or tennis ball off the stucco garage and pretending to be Charlie Gehringer, the famous Detroit Tiger second baseman. But one day a ball went awry and smashed through one of the garage windows. Mom heard the noise, came out and said "your Dad is not going to like that!" I believed her, but later went back to the game sure it couldn't happen again as I was a pretty straight thrower. But, it did happen again and I broke window #2. This time Mom came out and said, "Your Dad is going to kill you." I believed her and moped around waiting for him to come home from work. As soon as he hit the door, she cornered him and I knew what was being said.

I was behind the kitchen table and as Dad reached for me I took off, around the table and through the screen door as fast as I could run. I never looked back for several blocks, but when I did he wasn't in sight. I decided to walk to Scripps Library and "while" away some time. Soon it was starting to get dark, I left the library cold and hungry and decided to go home and take my whipping. As I went into the house, Dad said "get your jacket, we're going to the movies." I was in a state of shock as Dad, Mom, Sis and I went to the show. Afterwards, we stopped at the White Castle and got a bag full of those great little burgers. They were six for a quarter back then. I felt I learned that evening what forgiveness is all about. Later Mom told me that Dad said when he saw the frightened look on my face he figured I had been punished enough.

The only time in my life I actually got a real whipping was the time he caught me and a couple of other kids hitching a ride on a slow moving freight train. We lived only a few blocks from the switching tracks and coal loader and he had warned me not to ever jump a railroad car. That time he took me home by the ear, pulled down my cords and whipped me with a razor strop. Mom yelled, "Stop it, your going to kill our boy." Dad yelled back, "Be still woman, I know what I'm doing." In retrospect he was right, he did know what he was doing, and I never went near a train again without a ticket.

What Dad may not have known was the coal lumps we kids brought home on our wagons were not really "picked up along the tracks where they dropped off a railroad car." Actually, most were thrown off slow moving cars by the kids, including yours truly. Then there were the many Saturday mornings when we lined up outside the Sears and Montgomery Wards warehouses to have a turn in getting wooden packing crates from furniture and appliances to take home for the furnace or stove.

Dad was a man of very few words. When I was about 8 or 9 years of age, he came home from work one day to find Mom making supper. But she had tears in her eyes. He asked her what was wrong. After an initial denial of any thing wrong, she told him that Joe, the acquaintance from the flat above ours, had approached her while she was doing laundry in the basement. He attempted to kiss and fondle her. Without a word Dad climbed the stairs to the second floor and knocked on Joe's door. When he answered, Dad grabbed him by the shirt front, pulled him onto the landing and hit him in the face knocking him completely down the stairs. Dad walked over Joe's prostate form, slammed the door shut, sat down in his favorite chair with the newspaper and asked "What's for supper Mom?"

From the early teens in Detroit, my favorite memories involve Olympia Stadium, bicycling and the Boy Scouts. Olympia was within walking and running distance of my home. It was the scene of many of the sports and show activities of the time. The neighborhood gang and I learned early on that it was relatively easy to sneak into Olympia, especially after the game or show started. Without charge I was able to watch the Red Wings play hockey with some of the greatest players of that era, Gordie Howe, Ted Lindsay and Black-Jack Stewart, to name a few. On one occasion we were able to see Sonja Henie, the vivacious ice skating queen and her entire show. But our favorite spectator sport was the roller derby, which was very popular then. It had speed skating contests and team battles. Naturally, our favorites were the gal skaters, and we cheered lustily for the local favorites when they got into battle royals or knocked the opposing skater over the rail.

Back then we all had a bicycle and several, including myself, had a newspaper route. My mom and dad loved fishing and I inherited this trait and then some from them. On a Saturday, after my delivery route, I would strap my casting rod along my bike frame, tie a small tackle box on the rear wheel luggage carrier, and put my brown bag lunch Mom made for me into the basket and away I would go. Out Warren Avenue beyond the city limits and past River Rouge Park I would pedal to a small lake called Nankin Mills. It was formed by a dam on the Middle Rouge. In those days the Rouge stream system was not contaminated or polluted as today. In fact, the stream running into Nankin Mills ran clear like a Northern Michigan trout stream. I would spend all day hiking around and casting for bass on the pond. Warren Avenue was then a main street thoroughfare on the West side of Detroit and as such, had continuous traffic all day long. As I recall, it was approximately 14 miles one way to the Mill pond. There were no accidents, no problems, no accosting, over a half dozen or so trips. Mom never had to worry about her boy. Try to picture that occurring today. It was a different time.

One unusual event has always stood out in my mind. My best friend from school and the neighborhood was Dewey Cyr. We became acquainted in the first grade when we got into a shoving match over who was going to carry Liz Dox's books. Liz was our first puppy love. She was beautiful with the ever smiling crinkly eyes. All the boys loved her and most of the girls hated her. But, that's another story. Dewey and I both joined the Cub Scouts and later the Boy Scouts. Dewey was actually a year older than I and was therefore a bit ahead of me in the Scouts. There came a time at the Camp Howell Scout Reservation, where we were encamped with our Troop, for the special Order of the Arrow celebration. I had never been part of one or seen one before, but Dewey had and he painted a colorful picture for me. He left out a few details I learned later. It was a perfect summer night, and all the Troops were lined up single-file shoulder to shoulder partially encircling a huge hollow pasture. There was a massive bonfire in the center attended by several older Scouts, dressed in loin cloths and an apparent Chief, with massive headdress and all. We had all been instructed to face the bonfire, standing at parade rest, and to not move or change position.

As the Chief made several incantations and threw powder on the fire causing plumes of colored smoke, one of the "Braves" lit a torch and started to run around the perimeter of the hollow passing in front of each Troop. Every now and then we would hear him scream something and we were all cautioned to keep our eyes forward. As he neared our Troop we could hear the padding sound of his moccasins striking the ground and then as I caught a glimpse out of the corner of my eye, a hand of the "Brave" struck me a glancing blow in the chest, knocking me backwards on my butt as he screamed out. At that instant, my Troop leader's voice cautioned me to remain silent as someone blindfolded me. I was led a short distance and instructed to grab onto a rope which I did. I was led stumbling along a pathway, stopping and starting several times, until a voice advised me to let go of the rope, sit down and count to a hundred, remove the blindfold and remain at this location until someone came for me in the morning! I followed instructions and found myself sitting alone in the woods, completely lost without sight or sound of civilization. I knew this had to be some sort of initiation, but what?

Early in the morning a senior scout came, gave me a drink of water from his canteen and a slice of bread to eat. From there I was led to a group of other confused young scouts, and ultimately to a morning long work detail, shoveling and raking sand for the swimming beach. Later, we were given a fine lunch, an Indian name, a red arrow sash to wear with our uniform, and officially entered the "Order of the Arrow." I didn't understand the real significance of the ordeal then, but later I came to realize an honor had been bestowed upon me, and it was an event I never forgot. Of course, it was all setup by my life long friend, Dewey Cyr. I was beginning to learn what friends are for.

Like all boys, I got into a couple of fist fights but nothing serious until one night in my senior year in high school. Jack Callahan, our 135 lb. halfback on the football team and I had taken in a movie near home. While walking down the sidewalk we spied two "zoot suiters" coming our way. If you're not very old, you won't recognize the name. They were members of a loosely organized gang found in most large cities. They wore wild suits with huge lapels and long coats, over pants with baggy knees and tight cuffs at the bottom, and always a dress hat with large snap down brim. You could spot them a mile away and they meant trouble. These two were swarthy in appearance and in their early to mid-twenties. We gave them nearly all the side walk but that wasn't sufficient. They knocked us into the roadway anyway. Before I could tell Jack, "let's get the hell out of here," he put up his dukes only to get hit with a thundering right that knocked him into an open doorway. I looked around for the other one just in time to see him telegraph a wild swing. I was able to duck under it and hit him as hard as I could in the stomach. He doubled over and I waited for him to straighten up so I could clobber him. My mistake; he lunged into me in a perfect blocking position and sent me flying backwards. I heard the sound of crashing glass as shards fell beyond me and I found myself sliding across the floor of a super market in a bushel of apples. My new "Zoot Suit" acquaintance had knocked me through a huge front window of the store. As I pulled myself out through the broken window frame, I heard Jack yell "Hurry Russ, the cops are coming fast." Since my dad's name was Charles, my mother and everyone else called me by my middle name in those days, Russell, and I hated it. We ran into alleys, jumped fences, hid behind sheds and board fences and played hide and seek with the Detroit police cruiser for what seemed like an eternity. I said a prayer of thanks when they finally gave up and we made it home. This time I knew Dad would kill me if he had to pay for that window. I went through the pane so fast, I had only minor cuts and scratches. Naturally the bad guys, the zoot suiters, got away clean.

Our high school gang had time for one big escapade between our Junior and Senior years. Five of us saved what money we could and planned on a trip to Northern Michigan. None of us had ever been North of Pontiac, and certainly never in the so-called "Wonder land of the North." We found an advertisement in the Detroit News for a rental cabin on Otsego Lake, near Gaylord. According to the map US-27 and the Greyhound bus route ran very close to the lake. We went to visit the older couple who owned the cabin and rented it for one week. Mind you, this was in 1943, there were few tourists and little or no transportation. We took a gamble and it turned out to be one of the fantastic experiences of our young lives. We boarded the Greyhound late at night and awoke as the sun rose over the pines near Grayling. We thought we had died and gone to heaven. The bus then stopped at Otsego Lake, at the only nearby open business.

We found an elderly lady running the little store and boat livery. We confirmed the fact that our cabin was on the other side of the lake. What we found out for the first time was that the walk around the long lake to the cabin would be about five miles! But, we could rent a row boat and go straight across the lake in short order so we did.

The next morning we decided we would have to row back across the lake for supplies. It was a rather lengthy row and there were no volunteers. We cut cards and the two losers took our list and rowed across. They returned about two hours later with a story about the most beautiful girl in the world who worked there. She was the old lady's grand-daughter. Chuck Marceau and Pete McManamon made that first trip. Naturally, Barney Brewer, Dewey Cyr and I thought they were throwing us a line. But we weren't sure when they volunteered to go back to the store the next day. So, Barney and I decided to go this time. Wow – they weren't kidding. The young store keeper was 16 years old, beautiful and with a personality to match. From then on it was a row to make at least twice a day. We cut cards and the winners went across.

What a time we had on the lake, fishing, swimming, and just having a ball. After dinner we threw our dishes into the lake and dove for them to get them cleaned off for easy washing. We learned that Gaylord had a movie theatre, so all five of us, by now good friends with Granny and her grand-daughter, asked to take her to the Saturday movie. Since we had no transportation, we asked Granny to let us take her Ford rumble-seat coupe, and she gave us her blessing. Try to picture five young men and one pretty young lady driving into town and back, all in a rumble seat coupe. It would never happen today. But, this was a different time, and in my view a better time. We cut cards again to decide whose lap she would sit on going and coming!

I distinctly recall my first real date, a lovely French girl I had admired from afar. I finally got enough nerve to take her out. We went to a movie and rode the streetcar in Detroit to get there. No one had much money then so no one expected to spend much for any reason. I had figured out the exact cost for the evening, for the movie, popcorn, a chocolate coke afterwards and the round trip on the streetcar. We had a wonderful time and I never forgot my first date. After the war it was wonderful to find out she married one of my best friends from high school.

But back to that first date and my first big embarrassment of my young life, somehow, somewhere I lost a dime. As we left Pete's soda bar and took a stand at the streetcar stop, I discovered the loss. The fare was ten cents a piece and I only had one thin dime left. I apologized to Mary and gave her the one dime saying I would walk the four or five miles home. Then I heard a male voice say "Young man, I couldn't help but overhear your dilemma. Here's another dime, take it please." Those were the days. Detroit was different then.

Chasing Tail Lights to Forensic Ballistics

THE HIGH SCHOOL GANG L-R CHUCK, BARNEY, MIKE, FRED, PETE, RUSS (1943)

KWAJALEIN RADIO GANG (1945)
(RUSS IN CENTER)

It was 1944 and World War II waited for the younger members of the class to graduate. The older members of the Senior Class had already enlisted or were drafted. I graduated at age 17, had my 18th birthday at the Great Lakes Naval Training Center, through boot camp, radio (Morse code) sending and receiving school, and training with an amphibious group on the East coast.

The radio school was held at the White River Naval Armory in Indianapolis, Indiana. Next to the Armory was an old-fashioned amusement park with a roller skating rink. I spent most of my off-duty time there dance skating with Candy, the star gal of the arena. I had learned to skate well in Detroit. I promised her I would come back after the war but never made it. Then it was on to Noroton Heights, Connecticut, near Darien and Greenwich for the entire radioman contingent. Here they trained us in rushing into shore from landing craft with portable equipment and setting up on the beach. My very vivid memory there was going ashore with an Italian radioman from Queens, NY. He told me we were going to enjoy a real home cooked Italian dinner, made by his mother and sisters. We got there just in time to hear about the surrender of the Germans and instead of just the dinner, we had one heck of a party.

From there, they sent us to California where they confiscated our Navy gear and issued us Marine wool greens, a .30 caliber carbine, and even snow goggles. We pondered where in the Pacific we would use such gear. We found out when we got to Pearl Harbor that we were scheduled for the invasion of Japan. We thanked God when they dropped the atom bombs before we shipped out.

I was one of the lucky ones. One classmate was killed in action, two were wounded, one partially disabled, one (a Merchant Mariner) had two ships torpedoed out from under him. One of the more interesting events of that time occurred when several of the gang went from Detroit to Percy Jones Hospital to visit one of our wounded buddies. We had taken the train to Battle Creek and then back to Detroit. After returning, and while on the way to our car, one of our gang yelled out "Look at the crazy guy!" A young man ran directly toward us at breakneck speed on a zigzag course like a destroyer in battle. Then we simultaneously spotted a uniformed police officer chasing him with his revolver out. As we spotted flame from the muzzle we all yelled "hit the deck" at once. Just then the man grabbed his thigh and fell screaming onto the grass. The officer had hit him in the leg. It might have been a lucky shot, but in those days, the Detroit Police had the top police shooting team in the country, headed by Lt. Harry Reeves the famous Olympic Shooter.

All of my young life I dreamed of working outdoors, perhaps checking out trout streams for habitat, planting certain grasses or bushes to feed the wildlife, making counts of the Ruffed Grouse, etc. In other words, I wanted to work in the Conservation field. So, shortly after discharge from the Navy, I enrolled at the University of Michigan under the GI Bill. My chosen course work was heavily laden with botany and conservation type classes. The benefits lasted for two years, and then I was out of money and out of college for the time being.

I did have at least one other fanatic interest then. What a time it was to indulge in my love for football. This was in 1946 to 1948. These were glory years for the University of Michigan. They had a young but good team in 1946, and they were undefeated in 1947 and 1948.

One might recall the Rose Bowl of Jan. l, 1948, when they defeated Southern California 49-0. The team was known as the "Mad Magicians of Michigan." This was due to the ball handling and speed of the team. It was one of the last great single-wing football teams, coached by Fritz Crisler, now considered as one of the best of all time. As a student I was able to see all the home games. It was a real thrill.

During this time, one other important event helped shape my life and interests. At the University, I had a young roommate named Dale Zimmerman. He was from Imlay City, Michigan and I soon found out was crazy about birds and studying Ornithology at Michigan. One day he told me he was planning a trip to Northern Michigan to a village called Lovells. Near the little town was a beautiful lake, called Shupac Lake. He had learned a female Loon had been spotted nesting on the edge of the lake. He advised they were very wary and he was going to build a blind to set up a special camera with long distance telephoto lens to get photos of the Loon. He asked me if I would like to go along. I had told him about my love for fishing and he asked if I had ever fly fished for trout. I told him I had fished with flies for bass but never trout. He told me about the North Branch of the AuSable River, a beautiful trout stream running through the village so I should bring my rod and flies and go fishing while he waited out the Loon.

I still laugh when I recall walking down the river bank and attempting to fly fish there. I had no waders and knew nothing about this type of fishing. Shortly I heard a cough from behind and turned to view an elderly gentleman wearing waders, fishing jacket and carrying his fly rod. He said, "Son, what in the devil are you doing?" I sheepishly advised that I was trying to trout fish. He said, "Do you mind if I give you a little help?" He first clipped the huge Yellow Sally bass fly from my leader material and then clipped off my leader describing it as a hunk of rope. He fished around in his jacket and produced a loop of fine tapered leader and tied it to my fly line. Next he pulled out a fly box and produced a very small fly which he described as a "Royal Coachman." He advised that it was too late for a morning hatch and my best bet for a strike would be the little fly he tied on. He then smeared a small dab of white salve- like material he called "mucilin" onto his fingertips and rubbed it off on the little fly, mentioning it was needed to keep the hackles afloat. He finally told me to try casting with the new rig although he said it was too late and I would probably not have any luck. At that point in the river there was a small log jam and I attempted to cast my fly nearby. As luck would have it, my first cast alighted next to the jam and drifted along with the current until there was a flash and swirl and I was fighting a beautiful fish. As I had no waders I jumped into the river and finally caught hold of the 14 inch brook trout and pitched it onto the bank. I looked up in time to note my elderly adviser walking away shaking his head in wonderment.

Later, Dale gave me a pretty water color painting of two birds sitting on a Jack Pine limb. Recently, I changed the location of the painting on a different wall and it reminded me of Dale and the trip that caused me to be bitten by the trout fly fishing bug. Going on Internet, I located Dale A. Zimmerman at Western New Mexico University where he is Professor Emeritus and discovered he is famous in the field of Ornithology and several other natural science areas. But my favorite memory of Dale was the time we arranged to meet with our dates to attend the Forestry ball at U of M. Dale was late getting there from his home and his girl friend was fit to be tied. She described how they were traveling down the farm country dirt road when Dale suddenly slammed on the brakes, jumped out of the car and hurdled a barbed wire fence crying out "Oh my God, there goes an immature male Dendroica fuschia," or something like that. His date said she had to brush the brambles and dust off his suit so they could attend the dance. I knew then that he would be famous someday. There have been buildings and collections named after him. He is responsible for some of the bird drawings in Audubon's books.

Meanwhile our family had multiplied; there was my kid sister Geraldine (Gerry), two years younger, my brother Don, 15 years younger, and Mary Ann, 17 years younger. It was like two families in one. Don was born on the eve of Pearl Harbor and dad always claimed that suited him. When he was a teenager, he was hell on wheels and the family predicted he would get into real trouble.

Boy, were we wrong. Don joined the Navy, became an electronics technician, married a beautiful California girl named Lynn, and left the service to become a police officer. He went to college part time and earned a BS and Master's degree, eventually taking a position with the California Dept. of Justice and retired as an executive in charge of a computerized intelligence operation. Dad and mom were so proud of him now. He and Lynn have two lovely children, Kim and Kirk.

My sister Gerry married Bill Grenfell and they had three fine children, Janis, Jerry, and Tommy. Mary Ann married Terry McKinley and had three fine boys, Don, Shawn, and Perry. Later, she remarried Luther Rhodes a stalwart from Arkansas.

My immediate family consists of the miracle child Kathy, daughter Kim who presented me with three grandsons, Michael, Joseph, and Thomas. Mike currently is a computer whiz with the Air Force, Joey helps build yachts in Florida, and Tom is in the Navy aboard the USS George Washington (CV-73), operating out of Japan. My son Kurt, a Navy veteran and medical technologist, married a beautiful nurse Christine, who presented me with two lovely grand daughters, Chelsea and Lindsey. My "baby" daughter Kelly, the family artist and green thumb expert, currently cares for her father and sister Kathy.

Charles Meyers

I am blessed in that the family is still together in both spirit and love. Family is the most important thing on this earth, in my opinion. When I think back over the years, our family has to be considered a Navy carrier family. I served during World War II and the Korean War, Including service on the USS Leyte (CV-32). My son Kurt was a corpsman aboard the USS John F. Kennedy. My brother Don served aboard the USS Constellation, and my grandson Tom now serves on the USS George Washington. Well that's enough of the family tree, so on with the memories.

After the war ended, our units were broken up and we were transferred to various parts of the Pacific to man radio (Morse code) operating stations. I found myself dropped off at Kwajalein in the Marshall Islands, and remained there for about one year until I had my points earned for discharge.

THE SAILOR – 1944

Chasing Tail Lights to Forensic Ballistics

Mom & Dad's Kids – Don, MaryAnn, Geraldine, Charles (Russ)

Some of Hi-School Gang, Grown Up
L-R Dewey, Virg, Mary Jane, Marie, Mike, Fred, Pete

Charles Meyers

The Author's Family
L-R Back – Kathy, Nancy, Charles;
Front – Kelly, Kurt, Kim (circa '70)

Mom & Dad, Grandsons Mike, Joe, Tom,
Grand Daughters Chelsea & Lindey

Chasing Tail Lights to Forensic Ballistics

KURT & CHRISTINE & GRAND DAUGHTERS CHELSEA & LINDSEY

THE FAMILY
L-R BLAISE, TIM, MIKE WITH CHELSEA, KURT WITH LINDSEY; FRONT NANCY, KELLY, TOM, KATHY, KIM, JOE.

2

The Michigan State Police & The U.S.S. Leyte (CV-32)

It was 1948, I was broke and I had to go to work. Dad found a job for me in a Detroit automobile parts plant working on a line of automatic polishing buffs. It was hard work, but the pay was pretty good. However, it was so monotonous I thought it would drive me goofy. One day the line foreman approached me on break time. He asked me "Charlie, Jr., is this what you've planned for the rest of your life?" I told him "No, of course not, but I need the money." He then told me he knew of a job opening that didn't pay as much but offered a chance at a rewarding career. The State Police were requesting applicants for a new recruit school. I told him that I had never seen a State Policeman and didn't know there was such a thing. He told me they are called Troopers and that he had dreamed of becoming one of them. Then (1948) new Troopers had to be single and agree to remain so for at least two years! He met a young woman and fell in love. She told him to choose either her or the State Police, as she wouldn't wait. He said "I chose her and have been kicking my butt ever since."

I dropped in at the Detroit Headquarters Post of the Michigan State Police the following day. After a short interview with the Post

Sergeant, I was given application forms to fill out. Over a couple of months, my family, friends, school teachers, neighbors, etc. were interviewed at length by Officers from the Training Division Staff. I was required to take an intelligence test and perform properly in a test of agility and strength. Some weeks later, a telegram came to the house advising I was to report on the next Sunday evening to begin training. The Program lasted for ten weeks and I found it to be tougher than Navy boot camp. All trainees had to live in the training barracks and were allowed to go home every other week from Saturday after lunch till Sunday evening at 9:00pm sharp. Many trainees dropped out and we ended the Program with about 50% of the trainees left in attendance. I felt that the foreman better be right about this job or we would have a talk about it some day. As it turned out, he was right.

One interesting aside; in those years, specialty officers such as those in the Identification Bureau or Crime Laboratory had to come from within the ranks. It didn't matter if you had a degree or even post-graduate education you had to apply and go through the training and wait your chance to get into the Crime Laboratory. Of course, this discouraged some possible valuable talent, but we did have a few with science degrees that went through the program and were placed in the Laboratory after two or three years. This requirement was ended some years ago.

After Training I was assigned to the Gaylord Post (#73) in the Northern section of the Lower Peninsula. A Michigan State Police Trooper is on probation for six months after graduation. He is assigned a Senior Trooper to further his training and to watch over him. During this period the new Trooper could be fired for any reason; he has no Civil Service protection. The first day I was assigned to Trooper Robert Johnston, affectionately known as "The Wilbur Shaw of the Department." For those too young to know, Shaw was one of the earlier great race drivers in the USA. I soon learned that Bob was not only a fantastic driver but a very efficient officer in other ways as well. Training officers are usually selected because they stand out. I ascertained quickly that there was a lot that could be learned from such an officer.

After only a couple of months on the road I learned one of the many great lessons. On a weekend night patrol we stopped a suspicious vehicle with two men inside. They had pulled off the road in front of a couple lighted businesses and then drove back onto the highway. As we approached the car, Bob advised "Watch these guys Charlie, I don't like their actions." The passenger alighted as soon as we stopped their vehicle and pretended to clean the windshield with a rag. As I faced him Bob yelled "Get on him Charlie, they've got guns." As I jammed the suspect against the front quarter panel and searched him, out of the corner of my eyes I saw the other suspect fly out of the car, due to my partner's actions end up in the muddy ditch. My man had a blackjack in his rear pocket, but no gun. After they were both handcuffed and spread out in the car's headlights, Bob fished a loaded and cocked .45 automatic caliber Colt pistol from the front seat. We learned later that they were both ex-convicts, wanted in California for Armed Robbery. I felt Bob saved my life that night.

The months flew by with only one apparent problem. Bob was not satisfied with my driving or my reaction to the highway. One evening as I drove the patrol car along at about 45 or 50 miles/per/hour, without warning Bob suddenly shouted "Turn right raw ass." This term was one of the well known ones reserved for probationary Troopers. I slammed on the brakes as I checked the rear-view mirror, slid by the intersection with a small side road, backed up and turned right. Bob glared at me and said "Is that what I told you to do?" I said "No it wasn't Bob." About a week later, it happened again and with the same results. Now I felt some resentment from my senior officer and it really worried me. I vowed not to let it happen again. I didn't know what in hell "Wilbur Shaw" was up to, but I told myself the next time he pulled this stunt I was going to kill us both if I had to. A few days later as we approached a small dirt road that runs across to the Manistee River, Bob yelled out suddenly "Turn right raw ass." I threw the wheel hard around and the patrol car went into a wild skid, partially onto the dirt roadway. The car careened down the road from one side to the other, partly out-of-control and mowing down a couple of pine seedlings as we nearly went into an adjacent swamp. My heart was pounding and sweat formed on my brow as I fought the wheel, finally coming to a stop. I looked to my right expecting to see Bob frowning or glaring at me. But no, he had a big grin on his face as he said "now that's more like it, son." He directed me to take the patrol car to a nearby garage where the owner owed him a favor. Here, he and the garage man pulled and pounded the right front fender back into some semblance of its former self and straightened out the Van Auken guards that protected the radiator and grille. The one headlight had to be replaced and we were back on patrol. A week later the Post Commanding Officer had all the Troopers lined up on the driveway as he demanded "Alright, who screwed up the fender on 732 and didn't report it?" Of course, no one knew anything and after several threats he gave up and went back into the office. When people talk about the "brother-hood," this is what they mean.

My most tragic encounter while in Gaylord occurred when a Greyhound bus and a Houghton College bus with their hockey team aboard hit head-on in a blinding snow storm North of Gaylord. Another Trooper and I, along with a Conservation Officer, had to police this accident. We had six fatalities, twenty-four critical injuries, and thirty-six serious injuries. Unbelievably, the first vehicle appearing through the storm was a new ambulance being driven to a hospital in the Upper Peninsula. We loaded it to the roof and directed the driver to Little Traverse Hospital at Petoskey. Another break came from a new Kaiser-Frazier car agency in Gaylord. They had two cars, revolutionary at the time, with backs that opened up and seats folded to provide large storage space. The owner sent them out immediately and they hauled many of the more serious injured to the Hospital in Grayling. The amazing thing was that none of the critical injured died.

Now, recall the Bravery medal incident mentioned in the Foreword? That happened in November 1950, during deer season. A young Trooper from Southern Michigan was sent to Gaylord as part of a special detail for the very busy deer season in the area. Joe Feistamel and I were partners on night patrol. I was the senior officer since I had two and a half years experience, while Joe had about one year. It was a terrible night with snow and icy roads, and new snow coming in blowing winds. A radio broadcast advised us there had been an armed robbery at gunpoint in the southern part of our patrol area. The radio advised there were two robbers and that they fled the scene in a green Chevrolet, headed south toward the big cities. We headed south toward the scene to take the original report. A large semi-truck passed us headed north and we couldn't help but notice a car following the truck at about one car length. Very odd for the road condition and weather and I asked Joe if he got a good look at the car. He said, "Charlie, I think it was a green Chevrolet." I said, "Joe I think you're right." I spun the patrol car around and pursued the car to check it out.

They passed the truck and we followed suit. We got pretty close before they sped up and slid around on the slick road. We put our spotlights in their rear window in time to see one man climbing into the rear seat. He then knocked a hole through the rear window and shoved a rifle barrel through the hole. As fire spurted out of the rifle barrel, I notified the Post that we were chasing the suspects North on US-27 and they were shooting at us. Joe cranked down the right side window of the patrol car and shot back with his service revolver. It seemed funny at the time, as fire spurted out of the rifle barrel we ducked under the instrument panel and cracked heads. After a couple of shots we realized when you see the fire from the discharge, the bullet has already struck or missed its target. We stopped laughing then. Soon Joe advised his revolver was empty and he didn't want to mess with the spare ammunition in the glove box, so I unbuckled mine and gave it to him. About this time, they lost control and slid off the highway backwards, hit the ditch and flipped upside down. I rammed the patrol car into a snowdrift on the left side of the road. As I opened the driver door, I heard Joe yell "there goes one running and I'm after him Charlie."

I slid off the driver seat and grabbed the loose revolver lying in the middle of the front seat as I started across the highway. As I ran in a hunched position, I looked for any sign of the other suspect but couldn't see him. At about the center of the highway I screeched to a stop and looked at the revolver in my right hand. Like a sledge hammer blow, the thought came to me "damn it all, I've got Joe's gun and its empty!" I crouched low, opened up the small leather pouch on my Sam Browne uniform belt and dumped six .38 Special caliber cartridges into my hand. I ejected the empties out of the Colt revolver and attempted to insert fresh ammo into the cylinder of the firearm. In those days we didn't have speed loaders or that kind of today's convenience. In the blowing snow and cold I dropped several rounds onto the frozen highway but was able to get at least three into the revolver. I cocked the hammer putting one of the cartridges in line with the firing pin and continued around the upside down stolen Chevrolet. There was number two, crawling around in the snow, patting it down, apparently searching for his lost snub-nose .38 Smith & Wesson revolver. My Colt was now within three feet of his head, cocked and ready to fire. I imagined the loose cartridges in the weapon's cylinder were shaking and clicking, sounding like a rattlesnake ready to strike. At any rate, he got the message and threw his hands into the air as he surrendered. I distinctly recall the fear on his face as I shoved his head into the adjoining snow drift. Number two thought I was going to shoot him. For the first time in such a situation I felt glad I didn't have to shoot him. As I knelt on his back and handcuffed him I looked to see if there was any sign of my partner, Joe.

Next door to the accident location was a closed business with a night light illuminating the back yard. At the rear of the lot was a tool shed which stood out like an outhouse in the snow. Joe crept toward the shed and from my vantage point I saw suspect number one peeking around the corner. Just then Joe fired once more and the bullet made an ugly whine as it tore a chunk of wood out of the shed corner, about an inch above the suspect's head. At that, number one decided it was time to surrender.

By the time we jailed the robbers and were done being complimented on the arrests by the rest of the Troopers, it was about 4:30 in the morning and Joe and I were exhausted. Finally we were able to go to bed in the Post upstairs facility. We were both single and we were required to live at the Post. It must have been about an hour later when I was awakened by someone kneeling on my chest and shaking my head. It was my former senior officer and trainer, Bob Johnston. He exclaimed "Charlie, congratulations on a fine job – and now I want to confirm you – you are now a full fledged Trooper." What a guy. This act by him was related to the end of my probationary period, some two years earlier. The official bulletin had been received from the Commissioner stating I was confirmed. I was upstairs in the Post getting ready for day patrol when Bob arrived and yelled up at me "Recruit, I'll tell you when you are confirmed as a real Trooper."

The next day, the Post Commander showed us three bullet holes in the patrol car; two through the windshield and one through the right front fender. He recommended we receive a bravery award for the night's action. We thought that was a nice thing for him to say, but what the devil, that's what a Trooper's job is all about. Of course, we were both young and still foolish.

A short time later I was transferred to the Ypsilanti Post, between Ann Arbor and the University of Michigan and the city of Detroit. This was a large and busy Post with a fine complement of Troopers and non-commissioned officers. In the area was a huge restaurant and truck stop called the Fifth Wheel, located adjacent to Michigan's first "super highway." It was the best place to eat nearest the Post and State Police officers could be found there much of the time. Early on I stopped there for lunch while on day patrol. In that time, Troopers worked a minimum of nine hour days, six days a week, and without any overtime. While eating, a gorgeous young waitress came up to me and said "Trooper, there's a gentleman at the counter who wishes to speak to you." I went over and was pleasantly surprised to find Bob, my old senior trooper, now in plain clothes. We had a great chat before I resumed patrol. About a week later, I ran into him again and he inquired "do you recall the young lady who sent you over to talk to me?" I replied "recall, are you kidding, who could forget her, she's the prettiest girl I've ever seen. But, I've noticed her before and she's kind of snooty and not very friendly." He said "don't let that act fool you, I know her family and she's actually quite shy. Besides she told me that she found you quite attractive and would like to meet you." What I didn't know was that Bob had told Nancy Smith that the new Trooper in town, Charlie Meyers was attracted to her but too shy to approach her. Of course, we were soon dating, eventually engaged and married. From that moment on my social and family life were cast in stone and remained so for more than fifty five years. Troopers, you know, can be very persuasive.

I distinctly recall several events in our young relationship. One day on patrol I stopped in for lunch and Nan went to the juke box and played a jumpy tune of the day called "Charlie Is My Darling." All the officers and local drivers in the restaurant started to clap and laugh. I decided to go along with the joke, so I climbed out of an open window while in full uniform. On another occasion while visiting at her home, we were romping around in the back yard. I threw her vertically up in the air and then caught her coming down. The only problem was the rhinestone decorations on her blouse that tore my cheek open. I really got kidded about how rough our relationship must be. At the time, I had purchased a new black Ford convertible with cherry red interior. I obtained a hand made Indian blanket from Arizona which was folded neatly on the rear seat. Nan told all our friends that I kept asking her if she would like to take a chance on an Indian blanket, and they all laughed of course. It wasn't true, I asked her only once and she laughed at me that time.

As with many police officers, the following years of service brought many challenges; speed filled chases, irate traffic violators, assistance to the public in various ways, arrests of criminals, both minor and major, presence at important events, etc. A number of incidents are stamped into my memory forever.

One was out of Ypsilanti when another Trooper and I, on night patrol, attempted to stop a car containing two individuals who committed a serious traffic violation. They tried to elude us, dumping their lights and traveling at high speed through the city of Ann Arbor, while running red lights at wide open speed. They finally sped into a residential district, turning several corners. We lost sight of them around one corner, but then saw a darkened car in a driveway by virtue of a brief blip of a brake light. We pulled in behind them and placed our spotlights on the car and the two individuals in the front seat. They were in their mid to late twenties and were staring straight ahead as if they didn't know we existed. We ordered them to put their hands up and exit the car. They never moved or looked in our direction. The driver had his hands locked on the steering wheel. The passenger sat like a statue, staring out the windshield, with his arms folded across his chest. I looked at my partner and could tell he felt the same way that I did. There was something terribly wrong with these two and we were in a dangerous situation. Although they had only committed a traffic violation and were guilty of attempting to elude us, we knew there was more to this stop than that.

After several repeated orders without any compliance, my partner, a big tough Trooper, pulled the passenger out the right door bodily, threw him face down on the driveway, and covered him with his side arm. In the meantime, I attempted to break the driver's hold on the wheel without success. He was big and strong and acted as if he didn't hear me. I finally broke his grip by smashing him in the wrist with my five-cell flashlight, breaking it beyond repair. As he let out a hardly noticeable moan, I threw him out on the driveway and covered him with my revolver. After a few choice words, I dare not mention here, and threatening to shoot him, I was finally able to handcuff him. If this had happened today and a cell or dash camera was on the scene, the press would have us fired and jailed for mistreating the poor innocent driver and passenger. After all, they had only committed a traffic violation. We learned later that they were brothers, ex-convicts, and were out on bond charged with fighting a Trooper at another Post and attempting to take his gun away and shoot him. It just happened that time they picked on a Trooper famous in the Department as one of the toughest on the road.

The next embarrassing and scary situation occurred while I was stationed at the Center Line Post, located three miles North of Eight Mile Road, the Detroit city limit for the East side. This was one of, if not the busiest Post in the State. Lots of excitement, many challenges, and a bit of danger were to be found there. It happened on a rainy, dull day patrol when I was accompanied by a recruit Trooper, assigned to me as his senior officer and trainer. It was the kind of day officers hate. There was little or no radio traffic, no complaints to answer, and very little traffic. You have probably heard police work described as hours of boredom, separated by seconds of terror. We were experiencing the former and had little work to show for it on our daily record. While cutting across the patrol area on a side road, we spotted a car sitting down the dirt secondary road, about a quarter mile distant. The vehicle's hood was up and several figures surrounded the car. I told the cub that we were going to see if we could offer assistance. At least this would give us another item for the patrol record sheet. We turned the corner and approached the vehicle, stopping behind it. There was a garage cloth on the fender with several tools. The driver was under the hood apparently trying to correct the problem. As I approached I checked the inside of the vehicle. It was apparently quite clean with only a black leather jacket lying on the front seat. The driver produced a valid driver's license and registration for the car and explained the fuel pump was giving him problems, but he knew how to fix it. We offered to call a tow truck but he assured us it wouldn't be necessary and thanked us for our offer of assistance. Neither he nor his companions registered any nervousness.

A few hours later, near the end of our shift, the radio reported an armed robbery at the Hazel Park race track with a large sum of money taken. As the various police units patrolled the area, no suspects were spotted or reported. This uneventful day was finally over.

A few weeks later, as we prepared for another patrol, writing down stolen car descriptions and wanted person notices, I was approached by Det. Jack Pletzke. Jack was a wonderful and intelligent man and one of the better detectives in the Department. He asked "Charlie, do you remember several weeks ago, while on day patrol, checking a car parked on a side road with the hood up?" I assured him that I certainly did, and advised that the car description and driver would be on our daily record. He said "that will help. Now I want you to look at several mug shots." He spread about ten photographs in front of me. I studied them and said "this one was the driver, and this other one was one of the passengers standing alongside the car." He said "that's great; you'll make a good court witness." He then told me how the detectives developed a suspect in the race track robberies. The suspect had confessed and told them all about the incident. When the detectives informed him that they weren't sure he was telling the truth, he advised they could check his story with the Troopers who checked out the gang's car a few hours before the robbery. He told them they were cutting holes out of baby pillow cases they used for masks when they spotted the patrol car turn the corner. I sort of gasped and remarked "I'm really embarrassed; you mean I had three robbers right in front of me and ignored them. What in hell is my cub going to think about me now?" Jack replied, "Charlie, don't be too embarrassed; you probably saved you and your recruit's lives. Our suspect tells us they had a sawed-off shotgun under the leather jacket on the front seat. You might recall the passenger door was open and they decided if the Troopers try to search the car or get suspicious, kill them."

Criminals and drunk/reckless drivers aren't the only dangers Troopers face on the road. Perhaps the weirdest incident of my road career happened on one of the most popular assignments in the entire State. One fall Saturday, I was once again assigned to assist with the traffic detail at the Michigan v. Ohio State football game. On this assignment, Troopers can get into the "Big House" after the kickoff, watch the game from a standing position, and leave before the end of the game to resume their assigned traffic control position. This day, my partner and I had one of the worst assignments, manning a control point where the main highway from Ohio streams into a connecting roadway leading to the Stadium. We had shifted the traffic flow so that there was an extra lane turning left to accommodate the late arrivals from Ohio getting to the game before kickoff.

At one point I noticed a local car, apparently trapped between Ohio drivers in the other two lanes. The woman driver was frantically attempting to work her way out of the rest of the traffic, by now all Buckeyes headed for the game. But, she had to continue into the left turn, occupying the middle lane of three lanes, and as the cars slowly approached me as I directed the traffic flow, she swerved slightly and it appeared that I was about to be crushed between her and the car on her right side. I slapped my hands on her quarter panel and leaped upwards landing on the hood of her car. As I sat up, erect now, I could see that she was crying hysterically. Somehow I had retained my police cap and I placed it properly positioned on my head as she continued to drive along at about 5-10 miles /per/hour. She finally was able to stop about 100 feet from the corner. I felt enraged but I knew it would be useless to bawl her out. For perhaps the only time in my life I determined the right thing to say immediately, as I stated, "Thanks for the ride, Ma'am!" I climbed down and walked back to my traffic control point without further ado. It took a couple of minutes before the horns stopped honking and she was able to drive on.

Meanwhile, Nancy and I were engaged and planning on getting married. But the United States Government had other ideas. After World War II, I had been approached by a Navy recruiter who advised me he was aware that I had considerable experience operating the radio in Morse code. He knew I had been assigned after the Japanese surrender to the Naval Air Base radio station in Kwajalein

(NDJ). He told me about a small contingent, composed mostly of low ranked sailors with little radio experience, who were attempting to learn how to receive and send Morse code from the Navy Reserve station on Belle Isle, Detroit. Belle Isle was a beautiful little island in the Detroit River, connected to the city by a very ornate bridge. It contained park facilities, swimming pools, boating and fishing areas and the Naval Station. He knew Radio Kwajalein was a major relay station between Guam and Pearl Harbor and the operators stationed there were very experienced in handling quantities of radio traffic. He talked me into joining the Naval Reserves and teaching recruit sailors Morse code at the little Reserve base. I had remained in the Reserves after joining the Michigan State Police. Now my Reserve enlistment had been extended involuntarily by President Truman and I received a notice to appear at Great Lakes Naval Training Center for assignment during the Korean War. One unusual aspect of all this Morse code sending and receiving was that you never forget it. I remember sitting on the bus, looking at ad signs and quickly spelling Budweiser as -... ..- -.. .-- . .. .-.

 I immediately contacted East Lansing Headquarters of the State Police and was told not to worry, they wouldn't take a Trooper. A few days later I was advised that Radioman was a critical rate in the war effort and that I had 48 hours to report to Great Lakes Training Center in Chicago. I kissed Nancy goodbye and reported as ordered. Within 72 hours I was aboard the aircraft carrier U.S.S. Leyte (CV-32), headed out to sea.

 I wasn't very happy about this decision, but I made the best of it and served 16 months as a lead radioman aboard the Leyte. The cruise was relatively uneventful. The Carrier had just returned from the Korean area and was now engaged in training exercises.

 However there were three memorable moments of this cruise. The first happened in the Mediterranean while the Sixth Fleet was at anchor near one port of call. A sudden storm of typhoon quality struck without warning. Several of the ships broke anchor chains and were sent adrift. The Leyte still had partial power, always on ready in the event of a sudden attack (possibly from the Russians at this time). The Officer of the Deck immediately upgraded the power and the Carrier was maneuvered back and forth on her bow and stern anchors to avoid colliding with other ships from the Fleet. One, an oil tanker, came within feet of striking the ship. Afterwards, the Deck Officer received a citation for his handling of the Carrier in this situation, with all hands on deck in dress uniform to witness the award. It was very impressive.

The second situation could have been a tragedy for me. I had just finished the late watch on the radio circuits. On the Leyte the radio shack was high up in the superstructure, some distance above the flight deck. The ship had been gliding along with no apparent pitch or roll; the water was apparently smooth as glass at the moment. The radio gang compartment was just under the flight deck at the aft end of the ship and my usual habit was to walk the flight deck when there were no flight operations. After descending the ladder and opening the hatch, I was surprised to find one of the densest fogs in my experience. It caused me to reassess walking the flight deck. "If I descended one more deck I would be on the Hangar Deck; no fog but lots of equipment and planes." I decided to walk the flight deck, knowing there was a catwalk along both sides with a handrail to grasp and with the ocean smooth. I angled across the flight deck toward the starboard side, knowing our compartment was on that side. I felt sure that I could make it safely to the catwalk and then it would be easy to get to the rear or aft end of the ship. At about the time I expected the catwalk to show, the toe of my left shoe caught something, tripped me out and away from the catwalk. As I flew through the air, I recall having time for one instant thought; "I'm dead." I knew the catwalk was the last vestige of walking space and I would fall into the ocean, in the fog and in the dead of night, no one would hear a call for help. I probably wouldn't be missed until roll call the next morning.

But then I came to a crashing halt with a terrible sudden pain shooting through my mouth and face. By God's grace, I had fortunately landed on a collision net; a mesh of heavy rope and rubber cushions held in a metal cage and pinned so that it could be dropped at a moment's notice down the side of the ship. There were several of these on each side. One primary purpose was to use them in the event of an abandon ship, to allow the crew to crawl down them rather than jump from the flight deck, some fifty feet above the water's edge. One of the hard rubber cushions had smashed into my face, driving a couple of my teeth through my lip. But I was safe, bleeding all over my dungaree shirt, but alive!

This was the closest escape from the "Grim Reaper" in my young life. I wondered what tripped me. I then saw the curve of the hose (the goose-neck) on a flame extinguisher sticking up just above the flight deck. Some airdale (flight deck crewman) had stowed the extinguisher improperly and damned near cost me my life. I never told Nancy about this one until some years later.

My third memorable event was when returning across the Atlantic in December, just before Christmas. It was a bad time on the Carrier, and I saw what real sailors had to contend with. For several days we were running in heavy seas, pounding over the flight deck 50 feet high. The porthole below the flight deck on our compartment side gave a great view of the ocean, and the tiny Destroyer Escort running alongside our ship. She was battened down with only her smokestack uncovered. Every once in awhile she would appear on top of a huge swell, shaking like a dog shaking water off its back. And then she would disappear, not to be seen again for some time. We all wondered if she would make it back to Newport News and Norfolk but she did. Then we all knew why tin can sailors would tell us aircraft carrier Navy men that we didn't know what the oceans were really about.

The Radio officer had promised me Christmas leave for late December, 1951, and Nancy was so advised. She promptly advised me she was waiting no longer and we were to be married during my leave. When I protested this would be too much work for her, she stated "don't sweat it mate, no problem." And so, we were married on December 29th, 1951 in a beautiful little church, named St. Louis, in Belleville, Michigan. She was elegant in her white gown with the long train. The ceremony occurred during one of the most devastating snow storms in the history of the Detroit area. That didn't faze her. She had Deputies and Troopers to guide the wedding party and celebrants and County snow plows working to keep the drive and lot passable. What a gal!

While trooping out of the Center Line Post, Nancy and I had a disaster early in our marriage. Our first child Robin was about three months old when she died unexpectedly during the night. The doctors said it was crib death or what is now known as SIDS, Sudden Infant Death Syndrome. I thought it would kill Nancy, and it did take several months before she started to come out of that deadly spell.

We didn't even have life insurance on the baby. These things surely couldn't happen to us. The Troopers came to the rescue with the men and their wives pitching in to help us out. This is when I truly learned what the "brotherhood" is really about. Some of the men even put a little money in their cards, knowing we were broke and without insurance. One of my dear friends, Trooper Chris Swartzendruber pinned a $100 dollar bill to his card with a note, "Don't argue Charlie, take it and use it." That was a lot of money in the 50s. One of my school days friends was the daughter of a Detroit undertaker and she and her Dad took care of the funeral, gravesite and all. As the old saying goes "True friends are like diamonds, precious and rare, while false friends are like autumn leaves, found everywhere."

Then I was asked to go to Headquarters at East Lansing to act as a training officer in several upcoming recruit schools. This was considered an honor among police officers and we accepted.

At this juncture, a second child was born, a daughter named Kathy after a neighbor who helped so much when our first born died. We moved to a rented duplex in Lansing, Michigan, only a few miles from State Police Headquarters and the Training complex. It was six days a week, with many of the days involving 15 or 16 hours with the recruits, planning and setting-up training. It was hard work, but for me it was very rewarding. The Commissioner promised the Staff that we could have our pick of Posts for our next assignments as a reward.

This assignment was tough on Nancy, with a young child on her hands, but she never complained. In a short time, it got a whole lot tougher. We noticed Kathy seemed to be slow and behind other children her age and at times her behavior was beyond comprehension. We asked our doctor about her and he told us that he planned on having a meeting with us to discuss our little girl. He shocked us by advising he felt she was mentally retarded and he gave us a list of experts to see and have tests performed with her, concluding with the Children's Hospital at the University of Michigan. We followed his recommendations and ultimately found ourselves in the office of the top physician at the University of Michigan who had experience in this field. He asked Nancy if she wanted to have more children and she replied "God willing, certainly." He then told us Kathy was undoubtedly born brain damaged; she would have no memory; she would never be able to read or write; she would never be able to logic; her behavior would remain similar to what brought us there and the only thing for us to do would be to institutionalize her. He warned if we didn't Kathy would ruin our lives, our marriage, and the lives of any other children! Nancy grabbed my hand and practically jerked me out of his office saying as we went "You go to hell doctor!" The story of Kathy is a volume by itself that I will not attempt here. "Just a few facts madam," as Jack Webb would say in Dragnet long ago ", may suffice."

Kathy's mother vowed the Doctor's prognosis would not happen to her child. After nearly a lifetime of applied research on the subject, contact with a number of special schools, obtaining the services of a number of special teachers, including her cousin Gerry Smith a PhD in Special Education, the help of a wonderful young baby sitter, Christine Rey, and the services of the Mt. Pleasant Home and Training School, a model institution of some years ago, Kathy is now a lady of 55 years of age, who can read and write legibly, who has the best memory in the family and is more often than not the best behaved and most fun to be around. The Priest at our Parish, St. Anthony of Padua, Father Dennis Kress says she has a direct line to heaven. People of the Parish ask her to pray for them when they are ill or despair. So much for the mental health experts of yesteryear; Nancy, Kathy, the other children and I have enjoyed many moments of laughter kidding about the Doctor who knew so much.

However, I have to add there came a time when Kathy seemed to sharply regress and her behavior started to disintegrate. She was about 12 years old when this happened. She had been making wonderful progress, but seemed to be losing it. It was recommended that we voluntarily institutionalize her in a new program at the Mt. Pleasant Home and Training School in Mt. Pleasant, Michigan. It was then headed by Dr. John Todnik and his associate Jim Beall. They asked for her to be placed for two years and at the end of that approximate time period she would be allowed to return home when she requested it! With great trepidation, we took her there and left her sitting on a bed in the reception area. As we returned to the car, Nancy tearfully said, "Darn it, I forgot her coloring and work books she loves so much." I volunteered to return with them and did so. Kathy was sitting on the edge of her bed with tears streaming down her face. I asked her what was wrong and she told me she had a sore throat. All her young life, when troubled by anything her explanation was that of a sore throat. I gave her the books and left crying.

For nearly two years, we spent every other weekend with her, making it an outing for the family with hiking, fishing, swimming at a nearby river, etc. and always with a special picnic of her mother's best dishes. It was nearly two years later when we received a call from Kathy saying she wanted to come home. Arrangements were made with the Doctor and we went to get her. On the way home, she was quite talkative, telling us all about her experiences at the school. And then she said "Daddy, when you took me to Mt. Pleasant, you told me you were taking me to the college. Daddy, don't you know anything – that's not a college, it's an institution!" Nancy and I both exclaimed "my God, how did she learn to use a word like that?" We couldn't stop laughing all the way home. She has been a joy ever since. Of course the College, Central Michigan University, has a Special Education program where students spend part of their time at the Home and Training School, actually working with the Retarded.

TROOPER ROBERT (WILBUR SHAW)
JOHNSTON – 1948

Chasing Tail Lights to Forensic Ballistics

YOUNG (RECRUIT) TROOPER
@ GAYLORD – 1948

CPL. MICKEY KUKLER
AND OLD PATROL CAR - 1948

Charles Meyers

AUTHOR GREETED BY LT. LEROY SMITH, CRIME LAB. CO – 1956

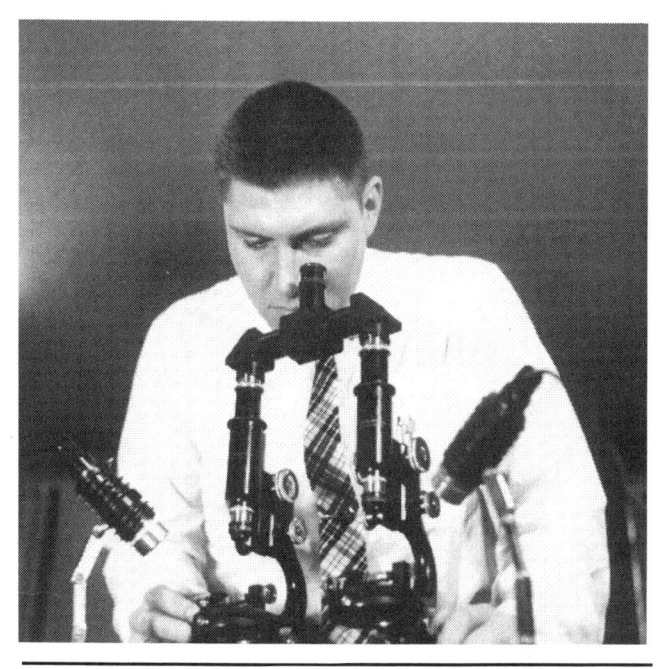

THE BEGINNER – LOOKING THROUGH THE OLD
COMPARISON MICROSCOPE – 1956

3

The Crime Laboratory - in the Beginning

Now on to my life long profession; I eventually became a forensic scientist, crime scene investigator, crime laboratory analyst, and consultant. When my duties as a training officer ended, the Commissioner advised me that I wasn't about to be sent to the Post of my choice as promised, but rather, if willing, I would be promoted to the next higher rank and assigned to the Crime Laboratory in East Lansing. Wow, although I had no idea what this entailed it meant no move and more pay. You bet I accepted it.

The Michigan State Police Crime Laboratory was established in 1932, and was one of the earliest in the United States. It sprang out of the older Bureau of Identification, housing one of the largest collections of master fingerprints in the world. The Department was fortunate to operate under State law requiring all criminals be finger printed and the original prints be forwarded to the Michigan State Police for classification and retention in their Master Files. It was believed that only the FBI files were larger. The original latent fingerprint experts of the Laboratory were brought over from the Bureau. One, Emil Wendling age 101, just passed away after attending the annual retirement dinner for the Department. Another original member of the Bureau, Leroy F. Smith, a former school teacher, was assigned to the new Laboratory and became its first Director. Smitty, as he was affectionately known, was still Director when I was promoted to the Crime Laboratory.

On the first morning of my new position, I became acquainted with Smitty and his major assistant, Wallace VanStratt, or Wally as he was known. I didn't know how to take Smitty at first, but I soon learned he was a wonderful man, very intelligent, with a remarkable memory for detail and a bit mischievous at times. But that first morning I didn't know what to expect. As I introduced myself to the Director he wove a little tale. "As you know," he began ", all promotions in the Department come through Civil Service rules. The Commissioner must choose among the top three names on the Register for any position to be filled. After the recent promotional examinations and the portions weighted toward science and the Crime Laboratory you came in third. Well, number one was too old; number two was too fat; but you were just right, so we chose you." It took a couple of weeks to find out he was just pulling my leg to see the reaction. My mentor, Wally, let me know it was mainly due to the fact that I had a couple years of college and co-workers knew I planned on obtaining a degree with part-time work.

So now the work really began. Wally took me to the library stack of books and pointed out a number that I was required to read and digest. Of course, the books included Hatcher's and Gunthers' works on "Firearms Identification," as a starter. These were authored in 1935 and were considered hallmark texts in the area. As time progressed, there were others that I had to review, at least in part. The Laboratory had a collection of about 350 different handgun models at the time. In the beginning, both Smitty and Wally worked with me learning some of the secrets of various firearm types while indicating the parts of primary interest for comparison and identification. After a bit, I was given the job of removing every firearm from the collection, disassembling it, cleaning it, and returning to the collection. In the latter stages of my training, I was given the responsibility of designing a new set of structures to properly house and display our ever expanding collection. The cases were built by the prisoners at Jackson State Prison (the World's largest walled prison at the time). Then I had to oversee their installation by prison trustees working at Headquarters.

In the earlier years, extra jobs were not the exception. For example, the firearms experts in the Laboratory had to repair and re-blue the Departments revolvers, rifles and shotguns. You would be surprised how many officers leave the shotgun on the roof of the Patrol car and then drive out from under it!

After a short while, Wally set-up an itinerary for me to follow with reservations at nearly all of the firearms and ammunition factories on the East Coast (at least they were all there in 1956). It is a standard practice to have trainees in Firearms Identification go through the factories on supervised visits, usually with a factory expert or even owner, to acquaint oneself with the methods of manufacture. Special emphasis is placed on the machinery used to make key parts useful in the comparison process, such as the drill, reamer, rifling broach, etc., used in barrel manufacture. Well, in 1956 the Department sent me to the East Coast for a three week visit to various installations. They provided a State car for transportation, three dollars a day for meals and an allowance of up to ten dollars a day for a room. I soon found out that the motels all charged more than my allowance. I found a rooming house that I could afford. It was an old clapboard sided former home with a number of small bedrooms and one shared bath. It was in Bridgeport, Ct. and that became my headquarters for most of my trip. It was a fabulous experience I never forgot. In several plants the owner or superintendent took me out to lunch and/or dinner. I was invited to several homes to glory over the owner's fabulous gun collection. I doubt that this experience is quite the same today. In this age, a number of the top companies provide training sessions and seminars for interested trainees and examiners to take part.

Back in the Laboratory, I spent many days and nights typing notes from the trip and reading and copying notes from my mentors, Leroy Smith and Wallace VanStratt. Smitty in particular had volumes of notes he had collected over the years. Much was copied from long ago publications and included items such as the proof marks from most of the industrialized nations of the world. One extensive collection included the coded markings from all the Nazi controlled factories throughout Europe, found on various firearms they manufactured. Many years later, in a discussion with David Byron, the author of a valuable work entitled "Gun Marks," he confided that he had been unable to find an authoritative copy of the German firearm coded markings, so I made a copy of Smitty's notes for him, which he thanked me for in his foreword.

Then it was the meat and potatoes of firearms identification; the comparison microscope and the evaluation and comparison of markings on bullets and cartridge cases. In those early years we had one such microscope. It was composed of two biological Bausch and Lomb microscopes, mounted on a wood platform, spaced appropriately to accept a microscopic bridge made by Zeiss, the famous German lens maker. In this manner, the examiner can see two images side-by-side at the same magnification, separated by a fine line known as the hairline divider. Thus the analyst can compare the markings on two bullets, one from the victim and one a test from the suspected firearm. The fine striations imparted to the bullets' bearing surfaces by imperfections or foreign material in the bore can then be examined to determine whether they compare in a remarkable fashion in shape, depth, width, light diffusion, etc., and occupy the same exact spaces on the bullets' surfaces.

Back then we took photographs through the microscope optics, known as photomicrographs, only on rare occasions, usually for use as demonstrations in lectures before attorneys, criminal investigators, etc. There were many reasons given for this practice, but in actuality, it was time consuming and difficult. Picture an analyst carefully focusing on the desired markings, placing a metal tube over the eyepiece and mounting a camera thereon. Then place a black hood over your head to block out any incipient lighting, refocus through the camera, and shoot a roll of film, hoping that one decent image will be found on the resulting negatives. The entire setup took a space of @ 2 feet wide by 2.5 feet high. In the Crime Laboratory world of today, the comparison microscope and its power actuated stand takes considerable floor space and towers over the seated analyst's head, while the photo accoutrements take more table space than the old microscope system. Of course it's nice to be able to choose among several images, push a couple of buttons and receive a sharp color photograph showing exactly what is desired. But, I digress, sufficient to say that the equipment and training of this day for the most part is superior to what it was many years ago, although none of it is quite as impressive as the CSI shows of today would have us believe. We will have to discuss that subject more in another chapter as for the most part I am attempting to maintain a semblance of chronology.

Later, we purchased two small table model Martin Held, useable but not as well as hoped for, although the cost was far less than the Leitz or American Optical microscopes Next, we were fortunate to obtain a floor model Leitz microscope with large stage table, very handy for large tool marked objects, and with outstanding optics, although still monocular. Eventually the Firearms section microscope field was largely taken over by American Optical and/or Leitz. All of the comparison microscopes of today are binocular and have the capacity to choose among a number of objective lens, alter magnification and do so almost instantly.

Back to training and practice: most of my latter stages of training were spent in examining and comparing bullets, shells, and cartridge cases. Efforts were made to examine these items where different versions of the same firearm were used to prepare samples. In this way, bullets or cartridge cases known to have been fired in different weapons with the same class characteristics were examined to ascertain similarity or dissimilarity of markings. With bullets, the class characteristics include the type of rifling, the caliber, the number of lands and grooves, the width of the lands and grooves, and the direction of twist of the rifling. In the bore, the lands are raised elements or the remnants of the original bore while the grooves are the recessed areas that spiral through the barrel. Therefore, the bullets are spun about their long axis and spiral toward the target much like a football pass only much faster, of course.

Over and over, attempts at discerning similar markings in similar positions were unsuccessful. Whereas bullet and cartridge case markings imparted by discharge in the same firearm and from the same portions of the bore or other part were found to contain groups of microscopic markings that could not be differentiated and thus determined to "match", to use the popular expression.

Contrary to the practice today, my courtroom experience as an expert witness in training was practically non-existent. However, as an officer I had the opportunity to testify a number of times so was somewhat used to the procedure. Today trainees are subjected to moot courts and critique before they are sent into the arena on their own.

As my training progressed, I enrolled at Michigan State University, across the road from Headquarters. I started part time work to obtain a Bachelor's degree, formerly a daunting task for a poor boy without funds. It's interesting to note that my advisor from the University was Prof. Ralph Turner, well known in forensic circles. During his tenure, he had another student and I explore Photogrammetric Position Finding, which entailed a huge investigation of literature, followed by attempts at using it effectively at crime scenes. I also enjoyed criminal law classes with Marshall Houts, a famous legal scholar and participant in the Court of Last Resort. Today, it is a requirement for a degree with some scientific exposure in order to gain entrance in the training programs of the Crime Laboratory. That wasn't true in some disciplines when I entered the Laboratory. Since it was certainly desired, I was always proud of the fact that I, in later years, was instrumental in getting the Department to agree to allow officers assigned to the Crime Laboratory to exchange extra work hours for classroom hours spent at the University working on a degree.

When first assigned to the Laboratory, I found on occasion the crew would be called upon to go to the scene of a major homicide to conduct crime scene investigation. The team would usually consist of one or two members of the Laboratory staff, one or two from the Latent Print section, and one or two from the Dept. of Health Crime Laboratory staff. The Dept. of Health staff was headed by Dr. Clarence Muehlberger, famous in forensic circles for many years and still very active at this time. He was assisted by Dr. Edgar Kivela, who was well known and quite active in the American Academy of Forensic Sciences. AAFS as the Academy was known was still young but growing quickly and even then was considered as the benchmark society in forensics. If you were going to work around Muehlberger you had better have track shoes on as he did everything at a fast trot. For crime scene crews the Health Dept. usually sent Dr. Kivela and possibly an assistant. In those days, the popular acronym CSI wasn't in use as it is now. As to our staff, Wally and I got the nod. As time progressed and staff was enlarged, CSI turned from an occasional task to a steady requirement. It seemed that major crimes were involved more and more. Finally, standby duty for crime scene calls became a major duty for the Laboratories. And, of course, calls for this assistance more often than not came late at night, on weekends and during holidays.

In my beginning I found most of what I learned about CSI came from on-the-job training, although, I did have the opportunity to attend the Scientific Criminal Investigation class at the University of Louisville, where nearly all the teachers and lecturers were well recognized forensic scientists from all parts of the country. One day was spent with Dr. Muehlberger and was greatly enjoyed. A number of the forensic specialists had been members of the original Crime Laboratory at Northwestern University, starting in 1930. The "father" of firearms identification, Col. Calvin Goddard, is credited as being the moving force behind this creation.

My major problem in starting to train and then become part of the CSI unit was in learning to properly use the camera of the era. We were equipped with the Crown Graphic reflex camera, which still used flash bulbs for added illumination. We had a couple always ready to go. In Crime Scene Investigation complete coverage of the scene and all known evidence detail is absolutely essential. In addition, a later review of the pile of photos taken sometimes reveals evidence that had heretofore not been recognized or realized as to its importance. I recall one homicide in the Kalamazoo area where later review of photographs played a role in catching the murderer. During the search, a pile of miscellaneous items on top of a dresser attracted the crime scene photographer's attention. It looked as if someone had hurriedly placed material from a pocket, including small change, in the location. Among the miscellaneous was a newspaper clipping that showed clearly in the close-up photograph. Upon enlargement the paper and city were identified, leading detectives to the suspect. In another homicide, the newspaper played a huge role. The murder victim lay flat on his back on the floor. His bloodied head was covered with a sheet of newsprint spread out to completely cover his face (often a valuable psychological clue). The killer's fingerprints were found on the newspaper and in a position suggesting their deposit as the unfolded sheet was placed over the victim. This type of photographic detail is not only important to the proofs, but possibly the bell ringer at trial.

At about the time my training period was ending, nearly two years later, Smitty retired and went to live in a small community in Northern Michigan. Not long after we received a letter from him explaining the small county could not get anyone to run for Coroner, so they asked him to do it as a public service, and he agreed. Not long after, in the winter and after a huge snowfall, he was called on an unexplained death. The officer involved led him to a nearby lake where a missing man had been found on the lake ice. The old Director advised they had to wade through heavy snow for several hundred yards before they got to the body of the would-be ice fisherman. Smitty had taken his personal camera with him and explained he had to take photos because the officer's flash wasn't working, probably weak batteries. We laughed as he remarked he was used to that after his years in the Crime Laboratory – so often the police officer's cameras weren't working. But then it got hilarious as he explained he had the death certificate filled out as "dead from a heart attack" before he got to the victim. He said hiking through that damn deep snow darned near killed him! That sounded like the old man.

One other thing about the photographic end of CSI – we had to develop, print, enlarge if needed, the crime scene and laboratory photos. We had our own darkroom and equipment for this purpose. Now agencies have photographic laboratories to do any specialized work, although much of it is done through the amazing world of electronics today.

Having your own darkroom can lead to problems sometimes. In the old Laboratory, we developed a process of identifying each major case with some kind of adjective description. I will never forget a case in Central Michigan which became known to the staff as the St. John the Baptist case. You must bear in mind that the staff and I were all God fearing church members and would not do anything to desecrate the biblical story. However, the crime scene crew was called out late one night on a brutal murder of a woman. The scene basically involved the area of a side yard alongside a home in question, and a car parked nearby. In the yard was the headless body of a woman and various parts of her anatomy that had been cut off. In the trunk of the nearby car we found her missing head. She was about forty years of age, not pretty, and with long stringy dark hair hanging down. The killer had done a neat job of decapitation and the head sat erect on what remained of the neck. By this time, the Coroner had arrived with a hearse. He and his assistant rolled out a hospital type cot with a clean white sheet spread over it. We had finished with our search and gave him permission to remove the remains. He first carefully removed the head from the car trunk and set it upright on the sheet. He then began to search the yard, guided by one of the crew, for body parts. But, another staff member spotted the head on the white sheet and took a couple more photographs.

Not long after we left the scene and returned to the Laboratory. Our intrepid crew member busied himself with the photographic work, while another typed notes on the scene and evidence gathered. Later in the day, the photographic whiz called the crew together and showed one of his enlargements. It was of the victim's head on the white sheet surrounded by the darkness of night. It looked just like the paintings and sketches of St. John's head on a platter, as he was martyred. So, gruesome as it might sound, this became the St. John the Baptist case. Sad to say, but CSI crews sometimes get a little callous from the onslaught of homicide cases in this country.

One case I have never been able to forget comes to mind. No matter how callous you my think you are, if a child is a victim, its hard to take and forget. One weekend I was on call for crime scenes and I was contacted by the local forensic pathologist who said he was about to conduct an autopsy on a child victim and wanted someone to assist who was capable of taking sharp close-up photographs. By this time, I assured him I could fill the bill.

I went to the morgue area of the hospital and met the Doctor. On the white slab was the body of a small girl, about one year old, as I recall. This was the most beautiful child I have ever seen; perfect in every way and with the face of an angel. The pathologist explained that she was brought to emergency but was dead on arrival. Further he said "this is no accident, this is a homicide case." As he examined her body, he pointed out a number of crescent shaped scars, including several fresh ones. He said "those are all fingernail cuts. Please photograph each one and its position on her body." He then pointed out several small, round bright reddish areas, including one on the lips of her little vagina. He said "those are all cigarette burns, please do the same." By this time I was having trouble focusing the close-up lens on the Leica 35mm camera. Tears were fogging my vision. I have copies of those slides. But I have never shown them to anyone with the exception of a couple forensic pathologists. My advice, if you're not mentally tough, you might not want to get into CSI. To this very day, when I think of that case tears roll down my cheek. Who would do this and why? Not so well understood then, but perhaps better understood today.

This child was one half of a set of identical twins and her mother was the killer. She lived in a beautiful suburban home and apparently had everything a mother should desire. These two were her first children and she was a young pretty woman. The authorities said that the other child was very well behaved but that the dead twin cried a lot and the mother had a hard time understanding and controlling her. On the day in question, the mother took her out of the crib and slammed her to the floor in desperation. The child died of a ruptured spleen, the pathologist told me. The mother was sent to a facility for the insane. I believe today some would call that problem Post-Partum Depression.

As I neared the end of my training period, I accompanied my boss Wally to court in Lower Michigan. The purpose was to hear him testify in order to assist me as an expert witness; to learn how to properly present your credentials to the Judge so that he may decide to allow your opinion testimony as an expert witness. I was also glad to hear him testify and see how he presented himself in court. Wally was a fine witness which mirrored his activities in general. He was a polite but tough Dutch man, and still carried a Japanese sniper's bullet buried next to his spine. This caused him trouble in later life and ultimately partially crippled him.

The teen-age sniper case: As we alighted from the Courthouse, a mutual friend approached. It was a Deputy from the nearby Sheriff's office Identification staff. His name I believe was Don McLaughlin (darn my memory); we called him "Mac". He said he knew we would be there in court this morning and wanted to talk to us. He advised the area had a shooting problem which culminated in a woman's death. He stated further the original investigation indicated the shooting was apparently accidental, but he was worried about that theory and asked if we could accompany him to the scene and look it over. Having just come out of court, we were dressed in suit and tie and didn't have our usual array of equipment with us. But in those days we always carried a small evidence kit and a complete camera kit in the trunk of our cars. We followed him to the scene.

He had explained this was connected to a story in the city newspapers for weeks. It was about the "teen age sniper." According to the story, several weeks before a .22 caliber bullet crashed through the living room window of a large home in a beautiful subdivision. No one heard the shot or saw the shooter, but the police found small shoeprints of sneaker footwear in the winter snow and it was conjectured that a teenager maliciously shot out the window. Several days later the same thing happened at another home in the vicinity. And then a week later, it happened again. The city news heard about it and apparently needed a front page story, so the teen-aged sniper story was born.

In this case, the woman of the house was standing at the kitchen sink when a bullet crashed through the window, passed through the curtains and killed her. At first her husband was not aware that she had been shot. He and their two children, a boy 16 and a girl 14, were in the lower level of the tri-level home, in the family room when the wife left to go to the kitchen and make lunch. She didn't return so after awhile he went to see what was keeping her. He found her lying unconscious on the kitchen floor and called for medical help. She was rushed to the hospital and the early guess was that she may have suffered a severe stroke, possibly a brain aneurysm.

She was pronounced dead on arrival (DOA). X-rays of the head showed a dense object and associated "snowstorm" of dense particulate in her brain. The pathologist recovered a .22 caliber bullet and determined the bullet entrance was in the inside corner of her eye, not noticeable at first. Now the police discovered the bullet pathway through the window and storm window glass of the kitchen. Reconstruction discovered small sneaker tracks in the snow alongside a garage across the street and it was theorized this was where the shooter had stood. From that location the shooter would not have seen the woman standing inside at the sink, so it was theorized this was another prank shooting with disastrous consequences.

Chasing Tail Lights to Forensic Ballistics

I had already learned from another case that one has to be careful in judging bullet paths from bullet holes. I touched the edges of the holes in outer and inner glass with my fingertips, discerning much of the inner entrance was gone, probably due to the bullet attempting to expand from the outer entrance site. Bullet holes through glass and bone are usually smooth on the outer side with a roughened or cratered area on the inside or exit side. This shooting involved a .22 caliber soft lead projectile that is easily damaged by penetrating glass or the skull. We were able to find at the entrance site a small perimeter, relatively intact, that showed the bullet was traveling at some upwards angle as it passed through the glass.

From this vantage point, Wally and I traced the bullet's path back to the point where it disappeared in the front yard snow! The firearm had to have been held along this line. There were no shooter tracks in the relatively fresh snow but there was a cleared sidewalk next to the kitchen window. This seemed to be the only location the shot could have been fired from. Black appearing specks on the window glass were found to be particles of gunpowder residue. This confirmed the fact that the shooter was within a couple of feet of the window when the shot was fired. The culprit had to have seen the woman at the sink. This was no accident, this was murder!

Investigators soon discovered the 16 year old son had stolen a .22 caliber handgun while with another neighboring boy. He admitted all the shootings, stating that he was attempting to setup a story about an accidental shooting so he could kill his mother without being detected! The boy claimed the mother was too strict and he felt like he was being smothered. This one might have passed as an accidental shooting if a Deputy with CSI background hadn't been involved. Some cases are unbelievable but they happen all too often.

A few weeks later Wally informed me that I was being released. I was on my own to work cases in the firearms and tool mark discipline and go to court to testify when needed. I was excited about the progress but a little nervous too. Before long I was buried in case work and court appearances all over the State, broken only by the occasional crime scene requirement.

At this time Michigan had two crime laboratories covering the entire field of work, one in the State Police handling all the physical identification areas such as firearms, tool marks, shoe prints, tire tracks, latent fingerprints, photography, physical matches, etc. It was a few years before we entered the drug analysis, serology, hairs and fibers and trace evidence areas, and began the expansion into satellite laboratories throughout the State. This was a joint effort by the two laboratories which were eventually merged into one system under the State Police. But that was all in the distant future. Right now I worked cases from the city of Detroit perimeter to the far reaches of the Upper Peninsula and this became a grind, although I loved the work, all the travel took its toll. And, in between time I attended college classes at M.S.U. This was doubly hard on my wife, but she was always the good soldier and never complained, well almost never.

On one long trip I testified at a murder trial in the morning in Ann Arbor, testified after lunch on another homicide case in Lansing, then drove hundreds of miles to the western Upper Peninsula to testify in a third murder trial the following morning. When I returned home I was a basket case for a day or two, but then was back at it.

I distinctly remember one of my first court cases. It was a simple Conservation violation, a misdemeanor, larceny of a coyote from a trap! It could hardly be considered a capital crime. Trappers collected $20.00 for a set of Coyote ears back then. In this case, someone stole the critter from a trap leaving behind a spent shotgun shell used to kill the animal. The accused was represented by an older attorney, a former Prosecutor in the UP. I barely read the original report on this one. After all it was about the larceny of a coyote. As he started cross-examination I noticed a stack of books on the table in front of him. At times he referred to one of them. After a couple of hours of grueling testimony, it was finally over and the Judge ordered a recess. Out in the hallway the old attorney approached me and with a slight smile asked "Well, how did I do son?" I replied "you know how I did - you darned near killed me up there." He grinned as he said "well an old acquaintance of yours fed me some information and book titles. He told me to give that young rookie from Michigan a good going over." I said "well it worked, who did it by the way?" He advised me it was an old buddy of his, Charlie Wilson, Director of the Wisconsin Crime Laboratory. Charlie was well known in forensic circles. He was one of the members of the original Crime Laboratory at Northwestern University (circa 1930). I never had a chance to thank Charlie, but it was the first and last time I went to court not completely prepared, no matter what kind of case it might be.

My early testimony days ran into a few snags and a little humor, although my testimony as an expert has never been refused by the court. Flint had a defense attorney notorious for defending every indigent killer he could get his hands on. The first time I faced him he crossed me regarding my background qualifications. He started "Mr. Meyers, as I understand your testimony, you do not have a college degree but are working toward one. Is that correct? Now, let me ask you when you first entered college at the University of Michigan. As I understand it, that was in 1946. It is now 1959. So, you have been in college for 13 years and still don't have a degree?" I tried to correct him on that statement but he interrupted saying ", that won't be necessary;" no more questions your honor." The next couple of times I testified with him he asked me, "Mr. Meyers, did you get that degree yet?" I would have to say "no sir." One year I was testifying in yet another homicide in Flint (we had many from Flint, Michigan in those days), and he was the defense attorney again. He asked "Charlie – did you ever get that degree (we were on a first name basis by then)?" I replied "yes I did, I received my Bachelor degree from Michigan State about one month ago." He gave me a big smile and wink, then turned to the Judge and said "I have no more questions of this witness, your Honor."

The courtroom can be a funny place sometime.

The airman pimp case: Another case that happened early in my courtroom career was from the Upper Peninsula. It happened to an enlisted airman from the big air base. He was acting as a pimp for a little local prostitute. It is alleged that they argued, probably over her take, and it ended with her killing him. The Prosecution theory was that he was coming after her and she took his deer rifle, a .35 Remington caliber, and shot him in the back as he retreated. The defense claimed she had retreated into the bedroom, got the loaded rifle out of the closet and shot him in the chest as he advanced toward her, and that she was in fear for her life. She was about 5'2" and 100 lbs.; he was 6-2 and about 250 lbs. Needless to say, but that .35 Remington bullet hardly slowed going through the big man. The entire case hinged on which way the bullet traveled, front to back or back to front. In this case, the analysis was that of determination of firearms residues. When a firearm is discharged, along with the bullet a quantity of residue from the fired case and the bore is emitted from the barrel. Examination of the victim's clothing should show which way the bullet perforated the clothing and body. The great majority of such residue would be found on the clothing and body underneath at the entrance site. I found such residues in great quantity on the front of the man's button down shirt adjacent to the entrance hole. On the back of the shirt I found a section of tissue on the undersurface with a trace of residue. This is what I testified to at her murder trial, so in essence although I was listed as a Prosecution witness my opinions favored the defense. Although this is not common it is certainly not rare. I summed up my opinion with a statement to the effect that the bullet passed from front through the back. The State attorney couldn't wait to get at me. He glared as he stated "Mr. Meyers you weren't here at the time of the Pathologist's testimony, but he testified that the bullet passed through the body from back to front. Mr. Meyers we are talking here about a Surgeon with 35 years of medical experience, and yet you are going to challenge his testimony. Can you explain your testimony in any other way to this jury?" As he talked my mind was racing, knowing what the punch-line query would be? I finally answered his question this way; "the only other solution, based on my tests, would be if he were wearing his shirt backwards!" Now his smirk turned to a terrible scowl, and I knew I had wounded him badly. The prostitute was found not guilty in that case.

Now, if you think that endeared the defense attorney to me for life, you are badly mistaken. Twice in later years I faced him with testimony favoring the Prosecution. In both instances, his opening line of cross-examination was "Mr. Meyers, we have faced each other in the courtroom before, haven't we?" I, of course, replied "yes sir, that's true." He then stated "in that first case, you contradicted the testimony of a medical doctor with 35 years of experience, isn't that true?" What could I say but "yes sir, that's also true."

The Prosecutor and Judge had no idea what this meant and there was no further questions or discussion along this line, but I think the jury got the idea; damn that s.o.b. Thankfully the evidence and my testimony were clear cut and basically uncontested in those cases.

Over many years, I testified in more than 1,000 judicial hearings and court cases. They ranged from District Court examinations, to Circuit Court , Military Court, and Federal Court trials.

In June of this year the Association of Firearm and Tool Mark Examiners (AFTE) met in Miami, Florida for the 40th anniversary of the group. Although I am retired and hadn't attended for several years I went because I received a special invitation and because I was staying in New Smyrna Beach, Fl. at the time. I received a special invitation as the 2nd President of the Association in 70-71. This group is important to mention because it develops and distributes more information on firearms and tool mark identification than any other source in the world. It has committees and working groups doing research in the field continually. Without this group, analysts in this discipline would be lost in this day and age. But like all groups its beginning was small, simple, and without much funding. Although, in the beginning it had some support from the firearms and ammunition industry and from some police agencies as well as the original participants.

For a number of years its original members had nearly all belonged to the American Academy of Forensic Sciences, the premier group in American forensic science. These members felt a little bit out in the cold as part of the Criminalistics Section of the Academy in that they were limited in discussion time and publication in the Academy Journal by virtue of their small presence in the huge Criminalistics Section, which embraced the majority of Crime Laboratory disciplines. So, each year at the Academy meeting, usually held in Chicago at the illustrious Drake Hotel, we gathered in a suite of rooms each evening for our own informal discussions and bull sessions. This was also necessitated by the fact some of us couldn't afford to stay at the Drake. Our Departmental allowance wouldn't begin to cover the hotel and dinner fees. I recall staying at the YMCA, some walking distance from the Drake. If you weren't awake when you hit the YMCA sidewalk, you certainly were within minutes. These meetings were always held in February and I ask if you ever walked the streets of Chicago, near the lakefront, in February? It was not fun, that's for sure.

The evening sessions in the hotel rooms were wonderful. Fun and information galore and some of the greats in the firearms and ammunition business were there to question in person about certain firearms and cartridges, etc. In addition there were representatives of several police agencies, and especially the Chicago Crime Laboratory. After all, this was in their backyard and they represented many of the older analysts who had been there from the beginning. And then there was Walter J. Howe, gunsmith and arms developer, editor of the technical sections of the American Rifleman, author and consultant on firearms matters. He was at once full of recent information, new ideas and a host extraordinaire. He was very intelligent and full of fun at the same time. In my entire lifetime, I never met another man who could cut to the heart of a matter as quickly and thoroughly. We knew the drinks and hors d'oeuvres in plentiful supply weren't furnished by the poor crime laboratory analysts present at these meetings, but by Walter and some of his industry friends like Burt Munhall of Federal Cartridge Corp., formerly with Munhall and H.P. White ballistic laboratories. During these meetings I was introduced to many of the top executives of the greatest firearm and ammunition companies of the world, along with some of the top authors of the world in the area of sporting arms and hunting, etc. What a thrill and what information one could learn just by staying sober and keeping your ears unplugged. Those were the days my friend and I wished they would never end. The analysts of today would have loved those sessions, although the annual meetings of AFTE are pretty great themselves in this new era.

Some of my friends say I'm long winded and the foregoing may be just a sample. But from that, picture 35 of these analysts and several of our sponsors together in a small conference room in the Chicago Police Headquarters in February of 1969. With Walter Howe, Burt Munhall and John Stauffer of the Department staff leading the way, AFTE was born. Although we had an argument whether Tool Mark in our association name could be used as one word Toolmark or two Tool Mark, we decided to use two words although our acronym should be AFTE not AFTME. I believe that was a wise decision, don't you.

Walter sent us back home with errands to run; develop a constitution, ethics laws, by-laws, etc. with the command that we meet next February in Chicago as a full fledged Association. In the meantime he had developed an AFTE Newsletter and agreed to publish it on his own.

I had become a member of the American Academy of Forensic Science in 1960 and was made a fellow of the Academy in 62. Now I was one of the 35 original participants who formed the Association of Firearm and Tool Mark Examiners in 1969, and I was justly proud. But, that wasn't to be the end of it.

At the meeting in 1970, all the required information had been assembled and Howe turned at the conference table and said to Munhall "Burt the next order of business is the officers for next year. We need a young man who has made no enemies in the forensic world and who represents an agency with a fine reputation to get things going." Burt glanced over at me and said "that's right, and Charlie he means you; your our next President." I stammered and stuttered as I protested saying that I had never done anything like that. But they agreed they would back me and that was that.

As soon as I returned to East Lansing, I went to a friend in the Department's Printing and Mailing Division and told him about my predicament; all these responsibilities and no money to work with. He said "tell me what you need Charlie." I prepared a list and gave him the information on AFTE. Within days I had application blanks, stationery with the AFTE logo, fancy certificates for members, etc. He even had a girl on his staff who did beautiful calligraphy and who agreed to do the new members names without charge.

By year's end, I believe we had about 70+ members and getting inquiries weekly. I then contacted the President and Meeting Chmn. of AAFS, found out they were meeting in Feb. 1971 in Phoenix and inquired if there was any chance we could meet with them at their expense! Bob Joling an attorney from Illinois contacted me and advised they would include our meeting info in their advertising and would pay for the meeting room and equipment, but we would have to stand the cost of our own banquet dinner. The only caveat was that we agree to let any AAFS members who desire in to catch our technical papers. No problem, I assured Bob, we're all in the same business. Next I contacted one of our new members, Joe Collier of the Phoenix Police Department and told him about the arrangements. Joe said let me work on the banquet. He called me back in a few days to advise me he made arrangements with the hotel for the same banquet as the Academy but at half the price. Next I contacted Dewayne Wolfer, head of the Los Angeles Crime Laboratory and he promised to get an interesting program together for us, and he did. The meeting was a great success. As each of our formal papers was presented the crowd grew bigger and the walls had to be moved to make more room. Later Bob Joling told me many AAFS members said the AFTE meeting was more interesting. Wow, we were really on our way.

The tourmaline murder case: Prior to the meeting I received a letter and clipping from Marshall Houts, who had been a professor of Criminal Law at Michigan State University. He was a well known lawyer and member of The Court of Last Resort. The note inquired "How's this for a leap into the Buck Rogers era." He also included a clipping from the Los Angeles paper with an extensive article about an unusual evidence claim. The gist of the article was that the testimony in a murder case by Dewayne Wolfer was far-fetched. As the current President of AFTE I was expected to investigate and bring ethics charges against Wolfer, if they were warranted.

The case involved the murder of a rich Los Angeles widow. On a trip to England with her new beau she had disappeared and her body never recovered. At one point in the investigation her bloody clothing had been found and she was presumed dead. The focus of the investigation was her so-called boy friend, a known scam artist who had apparently received a large sum of money from her. The investigators could not directly connect him with the murder, but they uncovered another man believed to be an accomplice and hired killer.

During the investigation the police were able to convince the accomplice that they had the goods on him and there was no sense in him going to the gas chamber when he could assist his case by giving up the real "killer." He told them a lengthy and almost unbelievable tale. However, there was little that could be confirmed. They asked him if there wasn't some fact that might be confirmed. He then told them about the victim's huge emerald ring. He knew it was a big mistake, one professional killers shunned, to take any valuables from the victim. If it were discovered and traced it could lead to their arrest. But the victim had a huge emerald ring on her finger he just couldn't resist. He felt it had to be priceless and could make him rich. So before he disposed of her body, he removed the ring and brought it back to the United States. What he didn't know was that the ring was actually an emerald cut Tourmaline stone. It was still valuable but not nearly so as a real emerald.

After some contemplation, he reluctantly decided he dare not take the risk of trying to sell or fence the ring. He decided to break it up and sell the pieces. There would be not nearly as much money in it for him but the stone wouldn't be traceable. He knew jewelers kept precise measurements and photos of such valuable gem stones. He got rid of the band, took the gem into the garage and laid it on a soft cloth on top of his large vise. He looked for the heavy duty hammer but couldn't find it so he selected a large adjustable wrench. He then struck the gemstone a fierce blow hoping that it would crack into several pieces and little would be lost. But the heavy duty wrench merely bounced off as the gemstone bounced around still intact and not even damaged. Now he was frightened as he took the gem and threw it in a deep body of water where it could never be found. What he didn't know was the "emerald" was actually a Tourmaline, which has a hardness rating approaching diamonds. As the detectives frowned in disbelief he told them, there is one thing you could check to help you believe my story. He went on to tell them the gem had left a deep "scratch" in the head of the wrench, and he still had the wrench. The killer took them to his garage and produced a wrench with a visible scratch or scar on the head. This was taken to Wolfer, head of the Los Angeles Crime Laboratory.

Dewayne examined the wrench with the stereomicroscope and found the scratch to be a somewhat deep impressed marking in the steel surface. He then took the object to Cal Tech which had a top-level Scanning Electron Microscope in their laboratory. A section of the wrench with the impression was removed to facilitate the examination. It turned out to be as he thought – the impression revealed a shiny smooth surface with no visible striations one would usually see or even imperfections from the instrument or "tool" used. But it did display an incised line along the bottom of the impression, and angled surfaces in the ends of the impression with angled facets such as would be found on a large polished gemstone. Photographs were taken and measurements made which were confirmed by the jeweler as matching those of the Tourmaline ring he had made for the victim! So Wolfer's testimony in the murder trial was no "junk science" or leap into a Buck Rogers scenario but entirely factual. It was one of, if not the earliest use of the SEM (scanning electron microscope) to compare "tool marks."

At the 1971 meeting of AFTE in Phoenix, he told me all about the case and showed me the SEM photographs of the impression. I was dutifully impressed. One has to know that Wolfer had been under attack by politicians and attorneys in California for a variety of reasons. He was the expert who analyzed and compared the ballistics evidence in the assassination of Robert Kennedy. Most know about the terrible murder, but most don't know about the group, including several so-called "experts," who alleged there was a second gun and evidence had been covered up by Wolfer and the investigators. The allegations were disproved by a select panel of experts, empowered by the U. S. Government to re-examine the evidence.

4

CSI – Then and Now

Today Crime Scene Investigation is often conducted by a special unit of the larger police agencies although they are closely connected with the Crime Laboratory for obvious reasons. It is essential and obvious that the Laboratory cannot work effectively without the physical evidence to analyze. Should small agencies be involved in major crime cases, it is extremely helpful if they have at least one individual on staff trained in crime scene investigation. Not only will a wider variety of trace materials be brought to the laboratory, but it will be preserved, packaged, identified and submitted properly.

In my experience the primary reason for a botched criminal investigation was either failure to preserve the scene and/or failure to process and protect the evidence properly. Sad to say after all these learning years, but there are still Police Departments who will jeopardize their case rather than call for Crime Scene Investigators or Crime Laboratory Analysts from the usually well equipped and well staffed State Laboratories or the Federal Bureau of Investigation.

In Michigan we tried to combat the problem with training classes for local criminal investigators. We hoped they would improve in evidence handling and call if there was something about the case that raised a red flag. It worked to a degree but not as well as we had hoped for.

This basic proposition has always been true. Even in "the good old days" this was evident. In my experience this constituted an ever lasting training problem for the Crime Laboratories and their staff. It seemed that as soon as one experienced layer of investigators were promoted, retired, or were placed in other jobs, the next group were usually woefully lacking in understanding evidence problems, especially as applied to trace materials. Trying to keep ahead of the need took an awful lot of time away from the laboratory specialists. It eventually became clear that some of the larger departments were depending on us to do the basic training for them.

With the advent of more specialized crime scene units, including their training in the proper search, recoding and handling of evidence this problem is undoubtedly improved. Although I have been retired from the Crime Laboratories per se for twenty years, it is obvious that we still have problems, especially in the smaller agencies. The news media and TV have made more persons conscious of scientific criminal investigation. It sometimes looks like the general public now expect, even in the less populated areas, to see groups of special investigators arrayed in smocks, booties, latex gloves, etc. parading through a major crime scene. However, it really doesn't happen that often and there are still many major cases that go unsolved or not prosecuted due to screw-ups with physical evidence. Besides I have a pet peeve about some of the well equipped and trained CSI crews of today.

In "the good old days" we tried to be as careful as humanly possible at a major crime scene to not handle or even touch in the wrong way an item of physical evidence. Many years ago, we did not wear protective attire, although we did have work uniforms to protect us in dirty or bloody jobs.

For example, latex gloves were brought about primarily to protect CSI and Crime Laboratory workers from Hepatitis-B and/or Aids. But, they also protect the worker from depositing his/her own fingerprints at the scene. I have seen searchers handle evidence that should be completely protected for partial latent fingerprints. One might get the idea that latex gloves don't smudge prints. It seemed as if they may be more concerned with not leaving their own prints than finding new ones. The same thing might be said for bootees. Are they there to protect the searchers shoes or to prevent them from disturbing the blood, soil, shoe print patterns on the linoleum, or possibly deposit their own shoeprint somewhere. Perhaps it might be better to be more careful in handling evidence or walking through scenes rather than smudge and destroy fragile prints. The memory of one horrible crime scene is forever etched into my mind; a photograph of the police officer holding a bloody hammer in a handkerchief wrapped around his hand. The hammer had been used to bludgeon a child to death!

Even recently in my area of the country, the physical evidence gathered for trial was botched so badly that the trial of the murderer ended with a hung jury and the killer is walking the streets unless or until "new" evidence is discovered.

Another quick example of the frustration about the proper use of evidence: A detective walked into the Laboratory one day with a small vial containing a fired full metal jacketed bullet. It was removed from the chest of a jeweler who had been robbed and shot. He asked to talk to the firearms examiner and leave the item with him. When I noticed the date on the evidence vial I asked him why he had waited nearly a month to bring the bullet. He told me they thought this was a local job and were hoping to seize a .32 automatic pistol to have compared with the .32 automatic bullet taken from the victim.

A couple of hours later I examined the bullet in detail and you have to be quite knowledgeable about firearms to fully understand what I am about to say – just take my word for it. The bullet was actually a .30 Luger bullet, which closely resembles the .32 auto. caliber bullet. Furthermore the rifling characteristics were very unusual and distorted and I knew why. The .30 Luger cartridge is classed as a bottle-neck cartridge. The outer case dimensions are that of the 9mm Luger caliber. The rifling distortion on the evidence bullet indicated this bullet was fired from a 9mm Luger pistol! This little fact was well known to firearms aficionados but not to most police officers. In other words, their large teams of detectives had been looking for the wrong caliber and type of firearm for about a month. What do they say about a "cold track?"

I could go on at length in this regard but rather I will mention a few cases where crime scene examinations produced some unusual but vital evidence. The first involved the kidnapping and brutal murder of a State Police Trooper.

The trooper and the shovel case: One of our Troopers working a single-man unit on day patrol received a message from his Post sending him to a small factory in the area reporting a breaking and entering the night before.

He responded to the call and talked to the owner and made a list of missing items. As a matter of course he asked the shop owner if he knew of any possible suspects. The man replied he had no suspects but there had been a stranger in the shop several days before who walked in unannounced and seemed to be looking things over. When approached the stranger advised he was just looking for work and was told there were no jobs available at this time. The man's actions were so strange that the owner jotted down his license number from an older model Cadillac he was driving. The owner however told the Trooper that he had destroyed the sheet from his desk notepad. The officer felt there probably wasn't anything to it, but just in case he picked up the notepad and used the old school trick, gently rubbing pencil carbon over the indented scrawl on the remaining pad. And by gosh, it worked and restored the entire license plate number.

As soon as he hit the road, the Officer radioed the number to the desk Cpl. who responded quickly with the name and address of the owner. Since it was only a short distance away he decided to check it out. He stopped in the little village and inquired for directions at a service station. The attendant advised the car belonged to an old harmless couple, well known in the area. The Trooper decided to check with them just in case someone else used their car or had taken it. Then too the shop owner may have gotten the number wrong or perhaps it was not involved in any way. He parked in front of the home and rang the front door bell. As the door opened, he was surprised to see a man in his 40s standing there with a pistol pointed at his chest. Only one other person saw him alive after that. A young girl noticed the State Police patrol car driving out of town with the Trooper at the wheel and a man sitting in the rear seat behind the Officer. When searching officers heard this description, they knew the Trooper was in real danger as the patrol units in those days did not have a protective grille or windshield behind the front seat. The last place you would place anyone in a Patrol car was in the back seat behind the driver.

The Post Corporal tried to contact the patrol unit several times by radio but received no answer. It was as if he disappeared not to be seen again. A search was started and units backtracked the missing Trooper but without success. A check of the address he was to contact revealed no one at home and neighbors advised the old couple were out of town. Eventually, investigators learned the couple had a cabin in Northern Michigan and obtained the address.

Troopers located the cabin and found the missing Cadillac in the drive. They silently crept up to the dwelling and slid inside, finding Alvin Knight sleeping with a revolver on the night stand next to him. He was piled on, handcuffed, and arrested. The officers were not surprised to find the .38 Special caliber firearm was marked with the Department logo and was issued to the missing Trooper. This happened in July during an extreme hot spell for Michigan. But where was our missing Trooper? The arrested subject would not tell the arresting officers anything and he maintained a stoic silence for days on end. A search of the car disclosed a short handle shovel with fresh dirt on the blade, a possibly ominous sign. A search of the cabin closet disclosed a gabardine shirt with several specks of dried blood on the cuff area and with a large number of weed seeds or stick tights.

Hoping against hope that our missing officer might have been tied to a tree or something like that, a huge search was instituted in the area where he was last seen. Due to the weather, we knew time was of the essence or even if still alive he might perish. Every spare officer was involved in the search as well as Boy Scouts, Conservation Officers, Park Rangers, etc. Two State Police aircraft were also involved in the search.

This was centered in an area of huge woodlots and swamps, old abandoned farms, etc., although in the southern part of the State the area was known as the most rugged terrain about. Finally one of our planes spotted the nearly hidden patrol car, mired down in an old bean field surrounded by brush and trees. As officers approached the patrol unit, the glint of shiny metal attracted one of the officers to a small creek crossing the area. There were two fired .38 Special caliber cartridge cases; later confirmed as fired in the missing Trooper's revolver. Another ominous sign, but we still have no missing officer.

Recall the stick tight weed seeds on the culprit's shirt. What role could they play in this search effort? In this case, keying them in Gray's manual shows these particular weed seeds are a relatively uncommon species in this area, although the genus is very common, so we watch and measure each batch of stick tights picked up on our fatigues as we search through the various swales and swamps hoping they might lead us to our Trooper. Interestingly, when we did recover the officer's remains, the swale involved yielded the only other stick tights of this species. So the theory was correct at least.

The only problem was that the search was concentrated out from the area of the abandoned patrol car. But our criminal, an ex-convict with a long record outsmarted us by partially burying and covering the body with brush some miles from where he later abandoned the car.

The most interesting crime scene evidence in this case though was the site near the body where Knight had buried the Trooper's uniform in the hope that the body would be unidentifiable when finally discovered and there would be no uniform to give up the secret. The digging was done in relatively damp fine grained clay soil. One of the crime scene team members, Dr. Kivela, spotted a clump that had apparently fallen from the shovel blade, remained intact and dried leaving some very distinctive tool marks from the shovel. A bucket of similar soil was removed from the site to compare with soil on the shovel from the Cadillac trunk and to use as test medium for tool markings made by the shovel. This produced an astounding "match"; the first known of this kind and used in a paper presented to the American Academy in 1961.

The pathologist in this case was Dr. Richard Olsen from Pontiac, Michigan. He was one of the best, if not the very best, forensic pathologist I have ever worked with. One of his favorite responses came as he was always asked by Detectives ", Doctor, can you tell us when the victim died?" His standard reply was to ask them when the victim was last seen alive and when the victim was known to be dead and he would then say "It was somewhere in between!" He would then explain he might be able to give them some idea after tests were completed, but that this process was complicated and precise answers are usually fraught with danger. Over the years I worked with several top experts in this field, including Dr. Dan Glaser of Kalamazoo who always had a corn cob pipe clenched between his teeth, Dr. Robert Hendrix of the U. of Michigan, and Dr. Thomas Hegert of Orlando, Florida.

Again, in this same case of the murdered Trooper, Dr. Olsen felt there could be a relatively large section of the fatal bullet to be found as it had deflected off his spine. He asked the radiologist to x-ray the area. After that staff member reviewed the x-rays he told Olsen there is no bullet fragment of any consequence there. Shortly after Olsen said "what do we have here," and extracted a large bullet section with some rifling marks on the side. He asked the radiologist to explain and he, looking again at the x-rays, said "if you look here Dr. Olsen, there is evidently some gas in the tissue at the site hiding that bullet." As he stomped off, visibly upset, Olsen looked at the crime scene crew and remarked "Gentlemen, isn't it nice to know that experts are human too?"

Crime scene investigators must not only be aware of the usual trace evidence but continually be on the lookout for the unusual. Despite the continual clamor over DNA, which is obviously of extreme importance, many major cases have been made with physical evidence long before DNA was available. And for that matter, are still being made today.

For a change of pace, I would like to mention Charlie Marzetti, who by the way was the only person to get through the square mile blockade around the above mentioned crime scene. The State Police had established an operations center on an old farm, nearly centered in the area. The Commissioner had ordered Troopers to insure no one and especially news reporters got into the crime scene area until after the crew completed its work. We had just left the crime scene and were gathered by a well with a pitcher pump and some nice cool water on this hot July day. I suddenly heard a loud pitched familiar voice cry out "Hey, is my buddy Charlie here?" I ducked around the porch corner and hid as the Chief of Detectives yelled out "Who in hell let that idiot in here – get him out of here!" So, let me tell you a little bit about my friend Charlie.

Chasing Tail Lights to Forensic Ballistics

About six years before the above incident I was alone on day patrol and stopped in a small diner for a hamburger and coffee. The place was nearly full of patrons but that changed suddenly. A slightly stooped young man, swarthy in complexion, with one arm apparently partially disabled, and dressed in soiled and greasy appearing overalls and an unshaven face approached me at the counter. As he did, a number of customers disappeared. I had the feeling they knew this guy but I didn't. He stuck out his hand to shake mine saying "My name's Charlie, what's yours?" I said "Mine is Charlie too." He then said "You're a State cop aren't you?" Of course I was in full uniform, so I didn't respond and he walked away.

The following day he walked into the State Police Post and said to the desk officer "Where is my buddy Charlie?" Thus began a weird friendship that lasted until I retired from the State Police.

Within a few weeks, he had learned the name of every Trooper at our Post; don't ask me how, no one ever learned all of Charlie's tricks. He bothered others at times, but I remained his favorite target. He got to be a complete pest. He even snuck in the Post late one night and scared the desk Corporal half to death. We decided we had to discourage him. At a Post meeting one day we heard him coming and put Moose on him. Moose was 6'5" and about 290 lbs. and as Charlie entered the reception area Moose grabbed him, spun him around, got hold of his pants and shirt, picked him up and threw him bodily over the railing onto the grass, and slammed the door shut. As he did Charlie got up and said "you better get the back door Moose, I'm coming around." We finally gave up trying to discourage him. A couple of us talked to him and got him to agree not to bother the desk officers unless it was important.

You might wonder how did this guy get around; well he drove an old model car his wealthy farmer parents had purchased for him and he had a driver's license (we checked). The bet around the Post was that his parents bribed someone in the license office. After a while Charlie got to be a legend among the Troops. You might run into him anywhere.

One night another Trooper and I were responding to a fatal car accident on M-53, our main highway north of the post. It was a terrible night, high winds and gusting cold rain with very poor visibility.

As we neared the scene I could see a faint light being waved, apparently as a warning of the upcoming crash site. As we rolled to a stop I rolled the driver window down to check out the traffic manager. It was Charlie with a little two cell flashlight. He looked in at me and said "Charlie, where in hell have you been? I've been waiting 15 minutes for you to get here!"

At about this time, a young girl had been abducted and killed in Detroit. It had been all over the news along with a sketch of the suspect done from a witness description. I know that for about a month Charlie went into the city to a point near the abduction site, carrying a copy of the sketch. He told me he was going to catch that mean man that did this. He didn't find him but you have to give him A for effort.

Charlie was obviously retarded, but he sure wasn't stupid. Over the years we all developed a fondness for him. You might say that he became the mascot for the Troopers from Center Line. The sad part was that his family was known to be wealthy and apparently didn't do much to help care for him. After I retired from the State Police I didn't see him. I felt a sense of sadness when I heard from one of my old friends from Center Line the word locally was his family finally had him committed.

Most people wouldn't understand but persons like Charlie seem to migrate to police officers. The cops, believe it or not, usually have more patience with problem people and treat them better than the general public!

In fact that brings to mind another individual with a special attachment to the Troopers. When I trooped in Gaylord, there was a garage service man doing odd jobs around the station, gassed and checked the car oil, etc. He was on the order of Charlie and was socially shunned by most. The Troops liked him as he gave the Patrol cars special attention, always cleaned the windows, etc.

But more importantly, he noticed everything that went on in the area and on several occasions gave us information that led to the solution of a local burglary or theft. One morning when the desk Corporal went out in front of the Post to run the flag up the pole, he found our friend lying there. He had a pistol in his outstretched right hand and a note in the left. In effect, the note said that he was tired of life and killed himself there because he didn't want the Troops to have to search for him or wonder what happened. The Troopers were the only real friends he ever had!

I have often thought that my Gaylord friend and my buddy Charlie gave me some advance preparation when my Kathy was born several years later.

Thinking back about CSI, I was directly involved for 13 years. By then I had advanced in the Laboratory to the point where I ordered myself off the routine schedule and played an administrative and teaching function in this regard. Over time I had assisted in the investigation of almost every kind of major crime imaginable; arson & murder, family disputes and murder, lover quarrels and murder, greed and the murder of an entire family of six, bank and jewel robbery, kidnapping and rape and murder, etc. Much of the gory details have thankfully been forgotten.

What is more vivid in my memory are the details of physical evidence; either unusual or of major importance in the crime solution and/or trials of the accused.

The nurse and the nylon-66: In a moderate size city in southern Michigan a young couple prepared for the days work. The young husband finished a rush breakfast snack and drove off to the garage. His young pretty wife had just finished dressing in her starched white nurse's uniform when she heard a knock at the front door. She answered the door and found a strange young man there. He immediately told her that his mother was ill and knowing that a nurse lived in the small home he wanted her advice. She told him to come in, sit down and tell her about the problem. But, after a few stammering attempts at conversation he admitted why he really was there. He told her that he had admired her from afar for some time and had fantasized about her on numerous occasions! He doubted that her husband could fulfill her sexual needs but felt that he was able to do more than that.

As he talked, the nurse was at first shocked and then visibly angered. She called him a crazy teenager and told him to get the hell out of her home. This only enraged him as he grabbed a heavy glass ashtray from the table and struck a vicious blow to her forehead. She fell to the floor, stunned and nearly unconscious. As she stirred slightly and moaned, the teen age young man ran out and down the street where he parked the car. He opened the trunk, took a rifle out and ran back to the house. He placed one well aimed shot into her face and upwards into her brain, and fled.

When her body was discovered the neighborhood was greatly alarmed and the detectives were perplexed by a possible motive. The victim hadn't been raped, the house hadn't been robbed, but she had obviously been struck by the broken ashtray. Was this due to some violent argument? It was perplexing and the husband had no motive and an iron clad alibi. This is the type of crime that can be difficult to solve. The only physical evidence was a fired .22 caliber cartridge case from the kitchen floor, the smashed bullet from her brain and some smudged and relatively useless fingerprints on the broken ashtray remnants. The bullet and cartridge case were rushed to the Crime Laboratory to see if they could offer any help.

In the firearms identification unit, the case was put on a rush basis due to the nature of the crime and no apparent suspects. The unit determined quickly that this was a standard .22 Long Rifle lead round nose bullet with the golden coating indicative of Remington ammunition at that time. The fired cartridge case was in agreement and was marked with the well known Remington head stamp (U). The class rifling characteristics were similar to a number of firearms in this caliber. The type and dimensions of the firing pin impression narrowed the search even further. Then I noticed a series of dot like markings in a rectangular shape indicative of the ejector location. At this time the only firearm that matched all of the class characteristics was a very popular .22 Long Rifle caliber semi-automatic rifle called the Remington Nylon-66 model. This information was passed to the investigators immediately. After several weeks of investigation without any success and the lead detective conferring with the Crime Lab, a new focus was placed on the murder weapon.

The detective team was shown photographs of the Nylon-66 rifle and they renewed the investigation with instructions to go to every home in this area seeking such a weapon. They spread out like spokes on a wheel and went on this new mission. After several days they thought they struck pay dirt. One detective found a home with a teen aged son who possessed a Nylon-66 rifle. They rushed it to the laboratory with great expectations but were advised the firearm demonstrated the same class characteristics but different individual characteristics than the evidence bullet and cartridge case. So the search went on. About ten days later I received another hurried call from the lead State Police detective, a personal friend of mine, who advised they had another rifle, owned by a man some distance away who had a nineteen year old son. The man of the family had allowed them to take the rifle for testing without hesitation. Once again the rifle was rushed to the Laboratory.

This time it was different. The individual characteristics of the bullet and the fired cartridge case matched the firearm extremely well. The detective was advised there was no question about it, this was the murder weapon. When confronted, the young man confessed stating in effect he hadn't intended to harm the nurse, but when she made fun of him he lost his temper and hit her with the ashtray. Then he was afraid he would be found out and sent to jail. He had to shut her up, so he killed her! How many of us would have guessed this was the motive for this murder. Many times homicides follow twisted and confusing facts that make them difficult to solve.

The child and the garbage bag case: Another interesting case where heretofore unknown or unpublicized crime scene evidence played a major role in convicting the murderer was in the kidnapping of a young girl from a school bus stop. The crime scene crew was from a local police agency which had a couple of CSI types on their identification team along with one from the County Prosecutor's office. The little girl's ravaged and murdered body was located in a dumping ground. Her body and clothing were partly wrapped in a large black plastic trash bag, the kind commonly purchased at the grocery store.

Although the officers found little substantial physical evidence, they wondered if the garbage bag from the body could be connected to some new bags of a similar type found in a suspect's home. We couldn't answer that question directly but told them to bring the evidence to the laboratory. We would certainly try.

The officers delivered a disheveled and soiled garbage bag from the victim and a nice clean new appearing box with several new bags still neatly folded and apparently untouched taken from a suspect. Obviously most of the bags had been used or taken out of the box. It was decided that the follow up investigation would be handled by a member of the micro/trace evidence unit and I representing the tool mark unit.

The first order of business was to contact the Corporation who had manufactured the bags. Our contact call was immediately followed by a return call from the legal division of the company, who when advised of the nature of the crime promised full cooperation including escorting us through the plant and the personal use of their research facility, one of the most modern in the world. With the support and financial backing of the Florida Department of Law Enforcement we made reservations to go to the Company plant on the East Coast and obtained air fare. In the meantime, we compared the evidence and new bags for method of manufacture, size, marking types from the manufacturing process, exact thickness, etc. and made tests of questioned and known material using Infra-Red Spectrophotometry. We could not differentiate between the bags, but that was merely a start and certainly not definitive.

Next we flew to the plant location. On the way from the nearby major city we stopped at the Research facility where samples from both questioned and known bags were subjected to wave length dispersive x-ray fluorescence (XRF). Again we could not differentiate between the samples. Scientists at the research center claimed this was important in that the Company used both virgin and scrap plastic mixed together to manufacture the bags and they can usually differentiate different batches by certain trace elements.

Then it was on to the plant where we watched the entire process used in the manufacture of the bags. We learned of a number of tool mark traces in the bags due to the heat sealing process, stretching the bags over drums to seal and cut them apart, and most importantly markings made as the molten plastic is forced through a die by high pressure air jets to form the bags. As the molten plastic material is literally blown through the die, it forms a huge balloon rising to near the plant ceiling, several stories in height. The balloon shape is maintained by huge air rings as the material rises from the die area. By the time it reaches its zenith it is cooled sufficiently to be collapsed, cut, heat sealed, folded and placed in boxes as the material descends.

We then learned that the plastic is not completely melted or uniform as it passes through the die, thereby leaving long vertical fine trails and some darker blobs of material in the plastic film of about .003" thickness. This can be seen by using transmitted light through the material, possibly on a light table or even at the window during daylight hours. These lines resemble striated tool markings and can be traced from one bag to the next coming off the same line. To the best of our knowledge this was the first reported examination of this type in this country. A literature search revealed several in England and Europe although they were limited in their information and testing.

The Micro analyst testified in the trial of the accused and it is claimed that the bag information significantly aided the case. Nearly thirty years later it was reported that trash bag analysis was instrumental in another murder trial and that the tests were conducted by the Orlando micro/trace analysis unit of the Florida Dept. of Law Enforcement!

The original case once again showed how important "unusual" evidence items from the crime scene can be if only the CSI personnel use their imagination. To paraphrase the old saying "if it takes the kitchen sink, so be it!"

One more example may be in order – this time to emphasize the importance of protecting fragile evidence; even that which might not seem fragile. One of the suburban Detroit area police departments employed a young man, well acquainted with the Michigan State Police Crime Laboratory. He was educated with a BS degree from Michigan State University. In addition, he had undergone some training in scientific criminal investigation and CSI. For the laboratory, he was a pleasure to work with. His evidence was always properly cared for, properly packaged, marked for identification, and posed no court problems.

The synagogue murder case: He came to the laboratory one day with one piece of evidence. It was a sheet of blank writing paper. The paper was lying flat on a bed of cotton, inside a box of slightly larger dimensions. Glancing at the sheet revealed nothing remarkable. He then explained the problem. Weeks before, the local synagogue was burglarized. The vault was broken and entered. The night watchman surprised the burglars and one of them crushed his skull with a crowbar. These were apparently professionals who wore gloves and left little if any evidence. Where they rifled through recesses in the vault they had thrown papers on the floor. On a sheet of new paper one had left a faint imprint of the heel of his shoe. This print in dust was barely visible in good light.

Further, another suburban police department had just caught a couple of burglars in action. They had broken into a vault and the method of operation was identical to that of the Synagogue. One of the arrested burglars had shoes with a heel like the pattern on the paper from the Synagogue vault. These shoes were submitted for comparison. Now our CSI friend asked "do you think you can do anything with this?" I broke one of my cardinal rules about not presupposing about evidence claims when I said "I doubt it, but I'll try."

Since the evidence heel print was composed of dust on paper, it was obvious that any amount of handling, any touching of the print, even changes in light or humidity might possibly alter it. The first object then was to record it. Several changes in lighting on the surface did not improve the evidence and in some cases made the markings more difficult to observe. Ultra violet and infra red were no help. But then I tried an old document examiner's trick and placed the box and paper content in front of a window allowing indirect North light illumination and the print appeared to be more visible. A number of photographs later I was satisfied with the results. You must remember, I'm talking about a case that happened about 50 years ago. In the modern world this project would undoubtedly be much simpler.

As time progressed and the evidence imprint was compared with test prints from the suspected heel it became more and more evident that faint as they may be there were numerous defects in the heel from wear and damage that compared favorably. Eventually I had to call the CSI whiz and tell him that I had been wrong and had to admit the dust imprint was made by the heel of the suspect's shoes.

The resulting murder trial was a three ring circus with the defense attorney threatening to bring an expert from Northwestern University who would prove I should have used plaster of Paris. I always wondered what book he read, or on the other hand could he read? The interesting thing about the legal aspects of the examination and trial was that the defendant was allowed to talk to me and told me "You are right – my shoes were there, but l wasn't wearing them!" Ed, the burglar and killer by law, sent me a Christmas card every year until I retired. He even sent me a news article from the prison's newspaper showing him up on the book racks. He had just been promoted to head librarian and was quite proud of his progress in Jackson prison. I always felt Ed was trying to tell us that he wasn't the one who killed the night watchman without actually confessing and implicating the actual killer, who was never charged with this crime. Why? There was no physical evidence to prove he was there.

CSI work wasn't all gory and scary and it sure wasn't much like the TV programs of today. We carried firearms due to the fact that we were sworn police officers. It had little if anything to do with the case and the pursuit of evidence. In about 50 years of forensic activity, I believed I talked to the defendant for a minute or two in two cases. And in one of those it was in a jail cell with the Prosecutor and defense attorney present. If we had attempted to take an active role in the actual investigation, interrogation, or arrest of the defendant, a detective would have told us to get the hell out of the way and take care of your responsibility, i.e., search for physical evidence. Furthermore we didn't hit on our partner(s); Of course they were all male then and most of the crew weren't handsome or dashing like the TV heroes of today. Some cases were kind of fun in a bizarre sort of way; which makes me think of "Archie."

Archie the mummy: I distinctly remember it was early on a Sunday morning when I received a call from dispatch that the Sheriff of a small rural County had called for crime scene assistance with an apparent homicide. I called another member of our crew, Art Kivela, who happened to be the brother of Dr. Ed Kivela of the Dept. of Health. Although Art had a degree majoring in physical anthropology, he was a State Police Officer! I was glad that he was available in that the meager description I received indicated his knowledge might be valuable in this case. One other thing about Art, he had a wicked sense of humor. We drove for more than an hour to get to the area and were then led to a large farm and a huge barn close to the secondary road. The Deputy took us deep into the barn's recesses and behind a huge stack of baled hay he pointed out the victim. The farmer had discovered the man when he moved some hay for feed. As soon as Art spotted the victim, he hurriedly played his flashlight over the sitting erect corpse. "Oh my God, he's mummified," Art cried out.

Obviously the victim had been dead for a long time, probably over most of the winter. His skin was hardened and parched in appearance. There were no eyes and little if any flesh left on the face. But there was still the remnant of a reddish moustache and wisps of red hair on the scalp. He was poorly dressed, obviously not sufficient for Michigan's bitter cold. He was sitting in a slightly hunched position as if he had gone to sleep there. Art said "I don't believe we have a crime here. This is probably the remains of some poor soul who crawled in here to get out of the weather and died, possibly from exposure." When the preliminary examination was completed we decided we would attempt to remove the remains as carefully as possible and take them back to Michigan State University to an anthropologist friend of Art's. We borrowed a large box from the farmer, carefully picked up Archie, still in the sitting posture and placed him erect in the box. We then put the box on the rear seat of the plain State car.

Art had been a heavy cigarette smoker but was trying to break or at least reduce the nicotine habit. He had a long cigarette holder with a filter inside. It looked exactly like the ones often see in pictures of President Roosevelt. He placed the cigarette holder in the normal smoking position between the jaws of our victim and stood back to admire his handiwork. "That's great, I think he and I are going to be longtime friends before this is done, so I'm going to name him Archie." So, this became the Archie case. But the day wasn't over yet. It was dark by the time we left to return to Headquarters with Archie. Since we were tired and hungry, I put a heavy foot on the accelerator pedal and we proceeded home. About half way back I noticed the lights of a vehicle swing out of a side road and start to follow us. I checked the speedometer and we were doing about twenty miles over the limit. I told Art there's a cop following us and we're about to be stopped. At that moment the red light (bubble gum machine we called it) started to spin so I slowed pulled off the road and stopped. I rolled down the car window and waited for the Trooper to approach. It was a young officer from the Headquarters Post. As he got to me he shone his light on me and said "darn it, I thought I recognized that car. What are you doing out here on Sunday night? And who do you have in the back seat," as he turned his light that way. His scream could probably be heard a mile away and he actually threw his flashlight into the air! He finished with "what in hell are you characters from the Crime Lab up to now? Get the hell out of here." And he stomped back to his patrol unit. Of course we made sure the story got around Headquarters; I don't think he ever lived that one down.

The serial killer: Some crime scenes are scary though for one reason or another. One occurred while the crew was checking the earthen basement of an abandoned farm house where the body of a raped and murdered young woman had been discovered. One of the crew set up the camera on a tripod to get photographs of one shoeprint that showed some detail and was probably that of the murderer. As is the custom, he laid a ruler next to the impression so that exact size could be maintained for comparison purposes. Like all our accessories, the ruler was marked "Michigan State Police Crime Lab." At that moment, the crew leader advised "We have been working long enough and it's getting late. Besides we haven't had any dinner. I don't know about you guys but I'm starving. I say lets knockoff, get some food and a room and come back in the early AM. The Sheriff has promised to leave a Deputy here to guard the scene." Everyone agreed that was a great idea. They had been working for about sixteen hours straight and had enough. The photographer carefully removed the tripod and camera, floodlights, etc. and the gang went to dinner. As they drove the photographer spoke out "damn it all, I forgot my ruler, its still lying there in the dirt. Oh well, it will still be there when we get back."

The next morning, the ruler was gone. In its place was the ear ring from a previous victim of the serial murderer. Apparently he sneaked by the Deputy in the dark, and made the switch. This killer was known to return to the scene of the crime. It's the kind of thing that makes the CSI crew a little bit nervous.

The above incident was related to a number of strange happenings in the string of crimes and their investigation. From the crime scene standpoint, I would like to mention one other from this long term investigation. While the CSI crew was checking out the possible location of one murder, which turned out to be one of the keys in the solution and conviction of the killer, they discovered something unusual again. In searching the basement of the home possibly involved, they discovered several small flecks of blood which turned out to be consistent with the latest victim. However, this was before DNA and would not be definitive. But then they discovered something else; something not usually considered. On the basement floor were numerous clumps of short hair clippings which they carefully collected.

Interestingly, the owners' of the house had four young sons. The father and boys all had crew cuts, so mom clipped their hair to save money. The basement was used as her "barbershop" but she forgot to clean up the hair before they left on vacation. The murder happened while they were gone. How important was this discovery? In the series of murders, the brutal killer stuffed something up the victims' vaginas. In the most recent one, the forensic pathologist, at autopsy, removed her panties from this recess; saying "We may have finally gotten a break in this case. Her body was probably lying in a barbershop. Look at all these clumps of short clipped hair on the panties!" Walter Holz of the Health Department Lab. examined the hairs and testified accordingly. His testimony was crucial in the proofs at trial.

Meanwhile, the Crime Lab began its expansion into the first satellite laboratory at Plymouth and it wasn't easy. It was the Commissioner pushing for more laboratories while the staff was pushing for additional personnel and updated equipment at the Central Laboratory. We had about five meetings to discuss plans for additional laboratories and developed a five year plan. All administrative personnel seem to love five year plans for some reason. But at the last meeting the Commissioner said, "Boys the talking is over. We are going to start our first satellite laboratory in Plymouth and you are going to decide how we can staff it until I can come up with added funding for new personnel. I have obtained a good building, the former Detroit Edison office building for $1.00 and we pay the taxes. It's a great building and you can't beat the price. A friend of mine arranged it for us. I have already determined we shall have our opening in spring, on April 1st. "

As we left that meeting I said to Wally, well he certainly picked the right date, April fool's day. Of course I didn't say that within ear shot of the boss. It turned out to be a real struggle, but we made it. We determined that the U. S. Government still had quantities of laboratory equipment, especially items like lab benches, tables and fume hoods, etc. in salvage. This was part of the equipment used by the Chrysler Tank Arsenal and General Motors during the war years. All of it was stainless steel and with a little cleanup was very serviceable. And we were able to get it for nearly nothing as it would be used for the State. Slowly we turned the office building into a serviceable laboratory with the help of the State Police civilian carpenter and building staff. And the Commissioner kept his word and squeezed out an additional appropriation for personnel. He even came up with funds for Ken Christensen, who would lead the new laboratory and I to go to Pittsburgh and interview the graduates of their specialized forensic program and we hired a couple promising people from that group. The big coup at this time was that we were able to lure a young top-drawer Serologist from the Miami laboratory. I'm not sure they ever forgave us completely for that one.

Yes, we did open on April 1st, April Fools day or not. This really wasn't surprising as this Commissioner usually got his way. I recall some years later, after he had retired, being required to attend a meeting of the State Training Commission. At the meeting all the members were very upset and wringing their hands as they had just been notified about a large reduction in State training funds by the Legislature. Just then the former Commissioner, Fred Davids, happened to pass by the meeting room. He was in the same building for a different meeting with a group he was working with on retirement.

As he spotted a number of Police Chiefs and command officers from the State Police that he knew so well, he stopped by to say hello. He became aware of the sour mood of the group almost immediately and asked what was wrong. We advised him of the cuts in the vitally needed police training program for all the State. He got up from his chair and said, "Give me a few minutes before you get back to your deliberations," and left the room. He returned in about ten minutes and told the group "Don't sweat it I just had the cuts reinstated!" He was a very persuasive Commissioner.

During the sixties, I was active in the planning and establishment of four additional laboratories under the State Police banner. Several members of the early CSI (Crime Scene Investigation) and CLA (Crime Laboratory Analysis) crew were directly involved in these operations and some ended their Michigan careers as Commanders of the respective laboratories; Ken Christensen at Plymouth and Northville, and later as my successor in charge of the Laboratory system, Paul Brabant one of the great latent fingerprint examiners at Warren, Herb Olney at Holland, Tom Nasser at Bridgeport, and later Laboratories were established at Grayling and Marquette. I had been promoted and placed in charge of the Headquarters Laboratory, but I still remained as head of the firearms and tool mark unit. In the good old days we didn't promote people and then take away their expertise which takes years to obtain; a little different than today. We always felt it didn't make sense to spend years and lots of money equipping a person to be an expert in his discipline and throwing it away to shuffle papers. I recall one of our commanders was almost always late with administrative reports but during the same period helping crack several big cases with his CSI/CLA expertise!

At about this time I was subpoenaed to testify in Eagle River, Michigan, the furthest city North in the State's Upper Peninsula. It was a bit of a thrill for me. The older laboratory officers kept a colored map on their desks with county seats marked in color where they had testified. I had the most but no one had ever testified in Keewenaw County. In fact this was to be the first murder trial in this part of God's country. It was a perfect time to take a little vacation so I got permission to do that and took the family in my personal car on the extremely long but beautiful trip into the northwestern UP. There was a pretty motel just outside the village with picnic tables on the sandy beach. It was a wonderful spot for the family and a beautiful day the next morning as I drove in to the courthouse.

As I returned late in the afternoon, having completed my testimony, I found the family in a festive mood and celebrating with another family at the motel. As I walked to the picnic tables they were all pointing at me and laughing out loud. I glanced at my suit trousers to make sure my fly was zippered, wondering what in hell is so funny? Nancy took charge at the moment as she explained the joke. After I left for court, the other family, including several children the ages of ours, was having breakfast at a picnic table. My kids asked Nancy if they could go out and play. She told them its okay, but don't you bother that other family having their breakfast. She looked out the window and they were all at the table eating. Nan was furious as she went out to round them up. But Mrs. Wielebenicki from Chicago said, "Please don't be angry, we couldn't help but spoil these lovely children when we heard the horrible story about their father!" Nan asked "what horrible story?" The lady said, "Please, the kids told us their dad was in court for murder." Nancy told me they couldn't stop laughing when she told them the father was a Lt. in the Michigan State Police and was in court to testify against a murderer.

I believe it was Mark Twain who said, "The difference between the right word and the wrong word is like the difference between lightning and the lightning bug."

The best thing about this event is that John and Jan Wielebenicki from the Eagle River meeting became very dear friends over most of our life. We visited them in Chicago and they visited us several times in Michigan. Even more important, they had a daughter who was mentally and physically crippled. This allowed Kathy and their daughter to send greetings and little gifts to each other for years.

We had one last thrill before we left Eagle River. The kids bugged me about going swimming. I tried to tell them you don't go swimming in Lake Superior in early June. In fact, it's tough nearly all year due to the bitter cold water. I finally gave in and told them to get their swim suits on. We ran down the beach and charged into the water, diving in immediately. As one, we all came out instantly screaming out loud. It was the shortest swim in our memory.

5

My Most Mind Boggling Homicide

In over 50 years of assisting in the investigation of homicides, one case stands out above all others. It involved the murder of an entire innocent family, mother, father, and four children. It happened in June of 1968 and it is still in the open case files of the Michigan State Police. As you read this account, please put yourself in the mind frame of a juror and decide, if you can, whether this case should be solved and closed, and if not, why not?

The family murder case: It was a beautiful summer day in the northern part of the Lower Peninsula of Michigan. School was out and the area secluded cabins were occupied by parents and laughing children. The high end cabins were far apart to provide maximum privacy, but close to Lake Michigan to afford beautiful views and appreciation of the clean air blowing in off the Great Lake. But now there was a faint stench moving with the breeze and one family had noticed it before. Now it was getting worse. It seemed to be coming from the vicinity of the Gooden family's lodge. So the neighbors decided there must be a dead animal under that porch or at least nearby. They had heard the Goodens had apparently left on an extended trip about a month ago, so they called the property caretaker and asked him to check it out.

Chasing Tail Lights to Forensic Ballistics

Eino Maki and his helper, Charlie the Indian, had the responsibility to care for the grounds and to assist homeowners.

They responded to the call. As soon as they neared the Gooden cabin, they could smell a strong and very disagreeable odor. They checked around the property and under the porch but found nothing. As they did, it was apparent the smell was coming from inside. Eino tried the doors and found them locked. He then located a pry bar from a nearby tool shed and forced one door open. As he opened the door the powerful odor from inside sickened him and myriads of blow flies exited. From the open doorway he could see into the living room area and he could see what appeared to be a body. It was mostly covered with a blanket. He and Charlie fled the scene, went to a phone and called the Sheriff's Department.

The Chief Deputy responded, soon to be followed by another. The Sheriff of the County was out of town. They noticed two cars, the Gooden family vehicles, parked and locked next to the cabin. There was a note taped to a window explaining the family was going to take a long trip. Some time previously the man of the house, Richard Gooden, had informed several people that the family was going to Kentucky and Florida to possibly purchase a couple of horses. The father fancied himself as an expert on horseflesh and wanted to raise a specific kind. They were supposed to fly out as guests of an individual who owned and operated a Lear Jet. Richard Gooden was a pilot and owned a small Cessna so he had friends who flew, including one, a Mr. Roberts who had been described as the owner of a Lear Jet. Now, however, it was time to invade the cabin and see what was going on. The deputies found a total of six bodies, the inside air a type of horrible smelling blue-gray haze and blow flies in great quantity. The Under-sheriff called the office and advised the dispatcher to call the Coroner to the scene and to call the State Police Crime Laboratory to request assistance.

Analysts from the Dept. of Health and State Police Laboratories, six in all, responded to the call. They reflected various disciplines as well as experienced CSI personnel. Upon arrival, the Under-sheriff briefed them on what he had found and told them the deputies had protected the scene and nothing had been disturbed. The crew donned their coverall fatigues and went to work. One member was designated to photograph every detail from the outside inward and another designated to take thorough notes on every detail.

The outside lights were still on and the two cars in the driveway entrance were locked and apparently untouched. The area near the cars showed the evidence of several rains and any possible tire or shoe prints had been washed away. The lodge was 1 ½ stories with a stone foundation and log siding. There were two entranceways at opposite ends of the living/dining area. The rear door window consisted of a number of small panes. One pane was mostly obscured by a paper napkin note with an inked message on it "Be back by 7-10, Gooden." Above the napkin was a paper note saying "We were here, the Stoegers." As the notes were carefully removed, guarding them for possible fingerprints, the investigators were surprised to find four small holes indicative of small caliber gunshots through the glass A search of the grounds nearby revealed four fired .22 caliber rim-fire cartridge cases of Remington manufacture, lying near each other and in a nearly straight row along side the building.

Upon entrance to the lodge, the CSI crew made note of the layout. On the ground floor, there was the dining/living room, a huge stone fireplace, a kitchen, bathroom, and two large bedrooms. There was a central hall providing access to the bath and bedrooms. The lodge was heated by a floor furnace, with the register in the middle of the hall. A stairway in one corner of the living room led to the upstairs bedroom.

On one couch there were three coats, a man's, a woman's, and a small child's. Next to the couch and near the rear door were three small camera cases. It appeared as if the occupants had prepared to leave. On the wooden table playing cards were arrayed as if solitaire was being played by two individuals.

A woman's body, apparently that of Mrs. Gooden, lay face down on the living room floor. Her body was mostly covered with a blanket. Her clothing was in disarray and part of the under clothes were actually cut. It looked as if she may have been raped or someone wanted it to look that way. It would be literally impossible to determine. All of the bodies were extremely decomposed. As it turned out, they had been dead for approximately a month.

The second body, Richard Gooden, husband and father, was lying face down on the hot air register in the center of the hall. The youngest son, Mark Gooden, age 12, was lying facedown on top of his father A small throw rug covered much of his body. Later, during the follow-up investigation, detectives wondered whether the covers over the mother and young son might be psychologically related to the killer. I often thought that might be the case.

Sarah, the young daughter, was lying face up in the hallway, next to her brother Mark. Robert, age 19, the oldest son, was face down, lying over the door threshold of the master bedroom with his legs into the hallway. The sixth victim, Greg, age 16, was lying on his back inside the master bedroom. It was apparent some of the body's had been moved from their original resting place and there were bloody trails to demonstrate this movement. Adjacent bloody shoeprints, long dried into the floor surface, raised hope that the murderer(s) might be caught from shoe impressions. The entire section of the floor was eventually removed and returned to the Crime Laboratory. Interestingly, only one set of shoeprints were found.

Investigators felt the bodies had been moved so that anyone peeking through curtain windows, etc. would not be able to see anything amiss. They of course checked this theory by trying to view the interior from the outside.

It was theorized that the older boys were playing solitaire when the attack occurred. The location of their bodies indicated they may have attempted to flee to the master bedroom closet which contained the family .22 caliber target rifle so they could defend the family.

The single set of bloody shoeprints indicated only one person might be involved. However, during the investigation some authorities could not believe that only one person could cause such deaths. Although it's hard to believe, history records many multiple killings where a number of victims were involved in one scene with one killer. There was Richard Specht in Chicago, Danny Rollings in Gainesville, Florida, and, the All American boy next door, Ted Bundy in Tallahassee, Florida; these are a few recent examples. It appears that surprise and sudden horrible fear plays a part in essentially paralyzing many victims of the mass killers.

Examination of the bodies at autopsy and of the premises revealed the older boys and the father had been shot multiple times while the mother and younger children had been shot once. In addition, the little girl had been bludgeoned in the head, possibly to finish her off. Remember that the Under-sheriff had advised the crime scene crew the lodge was protected and nothing disturbed. While in the area the CSI crew saw a local paper with headlines about the murders. The front page showed a photograph of the Under-sheriff standing in front of the lodge holding a bloody hammer in a handkerchief; shades of Dick Tracy, it's enough to make a grown man cry.

While it's in my mind, if I had a dollar for every crime scene with poor protection; oh well you know what I mean. The problem has provided a field day for defense attorneys far too many times.

The evidence showed two different firearms were involved in the shootings, one a .22 long rifle caliber semi-automatic rifle or pistol, the other a .25 automatic caliber semi-automatic pistol. This evidence was rushed to the laboratory where we determined the class characteristics of the firearms involved. From those we determined that the pistol was highly likely to be a .25 auto. caliber Beretta semi-automatic firearm. The .22 Long Rifle was more difficult as there were a number of possibilities in the beginning. Later it was determined that this firearm was likely the Armalite AR-7 survival weapon. This was a firearm originally made for the military but now popular among civilians. It was unique in that it easily broke-down in two separated sections and the barrel and receiver could be stored in the stock section and the whole thing even floated in the water!

Another oddity of this crime was the ammunition used with the Beretta pistol. They had no identifying headstamp as was the American custom and had a foreign primer system. We had no samples in our collection like it. A few calls were successful in locating information on this cartridge and samples from the FBI Crime Lab. It was .25 automatic (6.35mm) caliber SAKO very recently imported from Finland. As it turned out, all this information proved to be vital in this case and was immediately provided to the lead detectives from the Michigan State Police.

Detectives John Felton and Lloyd Summers were assigned to the case and stayed with it until the end; or was it the end? The first thing they attempted was to check the family, their friends, their business, their reputation in the community, etc. All local contacts and interviews in the vicinity of the crime scene had already been checked. There were various rumors floated about but nothing solid at all. They quickly learned that this was an upstanding upper middle class family with a home in a beautiful area of Southern Michigan. The mother and children were beyond reproach with envied reputation and scholastic achievement. If there was to be any link to the killer(s) it had to be through the father. Richard Gooden was a respected individual who owned an advertising agency which published a glossy and respected magazine with ads for various upscale businesses. He was a pilot and owned a small Cessna private aircraft. He was known by associates to be quite ambitious and yearned to become "bigger" in the business world. He was said to admire Howard Hughes and hoped someday to emulate him. Quickly the investigators found some things that greatly puzzled them.

During the original searches of the victim's effects the officers had found an onion skin paper copy of a document which carried a somewhat unusual message about a world wide management group bearing the name "The Superior Table." The message was signed by Mr. Roebert, the Director and in business style manner there were a series of names behind the cc: at the bottom ; Mr. George, Mr. Frank, Mr. Richard, Mr. Joseph, and Mr. Thomas. There was a red check mark by the name Mr. Richard indicating this was Richard Gooden's copy. And, it's apparent that the names are all first names not surnames. It certainly smacked of some secret society. More puzzling, a St. Christopher medal was found about the neck of the victim with a crudely etched inscription on the back "To Richard, my chosen son and heir." And, it was signed below "Roebert." The detectives wondered what the deuce are we getting into? Further, family friends recalled Richard had told them the family was flying on their vacation trip in Mr. Roberts Lear jet! To this day, no one has ever located the mysterious Mr. Roberts or Roebert or the Lear jet aircraft. Everyone registered in the U.S.A. was laboriously checked by investigators. Over time the officers wondered whether this and other information that came their way about Richard Gooden was a figment of his imagination, done to impress others that he was more important than true.

The name of Mr. Roberts came up again as part of a scheme directed by Richard Gooden that involved a multi-million dollar plan to purchase a small suburban airport, turn it into a relay center to Detroit International airport, provide helicopter shuttles, build a fine motel on the edge, and refurbish the airport to pass any regulations. When I heard about this one I had to laugh as I knew the airport owner personally. He was my younger sister's father-in-law. When the investigators talked to him, he was very truthful and skeptical of Gooden's intentions. He even described getting a call about this deal from a Mr. Roberts saying the voice sounded funny, almost like it was muffled. One thing for sure, if this plan was Gooden's intention, where would he get that kind of money and could it be related to the killings? Naturally, the Mafia was instantly considered as the police knew by now, he sure didn't have access to that kind of money. "Racket squad" officers were enlisted to contact sources and determine if there was any word about such a connection. It turned out to be negative, and possibly this was another of the victim's dreams.

Information about another big deal was soon discovered. Gooden announced he had a deal cooking and had to fly to San Francisco. He actually went to San Francisco officers discovered, but he had no contacts, took his meals in his room, and flew back to Michigan. During another announced flight, investigation revealed he never left the Detroit airport but stayed a few days in a motel. By now the State Police had officers traveling all over the country trying to track down Mr. Roberts and Gooden's deals. In the end, nothing was connected to his death except his local business right here in Michigan and its doubtful Mr. Roberts ever actually existed. The investigators did learn there were problems at the advertising business that might be connected to the deaths. Just prior to the murders, Gooden had called his secretary, his auditor, and his bank. There apparently was some type of financial problem. He even inquired of the bank whether they had received a $200,000.00 check he was expecting, and their answer to him had been negative and he seemed genuinely disturbed.

At this same investigative disclosure time, officers were interviewing and re-interviewing business associates and friends. One interview was of Gooden's associate and firm executive, Thomas Scroggins. As they talked to him, he suddenly asked them an unusual question,

"Did you ever find out exactly when the family was murdered?" As Det. Summers later told me," I thought it was funny and I glanced over at my partner. I could tell he felt the same way. But I took a gamble and told him the date we had pinned down as the definite murder day." Scroggins then, without any warning, lapsed into a story of his whereabouts that entire day, from about 9:30 in the morning until about 11:30 at night. As I looked at my partner his eyes told me that we were thinking the same way; we may very well be talking to the killer right now. I know how he felt, just from the hair rising on the back of my neck. Now, they had a real suspect. Of course the hours Scroggins described would nicely cover the time needed for the long trip and committing the horrible deed.

Later in the conversation, the detectives inquired whether he had any firearms. He told them at one time he had two .22 caliber rifles, "you know the Air Force survival gun." He said he got rid of them long ago; one went to a relative and the other to a friend in Chicago. When asked about handguns he replied that he had purchased two .25 Auto caliber Beretta pistols and two boxes of ammunition from a popular company in Central Michigan. Asked if he still had them, he said no, I gave one to my wife to use for protection and one to Richard Gooden along with the two boxes of ammunition for the pistol.

When they checked with the gun distributor, they found the company had the first two cases of SAKO ammunition ever imported into the State and they sold two boxes to Thomas Scroggins along with the Beretta pistols. As he promised Scroggins brought his wife's pistol to the detectives and they brought it immediately to the laboratory. A rush examination showed the class characteristics were identical to the homicide evidence but the individual characteristics differed; it was the right kind of pistol but not the one involved. Officers tracked down one of the rifles in Chicago. It had been given to a friend. It was the same story, the right kind of firearm but not the one involved. They attempted to obtain the other AR-7 rifle from Scroggins relative, who stated he was the firearms dealer who sold the rifles to Scroggins but none were ever returned to him, as Scroggins had stated. The officers checked his gun dealer's books and found they were very orderly and up to date, and that he had a good reputation for honesty. He had never received back the second rifle!

As the detectives and I discussed the firearms evidence, I asked "How likely would it be for an individual to possess two of each type firearm used in the murders, the unusual ammunition, and inexplicably one of each was missing?" Gooden's friends said they never heard of him having a firearm and in fact, he didn't like them. He had even written an anti-gun editorial in his own publication.

Now they decided they had to check out the extensive alibi. According to Scroggins, after he left the office on the day in question, he went to downtown Detroit to Cobo Hall where the builders show was in progress. One of Gooden's biggest advertisers was there with an impressive display. Scroggins got there in time to go to lunch with their client's executive officer. He advised the detectives he could remember that day well due to a record rainfall. He said he visited many of the other displays and hobnobbed with some parties, providing information on the advertising firm. After leaving, he claimed he went to dinner at a large restaurant. On the way home, he drove out of his way to the Gooden home, knowing they were on vacation, let himself in with a key that had been entrusted to him by his boss, and checked the basement for water damage. He stated further that the Goodens recently had water problems in the basement and he wanted to make sure it had been corrected. He stated further there was a small pool near the one basement wall and he wiped it up but noted no further damage. Finally, he said he got home late that evening and went straight to bed.

Det. Summers mused, "well he's got the date pegged correctly. That was the day of the record rainfall in Detroit. Many of the main road underpasses were completely flooded and the papers had pictures of cars stuck therein with water up to the windshields. I guess we had better check out the bathroom facility manufacturer he allegedly went to lunch with and spent several hours with "hobnobbing." He realized that most of the remainder of the alibi was the type that couldn't be disproved easily, if at all. So the detectives returned to their car and drove well into Ohio to the company plant and headquarters of Gooden's largest advertising account. There they contacted the executive whose name had been dropped by Scroggins and confided the reason for the visit. The company officer stated that he would more than welcome answering questions about a horrible murder like this. They told him about Scroggins' narrative of his travels on that fateful day. As he answered, their hearts sank when he quickly responded that Scroggins was there, they spent several hours together, and went to lunch together. This would be a complete vindication of their only suspect.

But then the executive had a puzzled look on his face as he said, "wait a minute. Now I recall that day of the record rainfall. That was on a Tuesday, wasn't it?" When they told him that was correct he really started talking as it all came back to him. He stated "Scroggins couldn't have visited with us on that afternoon. Due to the storm we had very few people in the Hall. As this was the last day of the display, we broke it down, picked up and were on our way back to Ohio that afternoon! Furthermore, I recall walking to a deli with Tom at lunch time. It was a beautiful sunny day. It was on Monday, the day before." The detectives now were excited thinking, "we're back in business, we are on to the killer." But, their next question and a vital one had to be, why – what could the motive be to murder an entire family? Undoubtedly it would fall into one of the standard reasons; sex, greed, robbery, or revenge. They knew this crime was not due to the inexplicable rage of a serial killer; there were just too many attempts at a cover up.

However, it is now interesting to note that long after the investigation ended, some interested and well educated parties theorized that Scroggins was actually a sociopathic type individual which was revealed by certain investigative information both directly and indirectly related to the murders. This plus more direct physical evidence linked Scroggins to the crime. It's hard to understand some people's minds. Here was a married man with children, on the surface a productive individual, but apparently with hidden traits, that were only seen in isolation. When I think about my experiences, it is not uncommon to find persons, particularly men who on the surface are family connected, successful in some way, and would never be thought of as a suspect in a brutal crime. A recent, highly publicized killer is a prime example. The media and TV were all over the stories of the BTK (bind, torture, and kill) incidents. Who was the killer? He turned out to be a fine family man and religious church worker, at least on the surface. Underneath, he was totally deranged. One of my

CSI cases was also a prime example. A young woman was abducted, brutally raped and strangled to death. After intensive investigation who was her killer? A young man apparently happily married and with two beautiful children was convicted of the murder; the question remained, why?

A lengthy search into the advertising company's records soon gave indications of fraud. Scroggins had been considered a whiz at the business by Gooden and as time passed he had been given more and more responsibility of running the business. But, the investigation revealed some of Scroggins' additional management duties were not given but apparently taken. In months prior to the murders, Gooden had busied himself with other interests and left much of the company care with Scroggins. During the interval Scroggins granted every one a raise. He granted himself a raise of several hundred percent! In addition, he had been playing a game with Company finances. When money was received he would shave off some and fail to pay suppliers, printers, etc., sometimes making partial payments from the totals. To summarize, investigators could show Scroggins had stolen in excess of $80,000.00 from the two Gooden companies.

It was theorized that when his bank calls indicated to Gooden that something was amiss, he knew Scroggins was responsible. Investigators learned that Scroggins called Richard Gooden at the cabin four or five times just prior to the killings. They believed he was attempting to thwart a criminal investigation and arrest. Further, they believed he drove to the lodge on that fateful day and probably begged Gooden not to expose him, but was rebuffed. Scroggins left for minutes then returned armed with the two missing firearms. First he killed Richard as he sat in his large easy chair. The window shots lined up with the chair and bullet damage from the .22 rifle. They believe he next killed or seriously wounded the older boys, the only real threat remaining. He then killed the mother and the two small children. He had to shut them up to avoid detection.

In addition, over time, Scroggins had been given three polygraphs (lie detector) and failed two of them. The other was inconclusive. Of course, this evidence cannot be used in a court of law. The examinations were given by a couple of the best examiners in the Country. Therefore, it buttressed the rest of the detectives' case.

Chasing Tail Lights to Forensic Ballistics

Now it was time to seek an arrest warrant. The lead detectives prepared a 700 page report on the total investigation and turned it over to the Prosecuting Attorney of the small county where the murders had occurred. After a short delay, he advised the detectives he would not authorize a warrant, declaring they could not prove Scroggins was at the crime scene. The investigators were crushed; they felt they had more than enough evidence to convict Scroggins. So, it was back to work.

Finally a break came their way. They learned of a young acquaintance of the suspect who had been in the military service during this interval, but had returned home just prior to the crime. They interviewed him, found that he was an outdoors type, liked firearms, and knew something vital. He told them that Scroggins had the second AR-7 rifle long after he supposedly gave it to his firearms dealer relative. Further, this same relative remembered he had been with the suspect one day when they went to family property and fired the rifle, shooting at targets. I learned of this aspect of the case when the lead officers came into the Crime Laboratory and turned over to me a paper sack full of .22 caliber fired cartridge cases. They had spent the previous day with a metal detector searching the family field where the firing range had been set up.

I carefully examined every one of the shells under the stereo microscope, looking for the class characteristics of the AR-7 rifle. I was able to separate twenty from the lot that looked promising. Most of the shells were severely stained from weather, soil and oxidation affects. After cleaning, I was able to find five that still displayed some fine markings from discharge. A few were in the firing pin area and there were a large number of striations continually repeated among the five cartridge cases. They were compared with the .22 caliber evidence cartridge cases (shells) using the comparison microscope where the two casings under examination (one from the murder scene and one from the Scroggins field) were examined side-by-side under magnification.

Some markings on the shells were caused by a blow from the firing pin on the rim of the cartridge where the explosive primer material is located. The other markings were created as the fired case was being extracted from the firing chamber. As the cartridge is discharged, the gaseous material under high pressure forces the bullet out of the case and out of the barrel. These same gases force the cartridge case to expand and thus fit tightly in the chamber. This is all part of the sealing process which prevents "blow-back" of the gas. As the case is extracted automatically to be ejected or thrown away from the firearm, imperfections in the chamber wall create clusters of fine scratch markings (striae) which are unique to the particular firearm. In this case, I was able to "match" five of the cases from the field with the crime scene evidence. I then proceeded to make photomicrographs (photos taken through the microscope lenses) for the detectives to take to the Prosecutor. We were sure this evidence would push the reluctant County Prosecutor off the fence.

The Prosecutor advised he would take it under consideration. After some delay, he advised the State Police that he still felt unable to issue an arrest warrant. We were shocked, as police officers we felt we had more than enough for arrest and probably enough evidence for conviction at trial. It was learned much later that the Prosecutor had a meeting with the Attorney General of the State. It was rumored that they discussed a different potential suspect; a local man who had displayed mental failings in the past and supposedly harbored ill feelings toward Richard Gooden. The lead detectives were totally in disbelief now. They had investigated the other man near the very beginning and said there was no reason to believe the local rumors about him.

The officers then decided to take another approach. They contacted the Prosecutor and his lead attorney from one of the large suburban areas where the Gooden's business, victims and suspect all resided. These two professional Prosecutors were considered the very best in the State. After they reviewed the evidence compiled and in the dossier, the lead Prosecutor stated in effect there was more than enough evidence for arrest and conviction in this case. Even further he advised "if I can't get a conviction in this case I will give up the practice of law!"

Michigan had provisions that would allow another attorney to try the case with the approval of the Attorney General. They went to his office only to be refused again. To this day, no one other than the Attorney General and the Prosecutor in the Northern County know why! As one of the lead detectives put it "the only thing I realized from this case was an ulcer." As they say in today's police jargon "the perp walked."

Eventually, the old company went into bankruptcy and was sold for a pittance. Guess who was the buyer? That's right, it was Thomas Scroggins. Within a couple years the business was gone. Not surprisingly several companies complained they were "short changed" by Scroggins during this period.

Five years had passed. Big City press printed front page articles on the murders on a couple of occasions. But as it seemed to be fading away, the story got new attention. It was reported that the downstate County Prosecutor and his lead Attorney were going to issue a murder warrant for Scroggins in that the murder plot and motives originated from the home County of the victims and Scroggins.

Before further action could be taken, Scroggins committed suicide with his wife's .25 automatic caliber Beretta pistol. He left a neat note for his mother stating he was guilty of theft, lying, being a cheat, but he didn't murder the family. It's amazing to me as I recall the many times brutal killers wanted a last word with their mother before their conviction or sentence. Under the neat note in an almost illegible scrawl in huge letters were the words "DEAR GOD FORGIVE ME."

6

The Late Years in Michigan

As the sixties drew to a close, I found myself promoted and in charge of the Crime Laboratory in East Lansing. My boss, the present Commander of the Laboratories throughout the State, was my old mentor, Wally VanStratt. He was entirely occupied with administrative work, or so it seemed. He was required to have an operation on his spine to remove the Japanese sniper's bullet. It left him partly paralyzed and doctors said he would never walk again. But, they didn't know the stubborn Dutchman. He worked out continuously, was in therapy, and every day at noon he would limp on his crutches over to the recruits swimming pool where he enjoyed water exercise. Eventually, he graduated to a cane and he almost never missed a day's work!

As administrative requirements increased my case load had to decrease but I stayed active working and assisting with some of the more difficult cases. Over the years I had also become responsible for training several young examiners, and this continuing duty kept me hopping.

During this phase, one of the more interesting homicide cases involved many State Police officers and the Crime Laboratory. It happened in an unlikely spot, in the East-central portion of the Upper Peninsula in a sparsely populated area.

The thrill killer and circumstantial evidence: A 16 year old teen-ager was promised a trout fishing trip with an older friend. The friend made arrangements to pick him up at the corner of a T intersection on the following morning. The boy departed early and walked to the corner to wait for the ride. There was an upturned sand barrel there so he assumed a seat on it. A short time later another older acquaintance, driving a large dump truck to a construction job, slowed and turned the corner onto the intersecting road. The driver spotted his young friend sitting on the barrel and waved to him. As he completed his turn, he could see his young pal wave back. At the same time, in his side view mirror he could see a man standing in front of the dense woods about a hundred feet behind. The man had something hanging around his neck. The driver conjectured "its probably one of those naturalist types or a bird watcher."

At the appointed hour the fisherman friend came to pick up the teen aged boy for the promised trip to the nearby trout streams. However, the boy wasn't there. Thinking he was delayed, he drove to the boy's nearby home and inquired, only to be told the boy had left long ago. As he drove back through town, he stopped at the service station and inquired if they had seen him. The attendant told him that the boy passed by walking quite some time ago. The puzzled fisherman returned to the corner to see if there was any sign of his fishing partner. While waiting he went to sit on the upturned sand barrel but stopped, wondering what caused the drag tracks through the weeds behind the barrel towards the woods. Curiosity got the better of him and he followed the drag trail until he stopped in his tracks. There was his fishing companion lying face up in the weeds. He appeared to be dead. Thus began the strangest case in the history of this Upper Peninsula of Michigan area.

Near this scene was a State Police Post and the Troopers were quickly notified. A call was immediately placed for Crime Laboratory assistance. The Troops kept every one away and protected the scene until the CSI crew arrived. As is often the case, this protection saved the day for solving this crime.

During this period, and while the CSI crew were starting to work the area, the truck driver returned and stopped to inquire what was going on. When told about the crime, he said that he might be of some assistance. He told the officers about seeing the young man sitting on the barrel that morning and about seeing the man by the woods in his mirror. They asked for a description and he told them "it was a white man of medium build. He was wearing a white T shirt and had something hanging about his neck. He also appeared to have very short hair."

The beginning investigation disclosed the victim had an apparent entrance bullet wound in the back of the head. It appeared he had been shot at close range, while he was sitting on the barrel. He fell off backwards and was dragged well into the weeds, where his body was dropped. Searchers found a cache of cigarette butts next to the woods where the killer had posted. They were Kools by brand. They were also able to pick up boot tracks in the sand near the body and to follow them into the woods to a two rut car trail where they disappeared. There were tire tracks in the well packed sand trail that showed some detail. They were photographed and the most detailed were lifted with plaster of Paris casts. The front tires were of common passenger car types, while the rear tires were "knobbies" or snow tires.

The boot tracks were another story. They were found through weeds and soft sand, and here were sufficient enough to determine type of sole and size, but lacking detail needed for identification. They were photographed using tripods and rulers so that actual size could later be determined. But, in addition to the shoeprints, an even more important detail could be observed in the soft sand. With nearly every step, the right boot toe area dug into the sand leaving a scooped out impression. The officers conjectured the killer might be gimpy or partly crippled. These impressions were photographed along with the shoe or boot imprints.

The local Troopers were instructed concerning the tire and boot imprints, the Kool cigarettes, and the truck driver's description. They were directed to go in all three directions from the intersection and examine every trail or dirt road leading from the highway, looking for tire imprints similar to the ones noted. The snow tires were well known in this North Country which was buried in snow in the winter time.

It wasn't long before the Post received a call from a patrol unit asking for back-up and advising they had found a fresh track of similar tires. The Troopers followed the tracks down a winding trail road ending at a small cabin. As they walked to the cabin they encircled an older model station wagon with the knobby tires. Inside the vehicle they spotted an opened package of Kool cigarettes lying on the dash, also a pair of binoculars on a leather cord. As they neared the cabin, the owner stepped out. He was a white man, wearing a white T shirt, of medium build, and had a crew cut. Without further ado, he was arrested, handcuffed and placed in the State Police unit. Troopers had the car towed to the Post garage for further inspection.

The suspect was identified as a sportsman type who lived in the Lower Peninsula, and was known as a loner in the area. He apparently had one friend, a local Indian guide for hunters and trout fishermen. A search of the cabin for boots like the impressions was negative. The rear tires of the station wagon were removed and taken to the Crime Laboratory for comparison along with photographs and plaster casts from the scene.

At autopsy, the local pathologist removed a smashed .22 caliber bullet from the victim's brain. The entrance site in the back of the head indicated a very close range shot. Apparently the victim was surprised by the attack. There was no connection between the victim and the suspect. This appeared to be a murder without apparent motive; probably a so-called thrill killing; i.e., a murder by someone yearning to find out what it feels like to kill some unrelated person!

The bullet was immediately delivered to the laboratory and rushed to examination by the firearms and tool mark unit. The bullet displayed class rifling characteristics similar to a very few firearms. Among these the likely choice would be that of a Smith and Wesson revolver. The suspect was determined to be a collector of firearms and at this time had sixteen handguns registered to him. A check of his home in the Lower Peninsula revealed only 15 firearms. The missing one happened to be a .22 caliber Smith and Wesson revolver, the "kit gun" version which was small and easily carried in a hiker or hunter's kit bag, thus the name. A check was also made at that location for any boots with soles similar to those at the scene, with negative results.

One break in the investigation came when the suspect's Indian friend mentioned to investigators that his friend some time back had purchased two pairs of military style jungle combat boots. Since they wore the same size, he gave a pair to the guide. He still had his pair and produced them. They were of the right size and with a sole and heel design like the evidence imprints. When investigators questioned the suspect he always had answers, but not the right ones. When asked about the missing boots, he explained that he had been trout fishing that very morning and his boots were quite wet and muddy, so he hanged them around the car fender antenna while driving home from the stream. They must have been pulled off by brush on the remote trail and thus lost.

When advised of the missing Smith and Wesson revolver, he also had a ready story. A few weeks before he said, he took his canoe into a beaver dam pond loaded with native brook trout. He had the revolver tucked in his waist band when he tied into a big trout, got excited and tipped the canoe over. His pretty little S & W revolver was lost in the pond as the canoe went over. The pond of course was silt-like with the bottom like quicksand. State Police divers tried to locate the firearm without success. Due to the pond's condition, they could not say it couldn't be there.

Next, the detectives checked back with the Crime Lab to see if they had any luck with the tires. The answer was negative, but there was an interesting note to the opinion. Lugs on the tire showed fresh damage, inconsistent with the evidence tracks. It appeared as if they had been recently cut with a type of sharp instrument. The suspect, a ready talker, had an answer to every question, including this one. He explained that on the very morning of the crime, on the fishing trip he had attempted to ford the feeder creek and became stuck. He had to rock the car back and forth to get out and the sharp pebbles in the creek bed must have damaged his rear or drive tires.

The County Prosecutor, however, charged him with murder although he felt it would be difficult to convict him. In this rural area, homicides were nearly non-existent and the Prosecutor felt he had little experience to try a case such as this. He went to the Attorney General and asked for assistance. The AGs representative was an older balding man with wire rimmed glasses. He didn't look impressive but he was sharp and between the two attorneys they did a masterful job of trying the case. Then it was time for cross-examination of the defendant. He demanded of his attorney that he be allowed to testify. Under direct examination the jury heard all of his convenient answers. The Prosecutor and Asst. Attorney General were prepared in advance for all of this.

They had an enlarged map of the region mounted on hardboard and placed on an easel well out in the courtroom so the Judge and jury could view it properly. The Prosecutor handed a pointer to the defendant and asked him to go to the easel as he wanted to inquire about the location of the fishing expedition. As the defendant arose and started across the room, both the Prosecutor and AG rose partway out of their chairs and stared intently at the shoes of the defendant. The hushed silence of the courtroom was broken by the soft shoe's dancing like sound as the defendant dragged the toe of his right shoe at nearly every step.

Obviously, the defendant was found guilty of first degree murder and sentenced to life imprisonment.

There was also one other fascinating part of this trial I must mention. The defense attorney who had objected to the introduction into evidence of the fatal bullet, did so only after examining the bullet carefully and stating "your honor there are no identifying marks on this evidence of the doctor or police." This Judge was known to be a stickler for marking evidence for identification. On that morning I received a call from the Judge who stated, "Officer Meyers, I am ordering you to gather one of your stereomicroscopes and a suitable lamp and bring them here forthwith." In those days the Judge's word was law and I replied, "Yes, your Honor," wondering what this was all about and knowing that is one long drive from Lansing to Newberry.

I did what I was told and was immediately ushered into the Judge's chambers. I set up the scope and light as he withdrew a smashed bullet from the vial. He asked me a few questions as I examined the bullet. I finally had to tell him there were no identifying initials on the evidence bullet. The Judge said "I may have to keep this out of evidence and deny questioning about it. But first you have to take the stand as soon as we herd the jury back into their seats."

As soon as I was seated and sworn, the Judge inquired whether I had microscopically examined the bullet and whether I had found any identifying initials thereon. I replied that I had not. But then the cagey old codger asked me a series of questions. "It's true isn't it that you are the lead firearms examiner in your laboratory and you've been at this business for a long time?" I replied "yes sir that's true." He went on "I understand that the evidence bullet in this case was brought directly to you. I further understand that you have had the opportunity to microscopically examine the evidence bullet on numerous occasions, isn't that so?" Again I replied "yes sir." "Isn't it also true," he asked ", on a number of occasions you had to compare this bullet with tests from a variety of seized firearms?" I replied "yes sir" and by now I was getting his drift. The next question was, "You have just examined microscopically People's proposed exhibit #7 haven't you?" I answered "yes sir." Finally the clutch question came, "Do you recall in all your experience ever seeing another bullet damaged in just this way and is there any doubt in your mind that this proposed exhibit is the same bullet?" I said "no sir." He then smiled at me and said "thank you Officer, you may go home now!" The canny old Judge had made all the record he needed. The court room can be a funny place some time. I knew that one of the CSI team must have coached him somewhat before I got there!

It was a time of rapid change in the Crime Laboratory system. There were Government funds made available to assist this change and we took advantage of them. One morning the Commissioner called me down to his office and immediately got to the point. He inquired "Charlie as you know we are nearing the end of the fiscal year. Any funds left available must be committed within the next six weeks. If you were to receive $500,000.00 dollars to spend on equipment could you handle it?" I immediately replied "Just try me sir." Now that's a lot of money today, but back then that was a fortune. To make a long story a lot shorter, I will only say that I spent darn near every red cent. It wasn't wasted on any foolish items. We were able to purchase equipment that vastly improved our capabilities. One of the main items I recall was a top drawer gas chromatograph/mass spectrometer. This is an instrument as common as dairy cows today but was in its very early use in the Crime Laboratory then. As I recall, we were the 6th or 7th laboratory in the Country to obtain one. It fit in perfectly in our laboratory expansion plans and we had the perfect candidate to set-up and use it. He was a graduate chemist who joined the State Police as a Trooper. As soon as he was on board the Department he stopped in the laboratory and talked to me, explaining the only reason he joined the State Police was to become a Crime Laboratory scientist and he implored me to get him into the laboratory as soon as possible. He became the youngest sworn Trooper to ever work In the Laboratory. His name was Don Collins and he was truly remarkable.

I have to laugh as I think of him and his beginning days in the Laboratory. I started him off with certain assignments to assist in his learning of the work and its requirements. As days progressed more learning was piled on and to prepare him for his planned final assignment. Each time, if I expected something to take weeks, he was done in days. Each time, he would bug me about how soon he could dig into case work and be an independent analyst. When I attempted to inquire of him about his training, he would say "I know all that stuff, and/or heck anyone can do that." Early on I thought he was very conceited and overly satisfied with his knowledge. It didn't take long before his fellow workers dubbed him "Super Don." It was a joke at first but within a short time became a statement of appreciation for his fantastic knowledge and abilities. Apart from work, he was a modest and unassuming young man, give him a job and he was a tiger. Until he retired and died, he was affectionately referred to only as "Super Don!"

It wasn't only his ability as a chemist and instrumental analyst, but he loved to fix things. It got so bad that he had little spare time for play. He was always busy fixing instruments, lawn mowers, automobile engines, etc. For several years the Department cancelled its expensive contracts for repair costs with the major instrument companies as "Super Don" became a full time trouble shooter and serviceman. As a supervisor and supporter I always thought of him as a dear friend and one of my personnel successes.

Then there was Mark Stolorow, another success story of considerable proportion. An Ann Arbor detective friend stopped at the laboratory one day with evidence and came by to talk to me. He said, "I've got a tip for you. We have a bright young man working as a Patrolman on the city police. He is also attending the University of Michigan and will graduate soon. I know he is interested in Forensic Science and you might want to grab him before he gets away to another State." I immediately went to the Commissioner, told him about the message and asked whether he could spring some personnel money even though our budget was completely depleted. This was to be contingent on interview and approval of the potential candidate. He said, "This one sounds good, if you like him grab him and I'll cover the cost till the new budget is aboard." We grabbed him and he eventually became our lead serologist at Plymouth/Northville. Mark was a young ambitious guy and after several years he moved on to a higher paying and more responsible position with the Illinois system. Later I overheard his name mentioned in conjunction with a major criminal case. His name was attached to Cellmark Diagnostics, one of the tops in DNA analysis throughout the world. I believe they said he was "Research Director." Wow, I knew he was bright.

Bob Stacey was another one of the rare Troopers in those years with a BS degree and a yearning to get into forensic science. Upon completing laboratory training, he was assigned to the Crime Laboratory at Warren, Michigan. Bob was a drug analyst and became a very good one. Meanwhile, the Health Department had hired a PhD chemist and assigned him to Warren as part of their commitment to the laboratory expansion plan. The CO of the Laboratory was an officer and latent print expert. He assigned the PhD to train in drug analysis under Bob. Within a short time I received a call from the Health Department stating I or my representative couldn't assign their PhD to train under a Trooper with only a BS degree! This was unseemly and embarrassing. I advised that their PhD had little or no experience in drug analysis whereas Bob Stacey had considerable and was considered a top analyst, BS degree or not. We ended up in a disagreement and had to resolve it in the Commissioner's office. It was agreed that Bob would train their man in drug analysis and he in turn would provide training to our chemists in Liquid Chromatography, as he was an acknowledged expert in this type of analysis.

Universities are not the only places where the PhD is the holy grail of education and practice. I'm not knocking advanced education and degrees. Of course, they are valuable, if properly applied. I've just seen too many instances where the PhD behind the name has unlocked doors and allowed intrusion into areas where they are not trained or competent. This is certainly true in the criminal law, in Circuit and Federal Courts, in Appeals Courts, etc. Some Judges seem to be unduly swayed by advanced education, failing to understand that the individual has little or no training and experience in the discipline under discussion.

As for Bob Stacey, after retirement from the State Police, he went on to be one of the leaders and investigators for ASCLD, the American Society of Crime Laboratory Directors, which has been so active in recent history in efforts to educate laboratories in good practices and determine whether individual laboratories can be certified as meeting such requirements. Later, for a time he was the Director of the Chicago Police Crime Laboratory, and last known was working in a high level position in the Federal Bureau of Investigation Laboratory. I ask you, can I really pick them?

Thinking about ASCLD, a bit of secret pride was that in my latter days with the MSP I was pleased to attend the formation meeting of the new group, held at College Station, Pennsylvania, home of Penn State University. Even more so, I especially enjoyed my arrival and exit. I talked the Commissioner into letting me fly there with our number one pilot Richard Brantner in the Department's new twin Cessna. Dick Brantner was also known for his shooting ability. He was twice the U.S. top Police shooter at Camp Perry, in addition to many other awards in various regional meets. The MSP had the top team and two other champion shooters of the era, Tprs. Robert Steinhurst and Elwyn Burnett. If my memory is correct, Dick was the first police officer in modern times to break the magical 2650 barrier, out of a possible perfect score of 2700. When we arrived at the airport, many of the other lab directors were there. I was so proud to step down from our shiny well marked MSP aircraft with the assistance of Trooper Brantner in his snappy uniform.

Another very good friend and analyst I must mention is Richard Bisbing. Dick had been working with the Dept. of Health as an analyst but wanted to work with us in the Michigan State Police system. So, I was fortunate enough to assist in the move and we became good friends as well as associates. Eventually, Dick was assigned to one of the new laboratories at Bridgeport. After leaving the Department, he went to work for the Mc Crone Research Institute in Chicago, a famous research facility. The company is named after Walter Mc Crone, often described as the top microscopist in the world. Walter claimed, and he could prove his assertions, that the great majority of trace evidence analyses could be made by using one of the many specialized microscopes. I, as well as many other analysts throughout the U.S. and other countries, was trained there in one or more of these specialties. I went there to learn the use of the Polarizing Microscope. When last I talked to Dick, he was an executive with the Mc Crone Group. Another of many friends and analysts I was pleased to work with during the MSP Crime Laboratory days.

I always took pride in the analysts, especially when I had a hand in their interviews and selection. However, I didn't have a perfect record in that regard. On and off through the years I have been chided or kidded about one.

A couple of associates and I comprised a panel interviewing prospective analysts. These were civilians, i.e. not sworn officers, who possessed the proper degrees and came recommended. One was a handsome young man, impeccably dressed and well spoken. He brought with him a record of his achievements. This was not unusual. We always asked for a Curriculum Vita from each applicant. It was the type that was unusual. He had been an officer in the Army and before discharge was a General's adjutant, a high honor. He presented us with a bound notebook containing a record of awards, citations and full length photographs in full uniform and with the General. Afterwards, one of my co-workers on the boards said, "Charlie, this guy is too good to be true!" As it turned out, he was right.

From the first moment we hired this man he was a pain in the buttocks. He professed to know more than his instructors. He demanded to be allowed to work independently before we felt he was ready. His arrogant attitude nettled his fellow workers, and every week or two he was in my office with a new complaint. At the time of my MSP retirement, he was working independently as an analyst and things seemed to be better. Within a couple years of my retirement, he accused another worker of having an affair with his wife. Next he went on record with the media accusing the Laboratory of mishandling evidence and finally sued the Department for a ton of money. He had brought chaos to the Laboratory and the Department. Every now and then when one of my friends from the Laboratory communicated with me they would ask, "Well, what do you think of the Adjutant now, Charlie? All I could do was to grit my teeth and reply, "Not much." All around the table would laugh at my expense. Oh well, as the football coach would say ", you can't win them all."

But, in 1970 the Commissioner called me down to his office. He advised me after the last promotional examination I was once again in the top three positions on the Register. He had already by-passed me for promotion twice as both he and I did not want me to leave the Laboratory. According to Civil Service rule he couldn't by-pass me for the third time without some definitive reason, and there was none.

Therefore, he was promoting me to Captain and placing me in charge of the Training Division. He stated "Charlie you have experience in training and I need someone there with a degree, so you are it."

I spent about 1 ½ years as CO of the Training Division. Those months were some of the most hectic of my life. A new recruit school was now starting. The United States Civil Rights division was busy evaluating everything we did. This was an era where many police agencies were accused of deliberately keeping black candidates from the ranks. We were no exception. A couple of candidates from a previous school complained we picked on them due to their race. We had several black candidates in the new school. I had to watch over them like a mother over a child, or so it seemed. One in particular complained almost every day and ended up in my office. So, it was my responsibility to monitor the tough training program and ensure it was fair.

The Division had just prior to my entering the scene completed a lot of preparatory work in establishing a formal record of the physical program. They had enlisted help of professionals such as trainers from Michigan State University and the Detroit Lions football team. The official physical requirements and practice of the program was typed and copies given to candidates to make them aware of the program and encourage them to train before entrance.

In the second or third week of training the new school of recruits, I became aware that a number had already dropped out. So, I decided to participate and the following morning I showed up at 6:00am in sweat togs, jumped into the ranks, went through the exercise routine, and finally the run just prior to breakfast in the Departmental dining hall. At this time I was 44 years old but still in pretty good shape, I thought. It darned near killed me. After breakfast I retraced the run route with a car and measured the distance. Later that morning I had the school commander send the physical leader to my office. I quickly became acquainted with one of the most interesting men I have known. In the beginning I had to chastise him and worry about him. Later, I can thankfully say, I was instrumental in assisting him in his first promotion. Eventually he rose to Captain and District Commander of the Eighth District (the Upper Peninsula).

His name was Gary McGhee and his nickname among the instructor staff was "the monster!" It didn't take too long to figure out why. In uniform, he came into my office, snapped to attention and gave me a salute saying, "Sir, you wanted to see me?" I told him that he undoubtedly was aware that I followed the exercise routine and run that morning. He said, "Yes sir." I said, "I went back and clocked the run distance. It was over 5 miles. Are you aware that our written policy calls for three miles at this early stage?" Still at rigid attention he answered "yes sir." I then asked him why he had done that even with me tagging along. He crisply said, "I thought they were ready, SIR." I couldn't suppress a half smile as I thought, "this guy is not going to try to BS you. He is the perfect example of why the school has always been tough and produces so many fine police officers who understand straight talk, discipline and professionalism." We finally had a little conversation about Civil Rights investigations and I cautioned him to try and be a little more careful about adhering to the Policy. As he left, I had to laugh out loud as I recalled near the end of the run when some were moaning and starting to drop out or fall behind, he started to run backwards, well out in front for all to see while he shouted out, "come on candy asses, keep it up!" I hoped he hadn't done that especially for me.

There were many exciting and interesting moments spent among these dedicated instructors that I will never forget. Near graduation time Nancy and I threw a party for the staff. We held it in our basement and I remember a contest where all the staff, including me, would dash across the basement floor, leap into the air and plant our feet on the side wall. One member would mark our highest spot reached as we took turns. Later Nancy remarked "you damned fool your going to kill yourself. You can't keep up with those young Troopers." I replied, "What's your excuse then for challenging the one show off to a walking on hands contest?" And Nancy won that one! Those were exciting days and often lots of fun.

Of course this was during the Viet Nam era and the resulting strife in the homeland. A demonstration on the MSU campus had gotten out of hand as demonstrators took over the Administration Building. It was something to see as a group of Troopers were called to break it up. In the lead was an old buddy of mine, Moose. He physically broke the human chain and pitched the lead trouble maker back in to the crowd. As is often the case, the worst ones are found out to not be a student, just a rowdy.

Not long after a huge group occupied much of the downtown district of East Lansing. They broke windows, damaged parked cars, set trash cans on fire, etc. It was night time and Operations notified the Division to get their Troopers ready to repel rioters. We had a Lt. CO of the recruit school staff, a Sgt. and several Troopers from staff and about 40 recruits, all with riot gear. I thought "what in hell am I doing – I haven't had riot training and I'm in charge." We were placed on a Department bus and dropped at a main intersection on the edge of campus and near Headquarters. We were told this was just a precaution. Most of the action was across campus and we probably wouldn't see any rioters. My top Sgt. George Gedda noticed the worried look on my face and whispered "don't worry Cap, we know what to do, we'll take care of it."

The Officers placed the entire staff across the intersection, curb to curb, standing at parade rest, with night sticks or riot batons as they call them now kept clenched in our fists behind our backs. In a very short time we heard the roar and din getting louder and a flying squad car stopped to inform us the rioters had broken through and were coming across the campus in our direction, so watch your step. Our officers cautioned the Troopers and recruits "don't move, stare straight ahead, and don't reply to any threats or filthy talk. These aren't felons and we will not go into action unless we are physically attacked." Thankfully, they were uncoordinated and with many stragglers when they reached us. There were a few bottles, soda cans, etc. thrown our way but no one was hit. Several of the nasty ones went face to face with us, calling us filthy names, etc. But several of the stragglers, as they passed through said, "you guys are great, what discipline – don't pay attention to those others, there aren't many like that." And then it was over.

The following day a large group on bicycles occupied the main street, from curb to curb, riding their bike just fast enough to keep it erect. As the roadway crossed the Red Cedar River Bridge, nearly holy territory to MSU students, a squad of Troopers met them, knocked them off the bikes and then threw the bicycles into the River. We caught some flack in the media over that one.

Eventually, I was subpoenaed to Detroit to face the Civil Rights judicial inquiry. Of course, they were interested in why we only had a few black Troopers.

I had to defend our training policy and assure them it was tough but race had nothing to do with it. As high a percentage of white recruits dropped out as black. I said, "Our main difficulty was to recruit blacks. "

We spent many hours at the various colleges and universities interviewing upcoming black graduates. Many told us openly that it wouldn't go over well in their communities for them to wear the uniform. There were others who told us State Troopers did not make enough money to make it worth their while.

Perhaps my major contribution to training was that I was instrumental in the planning phase for a new Training Academy. We were between Recruit Schools and I had sent the entire staff out to various sites getting information and plans for the new structure. We visited recently erected sites in a couple of States, and recently constructed swimming pools and gymnasiums at Colleges, etc. We got a lot of information from MSU, across the street from Headquarters. It was built shortly after my retirement, and it is a beautiful Academy. Every one's favorite training Sgt., George Gedda, died a very early death from Lou Gehrig's disease. I was extremely pleased the Department named the auditorium after him and placed a suitable plaque there.

Chasing Tail Lights to Forensic Ballistics

During the last weeks in Training, the recruits were on the range, firing for a final score. Their Coach, Les Doubleday, one of the finest we ever had, called me over to the range as I was walking back from Administration. He chided me for not being on the range for some time. We were all required to shoot at least once a month. He asked me to shoot along, but I had no firearm with me, so he let me use his new Colt Python revolver. I went along and was really impressed with this new firearm, right out of the box. I shot the best score of my career I had carried an expert badge for years but always yearned for that distinguished expert badge which only a few had. We went up to score the targets and Les exclaimed "Damn it, look it here – the old man missed "distinguished" by only one point. You see what a little experience and practice can do for you!" I was only 45 years old then, but for the Troops I was old.

After my short stint in Training, Wally retired and I was moved back into the Crime Laboratory as Commander of all the laboratories and staff, where I stayed until my retirement 1 ½ years later. It was pleasing that during Training and Laboratory command, every now and then one of the young examiners would ask me to look at a "tough bullet comparison." I spent all my spare time with staff or visiting the other laboratories.

It was rewarding for me to be asked to address the retirement party for John Stauffer of the Chicago Police Department Crime Laboratory. It was held in a huge ballroom with a large number of dignitaries present. I always maintained a close relationship with the agency during my career. I felt they were honored to have a Michigan State Police Captain praise one of their oldest and highly respected analysts.

One historic memory of those late years involved a request from the Commissioner to return to the Laboratory at Headquarters and assist with an unresolved problem in the Firearms unit. I stayed in a local motel and in the morning went to a small restaurant for breakfast. As I passed several full tables I heard a voice say "Capt. Meyers how are you?" I spun around to face a remarkable man, former Governor, now Chief Justice of the Michigan Supreme Court, G. Mennen Williams (Soapy). The six term famous Governor, heir to the Mennen family fortune (hence the nickname Soapy), had been introduced to me a couple of times over many years, and it was difficult to believe he would remember me. But, he was a very unusual man; handsome, very tall, about 6 feet 3 inches, I believe, and with a quick mind and fantastic memory. During his long years as Governor he developed a deep respect for the State Police and it showed. During his tenure, he addressed every graduating class of Troopers except one, and on that occasion he sent the Lt. Governor in his stead.

One experience solidified that relationship. Soapy was inspecting the State Prison system relative to pending legislation. His State Police driver and bodyguard went with him through Michigan's most secure prison at Marquette. In the kitchen area, three lifer convicts, including one known to be very dangerous, attempted to take the Governor hostage. One grabbed the Governor from behind threatening him with a potato masher while another stabbed the State Trooper, George Kerr, in the back with a large butcher knife. Kerr went down, seriously wounded but not out, rolled over pulling a hidden snubnose revolver from his waistband and shot the attacker, breaking up the attempted kidnapping.

The presence of the hidden revolver was a surprise to the convicts as firearms are not allowed inside the prison. What they didn't know was that George had two firearms he carried and had given one up at prison entrance as required by rule. Needless to say, but the Governor was thankful to Tpr. Kerr and the Michigan State Police in general.

I recall my first meeting with the Governor when on night patrol in Northern Michigan my partner and I were dispatched to a local roadhouse to provide security for Governor Williams. It was a well known place in the area and had live music on this night. We watched as "Soapy" called the square dances from the stage. It was a favorite hobby of his and he knew all the movements and calls. It was another one of the good old days.

CAPTAIN CHARLES R. MEYERS - 1971

7

Delta College & Edenville

During my last weeks with the State Police I had been to a couple of interviews for a new position. It would still be a long time before I could take long vacations from earning money. Within a couple of weeks from retirement I accepted a new position at Delta College in Michigan. They advised they would grant me an Assistant Professor position and a nice salary. The college administrator also inquired whether I had any experience at writing grant requests – this was the heyday for such requests. I advised him that I had written several and obtained finances. He also asked whether I might have any ideas for any expanded training programs in the criminal investigation field. I told him I hoped for such an opportunity. If the State needed anything it would be a specialized program in Crime Scene Investigation. Not just a few lectures, but an offer of a hands- on program taught by professionals over a length of time.

Delta College was a natural due to its location. It was named Delta College because it lay in the triangular and heavily populated areas between Saginaw, Bay City, and Midland, Michigan. Within six weeks I landed approval for a grant from the Federal Government who would provide the seed money, approval from my old department to allow analysts to cooperate and possibly earn a little extra money, through the new training program. I was also thrilled to get several of my old friends, pathologists and lawyers, to agree to assist in the program for a mere pittance and travel expenses.

The Crime Scene Investigation seminar and hands-on training program was scheduled to last a month. It was a great program, if I may say so, as the practical parts were handled by experts with lots of CSI background. It was one of the first, if not the first, to approach the problem this way. Students started the very first morning without any advice or warning as they were assembled into small groups, told to form a team. They were then told to attack a mock homicide scene they were taken to on the campus. The class size was limited just for this purpose. Outside the mock scene entrance was a rather complete evidence kit, including latent print supplies, evidence containers, etc. and a complete quality photographic kit with close-up lens, etc. (I believe it was Nikon 35 mm we used). Each group was accompanied by an instructor who took notes on all that happened. It got funny at times to witness the chaos.

The second day consisted of a critique on day one, the good and the bad and what might have been done differently. It also involved a written test on CSI, a type of pre-test. Likewise the last two days of the month long school were spent the same way as a post-test. This gave us the opportunity to gauge the improvement. It was an instant success and re-scheduled over and over with a long list of requests from various police departments to send students. Of course, as program administrator, I received extra pay; nothing wrong with that. And remember, this was in 1973!

In the regular two year program I taught either Police Patrol or Police Administration and Introduction to Criminalistics. I remember one of my very first students, a Patrolman from Saginaw, at the end of the course year provided me with a wonderfully drawn series of his own cartoons. They poked a little fun at various aspects of Patrol work. He was an exceptional artist and I wondered if he had missed his real calling. But, like most police officers, he preferred the grind, action, and service of police work.

The college was too far from our original home but we found a closer small home on the banks of the Titabawassee River that became a perfect little heaven. It was on a 5 acre lot with nearly

500 ft. of frontage on the beautiful river. Alongside the winding drive down to the home there was a huge variety of wonderful trees. The lot was bounded on one side by a bridge and on the other by a pretty little creek. The creek gully was bordered by large stands of spruce and cedar. There was a large metal workshop that displayed a power actuated chain fall. Everything was neat as a pin. And for the fisherman there was a cable operated dock that could be raised in the winter to avoid ice floes on the River. The old couple that had a sale by owner sign on the property advised they had a large farm on the River about a half mile down the highway and the property was just too much to care for. I finally asked how much they wanted and they said "oh well we'll take $35,000.00 for it." I darned near fainted as I said "It's sold."

We built an addition with a large bath, and turned a small enclosed porch into a bedroom for our son. We had three wonder fun-filled years there. We had many visitors, mainly due to the wonderful fishing in the area.

Our friends from Chicago, the Wielebenicki's, came several times as did my parents and other family members. Behind and to the side of the metal workshop was a large weed field. We cleared the property, obtained several old telephone poles from the local company and erected them behind the workshop. Edenville was a small village with a store, fire barn, barber shop, bait store and boat rental and several scattered homes. Since there was no local school or playground the wife and I built a baseball field on the vacant property. It didn't take long for the word to get around and soon there were organized games played and at times we had a couple dozen cars parked down the driveway. Nancy usually had Koolade and cookies or some treat for the local gang when they practiced and every kid in the region became our little buddies. It was wonderful fun.

Across the River and down the adjacent highway was a nice little town called Beaverton. They had a small movie house we attended often. Down the street was a restaurant which served the best pizza pie I have ever eaten in my life. You couldn't eat it without juice or melted cheese ending on your shirt or blouse. Mind you, I have eaten Pizza over all these years from East Coast to West Coast and in many of the major cities. It doesn't matter, Beaverton is still the best. It's been too long, but if I thought it was still there I would make the trip for a couple of those Pizzas.

Meanwhile, I drove the 18 miles to work every day, teaching at Delta College and working to help with our police centered programs. The community College was a very popular one with students from many sections of the United States and with a comparatively large Arab group. The College produced a special program for female police officers. It was very well received. I recall talking to a female Lt. from a large city department who confided that she was "scared to death," as she had just been promoted to head a homicide squad, even though her police experience was confined to that of a juvenile officer. She knew the primary reason for her new position was the absence of any female officers with such responsibility. It was a case of good old "Civil Rights" rearing its ugly head once again. Such confidences to the College staff were to acknowledge the female officers really appreciated the efforts to broaden their knowledge. The annual training sessions for strictly female officers was a model program at this time.

Another regular program annually presented at the College was a continuing education program for polygraph (lie detector) operators. This program was of special interest to me as I had a personal interest in Polygraphy. As MSP Laboratory Commander, I had supervisory control over our polygraph section. Michigan was very proud of this unit as the operators were specially selected, had attended the best training program in the Country and passed a six month probationary period afterwards, where their work was continually appraised and critiqued. They were quick to show any critics of the program, their accuracy percentages over many years were in excess of 90 percent.

I personally was aware of a number of murders solved by either their skill in interviewing the culprits and/or demonstrating to them that they were caught in lies that were critical. To me it was even more interesting to watch an operator prove by preliminary controlled questions or tricks that he could determine truth or deception, and then have the criminal confess without having the test completed. I watched through the one way glass as one operator convinced a gang killer that there was no way he could beat the operator and he might as well confess. Darned if he didn't confess!

Once in awhile, for a variety of reasons, the test came back as inconclusive or indeterminate. But, I found in nearly every homicide case they were involved, they got it right.

In one case that the officer reported as inconclusive, the suspect was a known arsonist and probably a mental case. After the preliminary interview, the polygrapher left the room for a moment. The suspect then zipped down his trousers and masturbated into his handkerchief, apparently to relax for the upcoming examination. It takes a lot of different kinds of people to make a world, as they say, and the veteran police officer sees many of them.

During the annual Polygraph program, many of the well recognized experts of the Country took part. It was rather surprising in a way that this small community college could support such programs. However, the small staff included two individuals who were well known and widely respected for their experience instructing officers. Interestingly, one acquaintance from the staff, a Prof. of Mathematics, was the father of an All-American football player and later professional Super Bowl winning coach, Tony Dungy.

Then an unusual incident occurred that produced howls of laughter all around the little village, as our place became known as the Polish car wash. I had worked till late afternoon and stopped at a little country store a short distance from home to pick up some bread and milk. The store was managed by an attractive Polish woman, who my daughters said tried to flirt with me. I never told them, but they were right, and I think Nancy sensed it too as she said on several occasions "for some reason, I just don't like that woman." As I shopped, the gal asked me if I heard what happened to my good car. When I told her no, she told me the car went into the river and had to be pulled out. When I got home with the groceries, I noticed our nearly new station wagon was sitting in the grass well off the drive with all the doors wide open. As I sat down at the supper table I noticed Nan and the kids all looking down at their food and none would look at me. I said "is something wrong?" "Oh no dad," the kids immediately replied. I then said I happened to look into the car after I arrived and wanted to know who put the big fish in the rear end.

Chasing Tail Lights to Forensic Ballistics

Now Nan and the kids all started to talk at once. It seemed that they had been shopping and mom parked the car off the driveway as the recent blacktop covering was still a bit soft. Suddenly one of the girls yelled out there goes our car as the station wagon rolled down the incline, broke off a small white pine on the river bank and then splashed into the Titabawassee. It floated past our fishing dock and then sank in about twenty feet of water. Nan called the Sheriff and he sent out a diver and wrecker and they pulled it out. By now we were all hysterical, laughing at the thought of the car riding down the River. I never did get why from then on neighbor kids called our place "the Polish car wash." Thankfully the insurance adjuster advised the parking pawl had broken and it wasn't Nan's fault.

It was a beautiful place with lots of birds and animals. I recall looking out the dining room bay window as we sat down to Thanksgiving dinner. Across the river three deer were having a drink and looking straight at us. But my favorite was the big beaver. My son Kurt and I were casting for bass in the tributary nearby when all of a sudden there was a terrible crashing sound in the water near our canoe. It was a huge mama beaver trying to scare us away from her nearby den. It was a great spot for bass at the time and we went back a couple of times and were greeted by Mrs. Beaver again, as she slapped the water with that huge flat tail.

On one 4th of July weekend the locals had a race down the river on floats. My kids built a float with my help and mounted on it several wooden boxes to sit on. They painted everything with white and red stripes and white stars on blue. They had a battery operated player on board and played patriotic music for the entire trip down river. We were all disappointed when they were awarded second prize. Like most parents we thought they were robbed. The preparations for the journey took a couple weeks and the parts cost plenty. But it was all worth it. They still talk about it and recall how they were robbed.

For the first time in her life, Nancy became a fisherwoman. She could sit on the dock and catch something nearly anytime she pleased. The "River" was home to many species, but her favorite was the grey channel catfish. They were good fighters and fine eating. She got in the habit of setting a pole on the end of the dock with a bell on it so she could hear it ring while she was cleaning house, cooking, etc.

Then one day a Conservation officer stopped by to advise her there was a State law against leaving lines in the water unattended. Her kid sister Kim was visiting so Nan and her decided to put the boat in the center of the River and anchor as they fished for a big one. I was in the shed when I heard Kim screaming. They landed a 9 lb. catfish and pulled it into the boat. Kim was so scared of the big fish with barbs and whiskers she was standing on the seat to keep her distance from the flopping critter. All I could do was stand on the dock and laugh at the great fishers.

During this period our family spent many holidays or weekends in Canada visiting Nancy's grandparents. Her grandpa had always been her favorite and I sometimes thought she loved him more than me. He was a little wiry man with a wicked sense of humor. He and grandma lived in an old farmhouse with a leaky tin roof. They still used well water and kept butter and milk in a bucket lowered far down the well just above the cool water. Grandpa had eight acres and tilled it by hand when he was in his early eighties. One early winter day, we arrived just in time for him to put me on one end of a huge crosscut saw. They still used wood for heating and cooking. We sawed till I thought I would pass out. Grandpa Great as he was known finally laid down his end saying "I am not the man I used to be. I thought, "thank God, you're killing me Grandpa."

Later he asked me if I would like to go target shoot, so I agreed. He went to his barn and took an old Cooey single shot .22 rifle off the wall and led me to the spillway where the water current was running swiftly under a thin sheet of clear ice. We walked onto the spillway and he handed me the loaded rifle and said, "Okay, you have an expert badge in shooting, hit that big bubble floating by." His old rifle had lost the front sight and was difficult to aim. I missed by about a foot. He reloaded and said here try it again. I missed again, so he took the rifle, reloaded and placed the shot through the center of a big floating bubble. I said, "Grandpa, how did you do that?" He said, "You have to learn to accommodate, son."

This brought to mind a couple of cases I worked with similar problems. One was alleged to be an accident and the other, murder. The first involved a hunter during pheasant season. The hunter flushed a cock pheasant or "rooster," as we always called them, raised his double shotgun and fired. He saw the bird drop somewhat in flight and feathers fly. He knew he had scored a hit. But the pheasant glided over the fence and into a neighboring corn field. He climbed the fence and went after it. He was new to the area and did not know that the owner of the next door farm was known to have a bad temper and didn't like hunters or trespassers. The neighbor was known to have threatened to shoot a hunter once before. As the hunter ran down a corn row after the wounded bird, the neighbor went into his barn and pulled an old single shot .22 rifle off the wall. He came out and fired one shot toward the hunter. The hunter let a yell and dropped in his tracks. The neighbor ran to the phone and called for help. As it turned out the hunter was lucky for the bullet struck him in mid-back and lodged next to his spine. Another inch over and he would have died or at least be paralyzed. The farmer claimed he only tried to scare him, not wound him.

I was asked to review the evidence and later testify. The rifle was very old, somewhat rusty, and was missing the rear sight elevator, the small notched piece of metal that adjusts the rear sight height. I conducted tests at the distance involved, about 200', and found the bullet striking the target about 4 feet below the aiming point. The farmer had claimed he attempted to fire the scare shot over the head of the hunter. My tests and testimony helped the farmer and the attempted murder charge was then changed to "careless use of a firearm resulting in injury." The Judge called me in his chambers after the hearing and congratulated me on my forthright testimony. As I walked down the hallway feeling rather proud of myself, I was approached by an elderly man in overalls who advised me that he thought my testimony was great but that he was a neighbor and knew the shooter well. On one occasion while visiting his neighbor he said they spotted a chicken hawk gliding over the chicken yard. The neighbor got the same rifle out of the barn and killed the hawk with one shot!

Later I was called by the Public Defender and asked to review a fatal shooting case for their office. It involved a poor area of the city. On a rainy night, quite late, the mother of one family was awakened by loud noses in the alleyway next to the home.

Her 16 year old teen age son was home and he went out to see what was keeping them awake. There was a fight in the alley involving a woman and two men. One of the men, apparently a pimp for the prostitute and the woman were struggling with a man they were trying to rob. The teen age boy grabbed his .22 rifle and ran to the back porch, fired one shot toward the group and the pimp died from the bullet which entered him at about the ear lobe and made its way into his brain.

The rifle was typical of many confiscated by police. The barrel was cut-down in length, the rifle was rusty, the front sight was missing due to the cut-off barrel, and most of the shoulder stock was also cut-off.

The Public Defender asked me if I would go to the scene with her and I quickly agreed. She pointed out the locations of the shooter and victim. It was raining at the time, there was no street light by the alley, and the distance was about 100 feet from shooter to victim. She told me the Prosecutor would not believe the story of the teen ager that he tried to shoot over the head of the pimp to scare him away, but was going to claim the defendant purposely killed the man.

The Prosecutor asked me whether I felt the shooter deliberately aimed and delivered the bullet to the head of the pimp, and I replied "due to the condition of the rifle, the weather, the lack of lighting, and the distance, I felt it was unlikely." What he could not hear was what I mumbled under my breath, "Even Grandpa Great couldn't make that shot!"

Back at our Edenville paradise, all was not heavenly. At times in the winter it was lovely with the fresh powdery snow gilding all the trees and covering the baseball field. The kids had a blast on sleds or toboggans sliding down the hill from the roadway and gathering speed toward the River. They usually were going so fast when they neared the river they had to dig in and swerve sideways to keep from flying off the bank onto the river ice. However, the drive was winding, descending and about five hundred feet long. Many mornings I was forced to warm the car and gun the engine as I tried to get enough speed to get out of the carport and up the drive so I could go to work. Sometimes I made it and sometimes I skidded too much. A few times I slid off into the ball field and had to have a wrecker winch me out. After one heavy snowfall, we awoke in the middle of the night hearing the roof creak on our new addition, under the weight of the snow. We had to climb up in the morning and shovel snow off to keep the roof from collapsing. And then I had to drive 18 miles one way to work, seeing cars and trucks in the ditch and piled into one another.

One Sunday night I was busy late at night trying to blow snow off the driveway so I could get out in the morning to go to work. The shear pin in the power take-off unit had broken and I was trying to replace it. I was sitting on the drive with a flashlight pinned under my chin as I attempted to get the pin through the shaft. It had turned colder and the wind was up and I was cold and shivering. I heard footsteps crunching through the snow as Nancy walked up behind me. I heard her voice as she said, "Charlie, are you tired of this white stuff yet? Have you ever thought of working in a warm climate?"

I had a good deal at Delta and after review I had just been granted tenure so I would be financially set for the rest of my life. But, to tell you the truth, I desperately missed firearms and tool mark identification, the courtroom battles, and the camaraderie.

In February I attended the AAFS annual meeting and lo and behold on the bulletin board was an advertisement for a firearm examiner in Florida, desired by the Florida Department of Law Enforcement. The contact at the meeting was a friend of Wally and a former analyst I knew from Wisconsin. I contacted him and he advised he was attempting to line up a few people for interviews. I told him I knew someone who might be interested. When he asked who it was I told him it was me. He told me if I wanted the job I could consider the interview over and it was mine. I told him I needed a few months to arrange the move. He said they would wait. I told him I needed to talk to my wife. She took 30 seconds to say "take it." Within three months we were on our way to Sanford, Florida to work in the State Crime Laboratory on the old Navy airbase.

8

Florida and the Crime Laboratory

We had made a deposit on a home in Maitland, Florida, near Orlando. It was a typical suburban Florida home with stucco outside, a palm tree in front, a small indoor pool in the rear with a tiny back yard surrounded by a six foot fence which kept you from seeing your neighbors. I needed a second car for work and we decided that I should get something special as a reward for my working years. My daughter Kim needed a car for transportation so we decided we would try to get two at a time, hoping for a price break. So, we went shopping with some money in the bank, for a change.

We checked several showrooms and lots without luck. Then we found a place that struck our fancy. All our life we lived with older cars and station wagons. The Chevrolet station wagon that was washed up after the Polish car wash was our 2nd new car in about twenty five years. I was at the age where men just have to do something foolish; sort of a 2nd childhood you know.

We ended our journey at a nearby Fiat dealership. They had a sporty small car with a wood luggage rack on the trunk that was a few years old and looked like new. On the showroom floor was a brand new Fiat Spider convertible.

Nan and I were dressed in old clothes and didn't look very Florida, if you know what I mean. An older salesman came out and we asked him about the used car on the lot. He acted like he was bored with these Yankee yokels and took a break to talk to another couple on the lot. He failed to come back. So, we rounded up a young salesman, asked about the car in the lot and the new convertible and told him to make us a price for the two of them. He did and we bought them both.

We snickered with each other as Mr. Snooty came in as the young guy was writing up the deal. The younger sales person told him that we had bought two cars, including the new convertible. You would have loved to see the look on his face. I was so bad in those days I even bought a jaunty sport cap to wear while driving the convertible with the top down. The new job, however, took that wild streak away very quickly.

When I reported to the Sanford (Central Florida) Crime Laboratory, I was given a warm welcome from staff who advised they really needed someone with my expertise. They told me they had an examiner named Bill Rathman. I had heard his name; he had been an examiner with the city of Cincinnati, Ohio. Bill died unexpectedly about two years before and they had been without a firearms and tool mark man since. The director showed me to the space reserved for me and I was rather pleased that it was roomy, and consisted of three divided rooms which should work out nicely. But then I looked around and failed to see any equipment or tools. I was shocked to find there were none. It was explained that after Bill died, Tallahassee came, i.e. examiners came from the headquarters laboratory and took all the equipment, ammunition supply, etc. away.

I thought this is a fine way to welcome your new analyst; you have had three months to get ready. My respect for the administration staff started to fade right away. I soon learned there were many good and friendly analysts on board. The following day I checked out a State car and drove to Tallahassee. There I found an old friend, Don Champagne, retired Royal Canadian Mounted Police firearms analyst. Don was a good examiner, with a wry sense of humor, but when it came to work he was tight as bark on a tree. He gave me a comparison microscope, an older American Optical version. He told me it was the one confiscated from Sanford. I doubted that but had no choice. I also asked for some ammunition for test purposes. He took two out of each box and placed them in coin envelopes as I marked them, thinking Don Old Buddy, you're a cheapskate.

The following morning I went into the micro/trace section and begged a stereomicroscope from them along with some old scavenged scope parts I later turned into a bullet measuring device to use under the stereo-scope along with a stage micrometer and eyepiece reticle. I brought my tools from home including gunsmith tools. I later replaced them with new tools purchased by the State. As the old saying goes "there is more than one way to skin a cat."

I also had a number of boxes of popular ammunition of the day for the .38 caliber and .22 caliber firearms. I used a number of mine before I obtained a quantity from the State. The next thing to do was to locate a cooperating supplier. I found a small sporting goods store in Sanford where the nice owner promised to get me any ammo I desired quickly in turn for the business. He turned out to be a good friend and helper. I then typed several pages of requisitions for over a thousand dollars worth of various cartridges and shot shells to stock for testing purposes.

Next I asked them where they kept the x-ray equipment only to be told they did not have any. By now it was getting obvious. These people were used to getting by on a shoestring. The next day I located information on the best portable x-ray package available and ordered one. Each time, the laboratory chief would come into my space and ask if I really needed this, what is it for, and it seems to be quite expensive. Each time I assured him we needed the material if we were to have a proper functioning firearms section. I found there was only a wood shoot box on legs for test firing. I told him to ask Tallahassee command if we could purchase a water tank.

During the early weeks, I used our swimming pool as my water tank; shooting a couple tests into it, then diving for the bullets on the bottom. In the meantime, Tallahassee advised it could not afford a water tank. I would have to make do. Most people know that water is so much denser than air (@ 800X). When I was young I watched those Tarzan movies where he would dive off the cliff or river bank and swim underwater while the bad guys shot dozens of times at him with military rifles. In a couple of films it actually showed bullets flying by at a slow speed. I thought that was just another Hollywood trick. But now I knew no trick need be involved. Even a high powered bullet can be significantly slowed to the point it's not dangerous after four or five feet of water. Of course the nice thing about water is that it will not scrub the markings from the barrel off the bullet sides. Whereas rags or cotton in a shoot box sometimes will do that especially when lead bullets are involved. However, I knew I dare not use the swimming pool often as my neighbors might want me investigated or complain about the racket.

Not long after, I test fired a 7mm rifle, shooting it into the wooden box. I had placed about six inches of wood board squares in the rear of the box just to be safe. When I fired the shot, even though I had carefully leveled the rifle, wood splinters flew out the back. I checked to see what happened. The bullet, a very hot load, had struck a knot in the center of the cotton rag waste causing it to rise and sneak out at the lid closing. I checked the back wall and found a nice neat round hole where the bullet exited the building. I went outside and there were no bodies lying in the street! I never found that test bullet. I then photographed the damage to the box and the hole in the steel building. I sent them to Tallahassee with an explanation and remarked I checked for bodies but failed to discover any.

Within two days they called me, advised they were really short of funds and asked if I could check locally and determine if a type of water tank could be built that would suffice and would not be very expensive. I was able to get a pipe manufacturing company near the laboratory to make a 4 ½ foot high, 14 inch diameter, 3/16 inch thick stainless steel vertical tank, balanced on steel hinges or bolts, and mounted on a steel slab with rollers. I sent them a bill for $1200 dollars, and they were pleased. We used it until we got the new laboratory in Orlando, where we had one of the fancy horizontal tanks that cost over $12,000 dollars.

By now I heard enough of our analysts complain about dealing with Tallahassee that I suggested at a staff meeting that they deserved a special name and I suggested Mecca or the Holy City. Our chief was not happy but for years the Headquarters laboratory was called "Mecca."

On another occasion I returned from vacation to find a new notice posted on the bulletin board for all analysts. It was about new orders for suitable clothes to be worn in the laboratory. Our chief seemed to like to give indirect orders to the staff and this was one I felt was uncalled for. I lost my temper and marched to his office. At the time, his assistant and one of our Directors from Tallahassee was in his office. I barged in anyway and in a loud voice told him I was sick of his childish memos and as to the latest one -"he could put it where the sun don't shine."

I could hear a cheer from the next door conference room where a number of the analysts were huddled. Later that day he came to the firearms office and advised me that what I did was improper and uncalled for. He asked what I had to say for myself. I told him that I agreed totally with what he said; what I did was improper, especially with the other administrators handy. He told me that I would have to be punished for the outburst and he was surprised when I told him that I expected it.

Several weeks went by and I stopped at his office and asked if he had decided on my punishment. He said that it was up to Tallahassee and they told him it had to be severe. I said thanks and left. A few weeks later I checked again and he told me he was waiting on Tallahassee, but it would be soon.

Again several weeks passed and I asked again. He looked at me and said "Look Charlie, if we can forget it, can you?" I told him that I certainly could. That was the end of my reprimand. When he gave up and left, the high command asked me if I would run the laboratory, with a nice increase in pay of course. I told them no way, leave me be, I am happier than a skunk eating cabbage doing firearms and tool marks. The only thing I ever loved more was my wonderful wife Nancy.

I really believe that I operate on even keel the great majority of times, but I have been known to tangle with higher administration. Back in the State Police I had a few problems like that and I always fancied myself as standing up for the folks, as Bill O Riley might say on Fox news.

It was a great amount of pleasure for me to find that my staff and analysts secretly called me "the bull." I was especially pleased when my secretary sewed a special microscope cover with a bull head replete with horns and presented it to me one birthday. The crowning event came when I introduced one of the first meetings of the Midwestern Association of Forensic Scientists in Lansing. Before I left the rostrum they presented me with a bull carved out of wood. It sits in an honored place on my desk.

My early days in Florida reminded me a lot of my early days in the Michigan Crime Laboratory. There was no firearms section at Tampa, Jacksonville, or Pensacola then. Tallahassee took care of the Northern Counties and city work while Sanford took care of the Central and Southern work and I testified in Ocala, Jacksonville, Orlando, Tampa, Melbourne, Palm Beach, Sarasota, Ft. Myers, Palatka, the Keys, and everywhere in between. Thankfully, Miami and Ft. Lauderdale had their own laboratories and firearms and tool mark sections. But I was back on the merry- go- round and was happy to see Florida expand their facilities with firearms analysts at Pensacola, Jacksonville and Tampa. During this interval, Tallahassee knew I needed help. They advised they had a young man on staff, who was partly trained and who was the son of the former analyst at Sanford. His name was Garry Rathman, and would I be interested in completing his training and having him on staff? I told them certainly and Garry was transferred back to Sanford, good for both of us as he was near his parents and family.

As I worked with Garry I found him to be lots of fun, and very intelligent. I believe Tallahassee had kept him under wraps a bit and he lacked a little confidence. This is normal in most trainees in the early stages. As time progressed, I found that he strongly wanted to forge ahead, and was just awaiting the go sign. The more I gave him tasks the more he wanted. He was a delight to work with and developed into a great examiner with a terrific microscopic eye for detail.

The two of us drove the rest of the laboratory crazy. I soon learned that Garry loved music and was really in to old music of my era, the 40s and 50s. We developed a little contest. As we were both sitting at the microscopes comparing bullets or cartridge cases, one of us would start to hum a song and the other one would try to remember or guess the title. The rest of the laboratory thought we were both a little crazy, I believe. However, there was one that did not. Her name was Nancy too and she was a serologist. Garry had let it be known that he was single and was going to stay that way. Nancy told her buddies that she had her eye on him and was going to marry him. I could have warned him, Nancys are like that and usually have their way. They were married and had a little boy that Garry and Nancy adored. Sadly cancer got Garry at a too young age. It might have been related to Agent Orange as Garry fought in Viet Nam and had been in areas where the chemical was deployed. Everyone that knew him was devastated and that included yours truly.

One event I will never forget was an annual meeting of AFTE held at the relatively new Michigan State Police Training Academy. The meeting was arranged by a couple of young analysts that I became good friends with over the years, Mike Arrowood and Jim Berglund. It was the best conducted meeting I had attended up to that time and the members had a wonderful time and left with much new information.

I flew with a delegation from Florida on a commercial jet. When we got to the airport there was a bus waiting to take us to the Academy. When we arrived a sharp, uniformed Trooper (Academy trainer) marched up to me, gave me a salute and said, "Captain, your bag sir." He picked up my bag and walked me in to the applause from the audience. When we left at the end of the week and were standing by the curb waiting for the bus, a State Police freshly polished patrol car drove up. The young Trooper got out, saluted me, took my bag and put it in the back seat as he said, "No disrespect sir, but no State Police Captain is riding a damn bus." As we drove off the group was howling with laughter.

Later, at the airport a number of them told me that you were right, Charlie, we have never seen a sharper outfit than the MSP. Of course, in Florida I used to brag about them all the time.

During my tenure with the Florida Department of Law Enforcement, I found myself involved in many interesting cases, mostly homicide. It is probably not a fair comparison but it always seemed that there were more in Florida than in Michigan. It may not be correct, maybe I was just getting older and it seemed that way.

The island murder case: One that I recall, primarily due to the State Attorney who tried the case, was one that occurred on the Gulf side when an attractive female realtor left her office just after lunch to meet a prospective client on the Island where they had a number of expensive homes. The man, George McNamara seemed quite interested and thus might lead to a sale and nice commission. The realtor, Helen Roberts told the secretary that she would be back later that day as she had papers to take care of for an upcoming closing. When she failed to return by dark, an assistant went looking for her. Her car was found parked at the model home and her body was found in the master bedroom. She had been raped and shot in the chest at close range.

At autopsy, the next day, a .38 special caliber jacketed hollow point bullet was removed from under the skin on her back where it came to rest. The bullet was rushed to the Laboratory. From the class rifling characteristics and data at that time, I was able to tell the investigators that there were only a few firearms with corresponding rifling characteristics and the only common one was a .38 special caliber Charter Arms revolver. As with all such preliminary opinions, a caveat stated no suspected firearm should be overlooked but submitted to the laboratory for comparison. This type of caution has always existed due to the fact that it is a physical impossibility to obtain tests and rifling data from every kind of firearm in the world. In this case the data from our laboratory and the FBI data bank were similar.

Investigation led detectives to a suspect with a prior criminal record, James Hamilton, and ultimately to a search of his apartment. There they found no firearm but they did find an ammo box with a couple of cartridges remaining. They were Winchester .38 special jacketed hollow points, of the exact same type as the evidence. An acquaintance of Hamilton advised that his friend had a Charter Arms revolver for such cartridges but he had gotten rid of it.

The firearm was never recovered and finally the evidence bullet and the cartridges were sent to the FBI Laboratory for analysis. They had developed an instrumental system for detecting certain trace materials found in lead bullet cores. They were the only Crime Laboratory capable of such analyses and in addition they had been engaged in research on this subject for several years. The analysis from the FBI came back with the opinion that they could not differentiate between the lead core material in the cartridges and fatal bullet and this indicated they were from the same batch or melt and therefore could have originated from the same box of ammunition.

As a trial date was set, the State Attorney handling the case contacted me and asked me to do him a favor in preparation for the trial. He stated in effect that he was aware that Winchester was a big company and the .38 special caliber was a popular one. He asked me to contact representatives from all the ammunition companies I could possibly contact and get an estimate of the number of .38 special cartridges they manufacture in a recent year. He wanted all this data compiled and sent to his office. He anticipated the defense attorney, a good one, would ask the FBI agent and myself to provide an estimate of the amount of these type cartridges Winchester would produce in that year. And of course the defense attorney asked if it was true that Winchester made many such cartridges and if I could tell him about how many. I can not remember that large number now but of course it was big. Then the State Attorney asked on rebuttal how many .38 caliber cartridges in total does Winchester make? Then after a few introductory questions he asked about how many .38 special cartridges might be produced by all known ammunition manufacturers in the year. Of course that number was staggering in comparison and seemed to impress on the jury that the defense argument was not that big of a deal. That was a new bit of reasoning for me but it apparently worked. And of course he had the testimony of the former room mate of the defendant about the possession of a Charter Arms revolver. The Agent and I were released and allowed to go home. But this trial still had a ways to go.

I had merely arrived home when the phone rang and it was the State Attorney. He said we have a bit of a problem. That afternoon, after we were released, the court officer went to the bench and whispered something in the ear of the Judge. The Judge immediately sent the jury out and called the attorneys into his chambers. He advised them the Sheriff had received some information and acted upon it to find a .38 Special caliber Charter Arms revolver lying in a conspicuous way in a dumpster near the court house. The officers were on there way to the Crime Laboratory and could I meet them there and start an instant comparison of that revolver with the fatal bullet. The Judge felt he dare not continue the trial without it. Once again, I felt obligated to do just that, but actually I was interested too and wondered what was happening. Thank God, the revolver was undamaged. It showed no indications of tampering and marked test bullets faithfully. I was satisfied this could not be the fatal weapon and so advised the officers and Judge.

Was this some type of defense ploy, a nasty joke, possibly a trick by an accomplice of the defendant? No one knows, but Hamilton was not benefited. He got life in prison.

The ex-cop killer case: One of the next homicides was a bit of a surprise for me. The killer turned out to be an ex-police officer with considerable experience in law enforcement, a degree background, and an instructor in the area law enforcement training program. It started when two deputies on routine night patrol spotted a car in a business parking lot, long after the time when the business was open. They decided to check it out. As they approached they noticed the driver window was rolled down and there was a man slumped over behind the wheel. He turned out to be the driver and owner of the car. He had been shot through the cheek and was obviously dead. Outside on the parking lot surface the officers found one .45 automatic caliber fired cartridge case. It appeared that nothing was amiss inside the car and he had apparently been shot from the exterior through the open window, suggesting it may have been the result of a discussion with one or more persons outside the car.

At autopsy the next day, the pathologist removed pieces of copper bullet jacket material, many minute round lead particles and a blue plastic cup or wad of some sort. No question about it, the victim had been shot with a Glaser Safety Slug, a recently made bullet designed for police use and not thought to be available to the general public as yet. This bullet type was designed for police use in that if one was fired at a felon, missed the mark, and struck the cement walk or road or hard object of any nature it would not deflect and kill or severely wound an innocent person. Rather, it would breakup into a myriad of small non-lethal pieces, thereby the name Safety Slug. It was composed of a hollow copper jacket, loaded with very fine shot, held in place with a plastic cap. Of course, the same bullet fired into the human body would disassemble into a large number of lethal objects with sufficient velocity to maim and kill.

The detectives discovered the victim was a local business person, a well known and respected insurance agent in the city. The only thing in his recent background that attracted their attention was the fact that he had dated a pretty secretary in town and was in competition for her graces. His main competition was a former police officer who taught at the nearby Academy. As they pulled up to his apartment complex they noticed him getting behind the wheel of his car. They walked to him and asked him questions about his whereabouts at the approximate time of the murder. He gave them an alibi, one difficult to prove or disprove. They asked him if he owned any handguns. He said that he did and advised he was licensed to carry and had his .45 automatic under the seat. He carefully produced a Star (Spanish mfd.) semi-automatic pistol. The officers asked him if they could take it for testing and he told them certainly. He was so cooperative and unflustered they thought they were probably barking up the wrong tree, but better have the pistol checked by the Crime Laboratory just in case.

In the Laboratory I had examined the jacket pieces and easily determined the class characteristics of the rifling were six lands and grooves left twist, with land and groove dimensions typical of the Colt or Colt pattern semi-automatic pistol. When the officers produced the Star pistol it was quickly eliminated on the basis of class characteristics.

An interview with the young woman who had dated the victim brought the Academy instructor back into the investigation. She told them she had also dated the ex-policeman, but had broken off with him as she felt he was insanely jealous. The victim had informed her that James Thomas, the ex-officer, had threatened him due to his interest in her.

The investigators got a break in the case when they learned that when Thomas was still on the force he had been a member of an anti-drug squad and at that time was known to carry a .45 automatic caliber Colt pistol. With this information they were able to obtain a search warrant for his apartment. No pistol was found, however several items of interest were seized. One was a box of .45 automatic fired cartridges. Apparently Thomas was one of the officers who retrieved his brass fired cartridge casings in order to reload them and save on ammunition. On a shelf in the coat closet they found a leather holster containing two extra magazines loaded with live unfired .45 automatic caliber PMC cartridges. The magazines were the type designed for the Colt pattern pistol. When the detectives asked him about the magazines he told them he carried a .45 auto. Colt pistol when he was on the drug squad, nine years previously. He sold the pistol to a young man on the squad who admired it, but forgot to give him the spare magazines. When asked, he was unable to remember the name of the officer, but that was nine years ago.

The investigators brought the items to the Crime Laboratory. I compared the box of fired cartridges with the evidence fired case from the scene. Lo and behold, the entire box of casings was identically marked and all were matched with the evidence case. This meant they could prove the wanted firearm had been in his possession for some time. How about the live rounds in the Colt type magazines? Contact was made with a technical representative from PMC, a South Korean ammunition concern, who advised they had only imported this cartridge into the United States for five years. Therefore the cartridges in the nine year old magazines and holster could have been here at the most for five years. When the detectives returned to arrest Thomas he had disappeared. Warrants for his arrest were obtained but two years passed before anything further developed.

The former girl friend came to the rescue as Thomas called her from out-of-state and renewed his interest in her. She played along and soon they were talking like lovers again. She was able to learn items about his new life and the type of job he had obtained. Although he did not tell her where he was he confided he was in an adjoining state. Listening to all these conversations were the investigators, with her consent. They learned he used a new name, had obtained a new social security number from records of a recently deceased person, etc. Finally, they had enough clues to guess where he was living and working and later spotted him on the street and arrested him.

He was returned to Florida, tried and convicted, and sentenced to life in prison. What is the old French saying - "beware of the woman?"

Firearms Identification embraces many functions, even though the bullet and cartridge case comparisons are the ones usually emphasized. It may include safety of the questioned firearm, repair of a broken firearm, bullet pathways and trajectories, x-rays of bullets, sounds and photography of discharges, powder and shot patterns, etc. But, it must be remembered that the actual comparison of bullets and cartridge cases with tests from suspected firearms is a form of tool mark identification. There are actually two types of tool marks; impressed where an object crushes a softer material leaving a negative image of its surface, and striated where an object is drawn or moved along a softer material leaving scratches or striae from its surface. Some authorities list a third type which is actually a combination of the other two. Instances of impressed markings being used in criminal investigation can be cited at least beyond two centuries Long before that the Chinese are credited with using thumb impressions in wax as a form of identification. Striated markings used in criminal cases can be cited back to at least 1900, to Dr. Kockel of Leipzig who wrote about such findings in great detail in the famous German journal Kriminalistik.

The Wallsink murders: One very interesting case in Central Florida involved cattle rustling, murder, and tool marks on the fatal bullet, barbed wire and on a broken lock. Many people do not know that Florida is a big cattle State. We usually think of swaying palms, orange groves and the oceans but there are many large ranches with large herds. On one of these Central Florida ranches, a sizeable number of cattle had become missing over a short span of time. Apparently someone was rustling cattle.

Ed Hill, the ranch foreman, and his assistant John Bogue were checking some of the outer reaches of the ranch when they spotted a pickup in an unlikely location. They stopped to check it out when they were approached by two ranch hands. They were completely taken by surprise when Russ Schmidt pulled a Dan Wesson .357 magnum caliber revolver from under his jacket and methodically shot them both.

Schmidt and his partner Ray Johnson, dumped the two bodies in the rear of their truck and drove a short distance to the wallsink. This sink hole was called wallsink due the nearly vertical sides. It was very deep and filled with dark water. Some years before neighbors had erected a barbed wire fence around the hole to keep wayward cattle or children from a watery death. Schmidt and Johnson obtained their bolt cutters from the truck bed, cut several strands of barbed wire and slid the bodies through and down into the sink hole. They knew the bodies would never be discovered here. As they were driving back to their residence Schmidt remembered the revolver and knowing a firearm could be traced decided to rid himself of the evidence, just in case. They drove to a nearby lake where a sandy bluff overlooked the deepest hole in the body of water. Schmidt threw the revolver into it, satisfied it was beyond discovery.

Ranch hands found the pickup truck of the missing foreman as they searched for him and his helper. They noticed spots of blood on leaves and drag marks for a short distance and theorized the missing men had been killed. They called for the Sheriff and Coroner to come to the scene.

Investigators early on felt the disappearance had to be related to the cattle rustling problem, due to the location of the crime and knowledge that the foreman was checking the ranch for evidence. The name of Ray Johnson was on their short list of suspects. He had a record and had been named as a potential suspect in the rustling. They picked him up and interviewed him about the disappearance. While doing so they noticed his obvious nervousness. They put the squeeze on him convincing Johnson they had the goods on him. They convinced him that the only way to keep out of old Sparky, the Florida electric chair, would be to cooperate and turn into a State witness. He followed suit exclaiming over and over that he had not wanted Schmidt to kill them but had little influence over him. He told the investigators he would lead them to the bodies and show them where his buddy had thrown the firearm.

A Department skin diver recovered the revolver and aided in the hookup to the bodies and their removal from the wallsink. Next the deputies brought the revolver, bolt cutters from the pickup bed, a lock with the shackle cut in two off the pasture gate and several lengths of cut barbed wire from the wall sink fence. The revolver was slightly rusted and inoperable, so it was placed in an oil bath to loosen the oxidized parts. After removal of marl from the barrel and slight rust from interior parts, the revolver was test fired and tests identified with the evidence bullets from the bodies. Next the bolt cutters were examined under the stereo microscope for trace evidence. Interestingly, even after this time lapse, I could see half moon scuffs on the cutting blade, one about the diameter of the lock shackle and the other the diameter of the wire. Tests cut through lead wire were almost perfect and matched the lock and the barbed wire cuts.

The trial of Schmidt, who would admit nothing, was a classic. The defense attorneys fought hard and accepted nothing, fighting every piece of evidence all the way. Finally, the defendant was found guilty of murder. About three years later I was subpoenaed to testify on this case again. The Appeals Court had ruled on a technicality and ordered a new sentence hearing. Such hearings where the jury hears certain facts and decides on a penalty to recommend to the Judge are recent additions in the scheme of things. Years ago, when the jury brought in the verdict their job was done. These sentencing hearings are like a mini-trial all over again and take up considerable time and cost tax payers lots of money. About ten years later I was subpoenaed to appear again for another hearing and the murderer was sentenced again. A few years ago, I was contacted again by the State Attorney in Florida to advise I may have to return and testify on the facts of this case one more time. However, that call was never followed up so I am hoping this case is finally over.

The dirty revolver: Sometimes I have been amazed when what seems to be a mystery turns out to be relatively simple, requiring only a little common sense to determine. I was asked to examine two firearms which were involved in a shootout and failed to properly function. One was a new imported 9mm semi-automatic pistol carried by a uniformed officer in a drug raid. The other was a .38 special caliber six shot snub-nose revolver (2 inch barrel) carried by the under-cover officer in the raid. A third officer in the raid also carried a 9mm pistol, which functioned perfectly and was used to kill the assailant.

Investigation revealed three officers entered a residence to serve a warrant for drug furnishing. Two were in uniform and carried the 9mm pistols as standard side arms. The third officer was in plain clothes and carried the revolver hidden in his waistband. They were met in the hallway by a man and his girl friend, the subjects named in the warrant. Unbeknown to the officers, a third person, an armed man with a .357 magnum caliber revolver, was hiding in the kitchen. As he came out of the kitchen, firearm leveled toward the officers, the first male subject in the hallway grabbed the first officer, apparently attempting to wrestle his firearm away and take him down. The male from the kitchen emptied his magnum revolver, firing all six shots. The first officer went down after firing only one shot from his pistol, now non-functional with a fired cartridge case in the chamber. The second officer, a plain clothes detective attempted to fire his snub nose revolver, but it failed to fire. The third officer fired all sixteen shots until his pistol was empty. He was effective in killing the assailant, but the other officer died with fifteen cartridges remaining.

What in heaven was wrong with the firearms of the two officers? There was nothing really wrong with the dead officer's pistol. Numerous tests confirmed that it operated as designed. As he fired the one shot he was in the grasp of the arrested man and the pistol was apparently trapped between their bodies as they struggled. As a semi-automatic weapon is fired the gas pressure that drives the bullet from the barrel also drives the slide backwards, pulling the fired cartridge case from the chamber (extraction) and throwing it out of the pistol (ejection). Any significant force restricting this rearward slide motion will cause it to not have sufficient rearward travel to extract the fired case and it will resume its normal forward position. This requires the pistol slide to be manually pulled rearward to eject the case and reload the weapon. As an old "wheel gun" (revolver) shooter friend used to say "at this point the pistol makes a good boat anchor."

What about the hidden snub-nose revolver of the detective? Disassembly was very instructive. The firearm had apparently been carried for some time hidden in clothing without inspection or cleaning. A large pad of cloth fibers, gunpowder residues, oil, grease, etc. had built up on the back side of the hammer and firearm frame, hidden from sight by the revolver side plate. The materials restricted the hammer from being placed in the cock position for discharge! One more reason regular inspection and cleaning a firearm is required.

Fats and the hit man: One of the weird Florida cases I worked on involved the killing of a lower echelon Mafia type by a professional killer or hit-man. A couple bass fishermen moving along a deep canal spotted a strange object under the water, barely visible in the depths. They used an anchor rope to secure it and pulled a large chest style freezer with locked lid into shore. A large screwdriver from the truck sufficed to break into the chest. There was no treasure, only the body of a heavily set well-dressed man in an advanced state of decomposition. One fisherman went to call the Sheriff while the other guarded the find. The local area had no missing person of this description. The pathologist removed the hands of the victim and turned them over to the Identification Bureau where technicians restored the fingers to a semblance of their original self. Fingerprints were obtained and the FBI answer showed the dead man to be John "Fats" Dinardo, who had a lengthy rap sheet over many years. A number of bullets were removed from his body that appeared to be in relatively good condition despite a slight fatty coating. The bullets were rushed to the Crime Laboratory for a determination of class characteristics and information on possible firearms. However, the bullets displayed no normal rifling traits, only large numbers of deeply scored markings along the bearing surfaces. The detectives were advised the caliber was .22 and the bullet markings indicated the use of a muffler or silencing device.

Surprisingly, a short time later, authorities were tipped that a professional killer was staying in a plush hotel on the opposite side of the State. There was an outstanding warrant for his arrest so he was picked up. He was arrested in his room without a struggle. In the room was a valise with several handguns and a silencer for one .22 caliber pistol with a threaded barrel. Tests with the silencer were easily identified with bullets from Fats.

This is the one time in my experience where a professional killer was identified through firearms identification. Although we had one case where a group of drug smugglers buried several firearms, covered with grease or cosmoline to prevent rust and wrapped in several layers of plastic. According to information, they were buried for several years to "cool off." After cleaning and test firing one of the handguns was identified with one unsolved shooting. Apparently the criminals had no idea that this type of evidence is maintained indefinitely.

By the early eighties we had moved into a new laboratory in Orlando, near the Federal Building. We had a roomy facility with a target range and a new horizontal water tank. For me, this was luxury and with no make-do or just get by. We had three examiners and a fine facility. We actually found time to do some badly need research.

Garry in particular was involved in several efforts resulting in papers for AFTE. We were aided by cooperation from our nearby forensic pathologist, a very good one, Dr. Thomas Hegert. The major problem for me was the drive from home to downtown Orlando, down the infamous I-4. Just one rubber-necker or gawker along the route would mean a delay of an hour or so.

Some time ago, Nancy and I bought an old home on Park Ave. in Sanford, the so-called scenic route to downtown and Lake Monroe (the St. Johns River system). We put a ton of work and a fair amount of dollars in renovation. We loved it and were not about to move to Orlando. To me Orlando was a nice place to visit but not to live in. I felt the same way about the sensation of the world, Disney World. We took the kids and grandkids there a few times but we were over the noise and thrill game.

When we first moved to Sanford, about 1978, it was pretty, quiet and tranquil along the waterway. By the late eighties it was slowly being swallowed by the megalopolis of Orlando and its suburbs. Of course, this made for more crime and business for the Crime Laboratory, but who needed it? I recall one day when Nan and I went shopping at a nearby supermarket in the middle of the day. That evening the news reported a robbery armed at that same market about a half hour after we left. In addition, the robbers fired one shot from a sawed off shotgun into the ceiling to get attention. Nancy remarked that it was a good thing we had left earlier or I would have butted in and got us shot. Then, there was one night when I heard a pounding at the front door. There was one young, disheveled and extremely nervous type on the porch. He yelled out for me to let him in as he needed a phone to get help for a car breakdown. I told him to get off my porch. He yelled back that I should let him in right away. I yelled to Nancy "honey, get my .45." He ran away and I found out the next morning that he was one of a trio of armed robbers who abandoned their stolen car down the block; so much for being a good neighbor.

9

The Courtroom

Everything we do in CSI (Crime Scene Investigation) and CLA (Crime Laboratory Analysis) is for the primary purpose of assisting the Judge and Jury in understanding the meaning and significance of the evidence related to the alleged crime. So, it is the most important part of the job. Testifying requires more than knowledge about the evidence. It nearly always requires some waiting, it can be educational (hopefully so for the Jury), it can be funny, it can be maddening and outrageous, it can be cruel.

Before I lapse into requirements for the witness, I would like to relate one of my personal favorite scenarios. It involved my favorite pathologist, Dr. Richard Olsen. He looked older than his years and walked with a slight stooped posture. His suit seemed to look a little wrinkled and he was nearly bald with wisps of short hair on top of his head. In other words he did not make an imposing looking witness. What most people could not see was the extremely muscular and fit man under the rumpled clothes. He had been a team wrestler in college. It was the first time I ever witnessed him testify. The defense attorney was a well known and well qualified one. The bailiff called Dr. Olsen to the stand. As he proceeded to walk in that direction, I glanced at the defense attorney and I noticed he had an odd, sort of incredulous look on his face. I could read his mind as he too wondered about this person being the famous Dr. Olsen. But then the Doctor took the stand and the Prosecutor asked him for his name. When he said "Dr. Richard Olsen," it reverberated throughout the courtroom with such force I swear the chandelier in the center of the ceiling actually trembled. I know I never copied from that loud and forceful voice, but I also know the Judge never had to ask me to speak up.

I know that sometimes I got a little long winded, and I remember one Judge in Brevard County who once interrupted me at the end of another of the Defense Attorneys argumentative queries and said ", Now Charlie, no dissertations please, just answer the question!" Over the years I found many occasions when court testimony was really enjoyable. If there is anything I hate to see, and I have seen too many in person and on TV, it is the expert witness who talks in a low monotone voice and gives the Jury the impression that he/she is hardly interested in the proceedings. When I hear expert testimony described as boring and uninteresting it really upsets me. It's no wonder the Jury sometimes places little stock in what they are hearing.

In more than 50 years of CSI and CLA activities in Forensic Science, I have testified as an expert witness on more than 1,000 occasions. The majority were routine. Many were merely corroborative of statements or other evidence; some however were vitally important to the case being heard. Some were cordial, but a few bitterly fought with personal innuendo thrown in. Most were professional with a Judge as guardian of protocol.

It might be a little enlightening to the uninitiated to describe several cases where the courtroom battle or antics played a prominent role. The first one I will describe is one of my favorites, at least from a humorous stand point.

The General: It was early spring, cold and with a light dusting of snow on the ground. The County Courthouse, located in an island enclosure surrounded by the main street of the normally quiet community, was bustling this day.

A murder trial, not the usual fare in this little town, was being held in front of a large local crowd. Arnold Gentry, the County Prosecuting Attorney, was relishing the opportunity to once again show off his lawyerly skills.

The trial should have been rather straight forward. It was not a complicated homicide. Hobie Smith, the defendant, was charged with killing his neighbor over an unpaid debt. The weapon of choice was an old bolt-action 12 gauge shotgun.

In the old brick courthouse, the main courtroom was full of spectators with a sprinkling of local reporters. Although the trial failed to promise much action, in this rural county the Prosecutor was the main attraction.

Prosecutor Arnold Gentry was known to the locals as simply "the General." He had served in World War II as a General in the Army Reserves, and thus was famous in the region. He was a big man with a loud booming voice which seemed to match his reputation as a fearless and relentless criminal prosecutor. Out-of-town police and forensic witnesses were rather surprised to hear him addressed as General Gentry, rather than as the Prosecutor or County Attorney.

The defense attorney was a local experienced lawyer, Richard Howell. He had recently been engaged in a bitter political battle in an effort to unseat Gentry. However the General was too popular to be beaten despite the ensuing mud slinging contest. Howell was a slightly built man with thinning hair and tiny wire-rimmed glasses. His appearance and posture indicated possible health problems, although his voice had an edge to it indicating he could be tough.

The State had proceeded through the case without a problem. It was now time to call the firearms expert to the stand. The bailiff sounded out "the State calls Charles Meyers to the stand." The Prosecutor introduced me to the Jury and asked for a brief resume of my qualifications to testify as an expert witness regarding firearms identification matters. Expert witnesses are permitted to render opinions regarding the examination of evidence within their discipline. After the Judge recognized me as an expert in firearms identification, the trial proceeded.

Within a brief period, the focal part of the examination was clearly at hand. Gentry handed me the murder weapon. I immediately checked the action to ensure that the shotgun was unloaded and safe. The Prosecutor then asked a series of typical questions asking me to describe the weapon for the Jury and whether it operated in a normal manner. He asked if there was a safety device and whether it was operable. Then he inquired how much pressure would be required to pull the trigger and fire the weapon. He then had me show the Jury the actions required to load and fire the shotgun. Shortly after that he turned to the defense table and advised him that he might inquire. The defense attorney arose and slowly approached the stand. There appeared to be a slight smirk on his face as he asked the first question. "Mr. Meyers are you familiar with firearm safety rules?" I replied that I was. He then asked if there was one common general rule applying to firearms and I told him that he might be referring to the rule to never point a firearm toward anyone as it might be loaded. At that he grinned like the cat that swallowed the canary as he stated, "Did you notice that when Mr. Gentry handed the firearm to you it was pointed directly at the Jury box?" At that Gentry sprang to his feet screaming "I object, I object, I object!" The Judge gaveled the yelling and laughing audience to silence and announced this is the perfect time for a lunch break.

As I stepped down from the stand Gentry grabbed my arm and told me that he was taking me to lunch and he was buying. Of course I had to go along with that plan. When we were settled in a booth at the restaurant across the square, he advised me, "We will pretend you are on the stand for re-direct and I will ask you certain questions and I want to hear your answers, okay?" The first question is, "Were you ever in the military?" I answered, "Yes, I was in the Navy during World War II and Korea." Gentry said, "Okay that may help. Then I will ask you, "Is it a fact that the bolt action shotgun in this case is similar to the military bolt action rifle in operating principle?" I replied, "Yes that would be correct." Then I will say, "When I handed you the shotgun, the bolt was open and pulled to the rear, is that correct?" I replied, "Yes that is also correct." Then I will ask, "When the firearm is in that condition it will not fire is that not true?" I replied, "Yes that is also true." He then asked, "Anyone who has been in the military would recognize that fact. Is that not true?" Before I could complete my answer, he grabbed my arm and said, "I want you to answer that question – yes, General that is accurate." I nearly chocked on part of my sandwich as I told him I could not do that, it would be unethical and unprofessional. Gentry became agitated as he said, "Charlie, we can not let the draft dodging s.o.b. get away with this; you have got to do it."

It took several minutes to calm him down, but he finally agreed it might not be necessary when I reminded him that everyone in that courtroom knew he was in the military and a General to boot.

It was another of the weird and sometimes humorous happenings in the court room, although Hobie Smith failed to see the humor since he was found guilty of second degree murder. It was probably the perfect verdict in this case.

The barrel switch: State Police detectives were investigating another drug related homicide. The victim had been shot once in the chest and the recovered bullet, a .32 automatic caliber full metal cased projectile, was in excellent condition for microscopic comparison. A priority examination of the fatal bullet in the Laboratory revealed it displayed class characteristics of six lands and grooves with widths and twist characteristic of several pistols with the FN Browning at the head of the list.

Within a few weeks Det. Lynford Adams appeared at the Laboratory with a 7.65mm caliber pistol barrel. While searching a room with a search warrant, they found no firearms but did find the barrel lying loose in the rear pocket of a pair of pants hanging in the closet, along with a quantity of drugs.

Examination of the barrel disclosed it to be a 7.65mm (.32 auto.) barrel of foreign manufacture and the design and proof markings identified it as made by FN in Belgium for the FN Browning pistol. A pistol of this type was pulled from the Laboratory collection and the evidence barrel substituted for the display weapon. Tests were fired and compared with the evidence bullet and identification made using the standard comparison microscopic technique of examining the evidence and test specimens side by side under the same degree of magnification and lighting.

Eventually it was time for trial. The Prosecutor was entranced with the substitution story and requested the display pistol be brought to show the jury. The Prosecutor dutifully qualified me as an expert in this discipline and then elicited testimony regarding the procedure used to obtain tests and the microscopic examination. With the permission of the Court he requested that I disassemble the pistol and illustrate the switch of the barrels. Knowing this can be tricky, although this is one of the simpler pistols to break down, I was very slow and cautious to complete the action. I wanted to avoid the embarrassment of losing my grip on a powerful spring and have it careen toward the Jury box.

Then it was time for cross examination. To my surprise the defense attorney made a big deal out of the disassembly of the pistol, indicating he had timed me and it took all of five minutes. He then looked at the Jury with a smug grin saying "I find it difficult to believe that a real expert would take that long for such a simple task."

Upon re-direct examination the Prosecutor asked "can you repeat this experiment in a more timely fashion?" I told him that I thought I could and to my surprise the Judge allowed another disassembly procedure, followed by another demanded by the defense with a precise explanation of each maneuver, etc. This was turning into a side show, but it finally stopped when the Judge stated "the Jury has seen enough I believe." He then asked if either attorney had any other questions for me, and when they said no, he excused me from the stand and further attendance.

I hesitated briefly, not sure how to properly proceed, and then addressed the Judge directly, "Your honor, I know this is out of order, but I have a problem." At that, the Judge sent the Jury out and asked of what my problem consisted. I told him, "Your honor I believe the barrel in the evidence bag is not the evidence one but rather the one brought in the Laboratory pistol." The Judge asked, "Is there a way you can quickly tell and if so do so." I quickly examined the so-called evidence barrel and told the Judge that it was in-correctly identified as the evidence barrel had my initials and case number etched into the steel. The Judge frowned and said, "Well switch them back." I did quickly before I left the stand.

Later, I wondered what if the switched barrel had gone un-noticed and another expert on appeal had conducted an examination, unknowingly, between the wrong barrel and the fatal bullet. He would have advised the Court that there was a mistaken identification and an injustice had been done. I wondered if this was an innocent mistake or a set-up gone awry. My suspicions were fueled by the most famous barrel switch in legal history. It involved .32 automatic Colt pistols, similar in design to the FN, in a case known to most criminal lawyers and forensic scientists. It was reported in the Montgomery book "Sacco and Vanzetti, the Murder and the Myth" about the infamous trial and hearings (circa 1923).

The plaster cast: One of the more hilarious events in a murder trial happened in a large courtroom in the Detroit suburbs. Both the Prosecutor and Defense were well known and at the top of their game, although they were marked contrasts. The County Prosecutor Joseph Daugherty was a study in class; conservative suit, white shirt and tie, reserved manner and polished speech. Whereas the defense attorney, Adam Liebowitz, was extremely colorful, with bold patterned suit, bright tie, and bombastic style. Although the case had not garnered a lot of publicity, the courtroom was full of spectators looking for action from the attorneys.

In this case I was responsible for the crime scene investigation and had just finished cross-examination. Prosecutor Daugherty stated "I have no further questions for this witness. The State now calls Ken Christensen to the stand."

After my crime laboratory associate had been sworn and qualified as an expert witness, the Prosecutor introduced a crucial exhibit, a plaster cast of a partial shoe impression found near the victim. The Prosecutor led Ken through a series of questions, including the companion photography, location, and preparation of the cast. He handed the cast to Ken and asked him to identify the same, which he did. This was followed by a series of questions and answers regarding the detail of specific imperfections or individual characteristics detected in the impression and shown in the cast, as compared to the shoe of the defendant. Finally the key question, "Mr. Christensen do you have an opinion regarding the source of the evidence impression?" Ken responded "yes sir, in my opinion the impression under the window was made by the left shoe identified as that of the defendant." Daugherty stated "thank you Mr. Christensen; your witness counsel."

Liebowitz arose, straightened his suit lapels and tie with a flourish, and approached the witness. He stopped at the desk of the Court Clerk and stared intently for a prolonged period looking at the plaster cast lying there. His studied and dramatic movements had produced a hush in the courtroom. Finally, he swept the cast from the table in a sweeping motion. He carried it down the table length to a desk lamp, where he examined the exposed surface of the plaster cast bending over and peering intently, while moving his head back and forth to alter the angle of vision. It appeared to be designed to impress the Jurors and audience and it did. By now you could hear a pin drop in that courtroom. Liebowitz had the attention of everybody in that room, including me. I pondered what he was up to.

Suddenly he swept the cast away from the table with an exaggerated flourish, insuring the Jurors were following his every move. He walked slowly out to the center aisle, under the huge chandelier, ablaze with lights. Again he spent considerable time studying the surface of the cast. Finally, he turned and approached the witness. I wondered what kind of trick he had up his sleeve.

"Mr. Christensen," he started, "as you no doubt have noticed I have studied this cast under the table lamp of the Clerk and even under yon chandelier." He actually used the old expression "yon." "You have testified regarding similar characteristics found in the cast and the shoe of the defendant, portions of a mold pattern, a cut here, a break there, and so forth. Yet, I fail to discern these illuminating features you so pointedly referred to under direct examination. Can you explain this anomaly to me and this learned Jury?" Ken replied, "Yes sir, I believe I can. Sir, you were holding the cast upside down!" Liebowitz quickly returned to his seat, buried his face in his hands, and whispered "no more from this witness."

Apparently his question was not a trick one. He had been looking at the upper surface of the cast and was fooled by the ripples and drips seen there from the pouring of the cast, along with scratch marks left by the CSI person to identify the cast. In any case, after the huge build-up this was one of the strangest happenings I have ever witnessed.

The patent leather shoe case: The trial resulting from this homicide turned out to have one of if not the most dramatic climaxes in my memory. It all started on a pretty spring evening when a young secretary in Central Michigan decided to walk home from work. Her journey took her through a small park in the city. During the day groups of children and mothers could be found there on the park playground. But now it was dusk and the park was deserted.

As the secretary passed a hedgerow of bushes, a burly shape emerged and grabbed her from behind. He muffled her screams with a hand over her mouth and his arm around her neck. She was dragged behind the bushes strangled, disrobed and raped. Her killer left the area unheard and unseen.

The following morning a park attendant found the victim lying behind the bushes and her clothing thrown into the nearby pond. The clothing was in the water in disarray and with one shoe. The other shoe, a new patent leather type was found on the pond bank close to the water's edge.

Crime scene investigators realized the patent leather shoes might be ideal for obtaining latent fingerprints so they were carefully handled and brought to the Crime Laboratory. The processing was done by a young industrious CSI member and latent fingerprint examiner, George Hein. "Big George," as he was sometimes called was nearly 6 ½ feet tall, large and strong. Although he was young in the forensic area he was known to be competent.

The shoe found on the bank revealed a small partial well defined print on the heel as the processing continued. The print was photographed in a number of ways, lifted for comparison, and the remaining original covered for protection. George called the city police and advised the detectives the print was not that of the victim, but undoubtedly of the killer. Over a period of time, known fingerprints from suspects were submitted to the Laboratory for comparison. Finally, one day George let out a war cry exclaiming, "This is the one. I have a matching print from a suspect."

In latent print comparison, once the class characteristics of the pattern are satisfied, the examiner critically analyzes the pattern for fine features, sometimes referred to as "Galton details." These features of the fingerprint pattern are so-called after Sir Francis Galton a noted anthropologist of the late 1800s. These characteristics include details such as the abrupt ending of a ridge, one ridge separating into two or more (called bifurcations), a complete opening in the ridge structure known as an enclosure, a very short but separate ridge, and a small ridge known as a dot. The location of these details is plotted along with their distance from other parts of the pattern and each other. In this case George said there were enough, but just enough, to satisfy the minimum criteria for positive identification. As it turned out this was the only physical evidence of the culprit.

As the County Prosecutor prepared for the trial, he assembled the CSI crew, representatives of the Crime Laboratory, and detectives to discuss the case. He confided he was concerned the only physical evidence of value was the partial latent fingerprint, and the analyst had a minimum amount of experience in the discipline. He suggested the State should attempt to locate another expert with considerable experience. The following discussion led to the name of Larry Stackable. He was one of the State Bureau of Identification oldest employees. His career dated back to the 20s. Larry had been a motorcycle officer with the Michigan State Police, but like many ended up injured and placed in a different job. He still walked with a limp after all these years. Larry was known to be blunt in his manners and had a strong voice he was not afraid to use. "The Bull" was his affectionate knick name. Years before he had been brought from the Bureau into the Crime Laboratory to do latent fingerprint processing and comparison. He was a liaison between the Bureau and the Crime Laboratory.

Larry was asked if he would be willing to compare the latent from the shoe with the suspect fingerprints and he agreed. After an examination of the two he advised that he agreed with George that it was a valid identification. So his name was added to the witness list.

At trial, Big George testified and did a fine job although the defense attorney attempted to minimize his opinion by pointing out his short tenure as an analyst. Next, the Prosecutor called the Bull to the stand and elicited testimony about his long years of service to the Identification Bureau and the Crime Laboratory, followed by his opinion in this case. Larry was then turned over to the defense attorney for cross-examination.

The defense attorney was a good one. An older, former prosecutor, he was aware much of the experience Larry discussed was in the early days of the Laboratory when case loads and identifications were small in number. He asked, "Sir, the Prosecutor makes much of the fact that you have forty years of experience in the fingerprint business, but is it not true that much of the experience was with the Identification Bureau, where your primary duty was the classification of fingerprints?" Larry replied that this was true. The attorney next asked, "Is it not also true that in those early days caseloads were small and identifications few and far between?" Larry acknowledged that was also correct. The defense then asked, "Tell this Judge and Jury just how many actual latent fingerprint comparisons you actually made during all those years." Larry replied, "I never kept such records or accounts."

What the Jury fails to realize is that the defense knows these facts from pre-trial depositions. Now, the attorney pressed harder "Oh come on now, certainly you can give this Jury some idea of that number." Larry replied again, "Sorry, but I never kept such records." The defense then sarcastically asked, "Are you refusing to even make an estimate, or are you too embarrassed to answer?" Larry turned to the Judge and said, "Your Honor I cannot answer the question the way it is posed, but there is another way I may be able to satisfy counsel." The Judge in exasperation said, "Witness answer any way you can."

Larry then described a crime scene investigation he had participated in over thirty years before. An elderly woman had been robbed and brutally bludgeoned to death. The scene was quite bloody he explained and he found a bloody fingerprint on a wash basin where the killer attempted to clean himself. This horrible crime was indelibly stamped into his memory as was the bloody fingerprint.

Upon return to Lansing, he directed that all master fingerprints from anyone convicted of any crime of violence be placed in his "In" basket before they would be filed. He then checked them against the evidence from the murder before they were placed in the master file. He concluded by stating "In that one case, I did keep records as solving this crime was an obsession. In that one case I have compared over 100,000 prints, does that answer the question satisfactorily?" The defense attorney wearily walked back to the defense table saying "no more questions of this witness."

The defendant was found guilty of first degree murder and sentenced to life in prison.

In most courts, the Judge effectively controls the trial, the witnesses, and the attorneys, although there are notable exceptions, such as the O.J. Simpson case. I was retired at the time of the notorious trial and made a point of watching the testimony of all the experts, both for the State and for the Defense. Obviously the Judge played to the cameras and appeared swayed by the famous reputations of defense counsels. I have appeared before some that had personal prejudices and failings, but I think that case took the cake, especially when you consider the impact of the double murder and famous defendant. The case was replete with examples of how-to and how-not-to testify as an expert witness. There were also several examples of misleading and even unethical testimony. It was not a hallmark case for crime scene investigation or crime laboratory analysis or for that matter for forensic science in general.

In my court experience of nearly fifty years, certain Judges have left a somewhat unique imprint for a variety of reasons and I would like o tell you about a few of them.

The tough judge: I traveled some distance to the Southern part of Florida and was waiting outside the courtroom to be called as a witness in a homicide trial. The State Attorney came out during recess and quickly went over questions he would ask. At one point he inquired, "Have you ever testified before this Judge before?" I told him that this was my first time in this court. He then advised me, "Let me give you a little word of advice, Judge Sherman rides hard on prosecution witnesses and expert witnesses in particular." I told him "thanks for the tip."

Not long later, the Court officer came into the hallway and said "Mr. Meyers you are on the stand."All went smoothly with my introduction, brief resume of my qualifications, and testimony regarding the bullet and firearm and their identification with one another.

In this homicide, the distance of discharge, or determination of how far the firearm muzzle was from the victim when fired was one of the issues. Part of the evidence was close-up photographs of the entrance bullet hole and surrounding gunshot residues. The State Attorney approached the witness stand and stated, "Witness I show you State exhibit 34 and ask if you can identify it?" This process is a necessary prerequisite before testimony on an exhibit can be received in evidence. He handed me an 8x10 inch enlarged color photograph depicting part of the body with entrance hole centered. I immediately flipped the photograph over and scanned the backside. Within seconds a loud voice boomed out, "Witness what in hell are you doing?" It was the voice of the Judge and he went on, "the State Attorney asked if you can identify this photograph and you are sitting there staring at the blank side?" I glanced at the bench and could see he appeared visibly angered. I said, "I am sorry Your Honor, but I was checking for my initials and case number as I treat photographs as any other evidence and mark them for identification on the back side." The Judge then asked, "Well, were they there?" I said, "No Your Honor." He then asked, "Have you ever seen this photograph before?" I replied, "No Your Honor."

At that the Judge whirled toward the State Attorney saying, "What are you doing showing this man a photograph he has never examined?" As the Prosecutor stammered and stuttered, the Judge exclaimed, "One more trick like that and you will be in contempt of this court, do you understand?"

Of course it was a simple mistake. The Prosecutor had another photograph, very similar to the first, which had been sent to the Crime Laboratory and was appropriately marked. It makes one wonder if the Jury knew what was going on.

The sleeping judge: One of my favorite old Judges in Central Michigan was trying a murder case; the kind that makes one wonder about the human condition. Two co-workers were discussing the Tigers ballgame of the previous evening. One remarked about how great it was to see the Tigers come through and win the game in the 10th inning. The other said something like you must have been watching a different game. They actually won in the 9th inning. The first insisted it was in the 10th and the second insisted it was in the 9th. The argument got heated and one called the other stupid. He responded by calling the first a dumb s.o.b. So the dumb one went out to the parking lot, got his 9mm pistol out, came back in the shop and shot the other one in the head. Well, he won the argument, but now he was being tried for murder. The only real question was the degree.

I was on the stand going through the perfunctory legal steps for admitting evidence and testifying thereon. The old Judge was sitting with his head partly lowered on his fingertips. From my vantage point I could see he was nodding to sleep. Just then the Prosecutor asked me whether I had been able to determine if the fired cartridge case was discharged in the 9mm pistol of the defendant.

The Judge suddenly sat erect and stated, "we all know the Crime Lab people can identify a bullet with the right gun, but they do not do that with the casings." He then turned to me with a puzzled expression on his face and asked, "Well, do you?" I said, "Yes your Honor, we do." By then he was awake and told the Prosecutor "well get on with it." The Jury had no idea what was happening.

Bat woman: In one of the busiest Counties in Michigan, there was a wonderful female Judge. She had been elected on her promise to get tough on violent criminals, and she lived up to the promise. She was very tall, thin, and graceful in her movements. She appeared to have a fetish about wearing her black robe and everywhere she was seen about the courthouse she was wearing it. As she quickly moved about the robe flowed out behind her and she garnered the nickname of "bat woman."

On this day she was hearing a homicide trial and the defense attorney was Tom Shapiro. He handled many of the County indigent defendants on homicide charges and was known to be well versed in the Criminal Law. However, he was known to get a little agitated and nervous in the courtroom. I was on the stand testifying regarding the so-called ballistics evidence. Shapiro was trying to machine gun me or ask repeated questions very quickly, a trick designed to confuse the witness. He had a pocketful of change and as he talked very fast he jingled the change in his pocket.

Suddenly there was a loud crashing sound as the Judge smashed her gavel down on the bench. You could hear a pin drop in that courtroom for a brief moment. The spell was broken by the crisp and clear voice of the Judge as she stated, "Mr. Shapiro – you rattle those coins one more time and you are in contempt and out of here. Do I make myself clear?"

Shapiro talked much slower and finished his cross-examination with both hands clasped tightly together in front of his stomach.

The outstanding Judge: Of all that I ever appeared before, my favorite was Judge James Breakey, a Circuit Judge in Washtenaw County, Michigan. Many police officers and trial lawyers of that day agreed with my opinion.

His old courtroom had a large clock above his bench that sounded off each passing minute with a barely noticeable click. The sound could be heard in the hushed courtroom and this one was usually very quiet. Just prior to 9:00am, the Court officer, clerk, and stenographer would take their place, quickly followed by the Prosecutor and Defense Attorney. As the last minute before 9:00am ticked off, the chamber doors would burst open and the Judge in his black robe would take his seat. While doing so he would stare at the prosecution and defense attorney tables to insure each side was present and ready to proceed. They had better be or they were in trouble and everyone in the courthouse knew it.

When he called a 15 minute recess it expired in the same fashion. Some thought he had a bit of an obsession with timeliness. But he tried more cases than anyone in the State, and witnesses were rarely caused to sit and wait for long periods as was so common in many courts.

Although he was efficient he was also known for legal brilliance. As my years in the criminal justice system wore on I wished there could be more like him.

10

Retirement II & Consulting

In 1989 I decided to retire for the 2nd time. I hoped to spend more time with my wife, children, and grandchildren. I also planned on doing a little consulting to keep my hand in and earn some extra money.

As to the consulting part, I had planned ahead for a long time. Over the years I built a library of reference material that rivaled many established crime laboratories. I had about 100 hard bound volumes and nearly that many soft cover books that pertained to some aspect of firearms and tool mark identification. They included some of the historical texts including an original Gunthers' "Firearms Identification" from 1935. The library also contained the American Academy of Forensic Science Journals from 1960 to present and Newsletters and Journals from the Association of Firearm and Tool Mark (AFTE), from 1969.

For some time, I had purchased and collected gun smith tools and paraphernalia, including bore scope, a quality metal detector, a complete camera kit, including 35mm Canon camera with wide angle, close-up lens and bellows attachment for extremely fine work such as tool marks, etc., and an old comparison microscope with all the original attachments. The comparison scope was one of the earliest made to use for bullet and cartridge case comparisons. It was a Spencer Lens Co. made in the thirties, monocular, with 5x eyepiece and 2.2x objective lenses. I contacted a representative of American Optical Co. which had taken over Spencer many years before and learned the objective tubes were threaded the same as the new A-O scopes. I was able to obtain two sets of matched objectives 5x and 10x. So I finally had a microscope with an 11x to 50x range, suitable for most comparisons. I had purchased a stereo microscope and made an adjustable stage with dial micrometer set up for measuring bullets and cartridge case markings, etc.

Without further detail, I was all set to go in business except for one thing. I needed something to catch the bullets. One day as I was searching catalogues for various bullet catchers and retrieval devices, a large pickup pulled up to the house. In the bed was the original welded steel tank I had built many years before to catch bullets in water. The Asst. Crime Laboratory Director with a couple of analysts removed the heavy tank apparatus and rolled it into my carport. He advised the old tank had been in salvage since the new laboratory operation and the use of the new fancy horizontal tank. Although the laboratory had given me a going away retirement party, they got permission from the top brass to give me the old tank as a late going away present. Just what I needed – I imagine Garry Rathman had something to do with this. Well now I was ready to go into business.

In a short time business found me as requests for my services started rolling in. I remained active in this role as a consultant and teacher for 15 years and continued my interest and some involvement for 5 more. As expected many calls for my assistance came from attorneys I knew from my Crime Laboratory days. But then the word got around and I received calls from many other areas. Some requests I accepted and some were rejected. There were some calls from attorneys who would preface their request with statements such as, "I need a ballistics expert to make a certain investigation and establish the following facts etc." At this point I would point out that I am qualified to do the prescribed work, but I would establish what facts or opinions are forthcoming from this examination. In other words, my report would specify exactly what I uncover, no matter which side it represented. Some would say fine, I only want the truth of the matter while others would say thank you for your time, but no thanks. Thankfully, the former were in the majority.

There came a time several years after my "retirement" when Nancy told me "you have gotten so busy, maybe you should just "un-retire" and go back to the Crime Laboratory." I finally told her I would attempt to slow down and reduce the work so we would have more time together, and there would be more time to take the grandsons fishing. During this period I had the opportunity to re-examine evidence and consult with attorneys from ten States from Michigan to Florida and even Los Angeles, California. Most were for the defense, and most involved so-called indigents and their Public Defenders. However there were a few from the Prosecution for various reasons.

The dying shark: One of the more interesting cases was a civil case that involved a lot of time and an "expert" for the defense who was more than interesting. The call was from an attorney in one of the larger cities in Florida. He advised he needed to consult with a tool mark expert and I assured him he was talking to the right man. He described a case where a huge Corporation was being sued for a small fortune. The company he represented leased a truck that was alleged to have caused an accident resulting in the victim becoming paraplegic.

He described the accident as such: On a cool foggy morning, a young man was driving to work on his motorcycle. He was traveling on a two lane highway and the visibility was limited. As he traversed a curve, a large truck entered the highway from a side road and he was unable to avoid it, striking the left rear corner. When he awoke in the hospital he discovered he suffered devastating injuries and was paraplegic. The police had investigated the accident but never uncovered the truck involved. Officers conjectured the truck driver may not have known he hit anyone due to the conditions and a brushing accident with a motorcycle in the fog.

Now, two years later, the complainant legal firm advised they had an expert who had found the truck trailer wheel involved in the incident and could prove it by tool marks. Further, attorney Allen Robinson advised the tool mark expert involved had claimed to be among the best in the country. He asked me if I would want to work with them, and I told him I could hardly wait.

Chasing Tail Lights to Forensic Ballistics

I was saturated with pre-trial depositions from the tool mark expert, reports, and a pile of 35mm transparencies that were copied from his originals. There were also several enlarged color prints that purported to show matching tool marks; one set allegedly from the motorcycle frame and the other from the truck trailer wheel. The prints had been enlarged from transparencies taken through the microscope and displayed a number of problems. There were obviously faults in the original photographs that showed somewhat fuzzy detail in the original transparencies. Now they were enlarged which only made them more fuzzy and indistinguishable. In photography this is referred to as empty magnification. However, one consequence of this type of photography is that markings seem to blend together, making it difficult to distinguish between them based on their shape, size, or exact position. One immediately wonders whether this is accidental or done on purpose, making it difficult for a juror to distinguish between the markings.

However, as I studied the enlargements; copies of which would be shown as evidence in the trial, I noticed something very interesting. They had been described as different matches from several different locations on the motorcycle. However two exhibits displayed fuzzy blobs, apparent defects in the photographs that appeared exactly the same although in different positions. The largest defect was nearly oval in shape and on its side with an appendage that looked immediately to a Floridian like a shark fin cutting the water. In the one print the fin was erect but in the second the fin was upside down. From those positions one could trace other microscopic defects that matched entirely except they were up side down and reversed. There was no question about it, someone had taken the one transparency, reversed it to the other side of the hairline and turned it upside down in an attempt to make another "match." I knew the entire procedure was improper and indicated either incompetency or an attempted scam. But, to the non-tool mark expert it would be easier to just demonstrate it. So, I copied the original prints and prepared my own exhibit showing the unlikely comparisons.

I of course showed the exhibit to attorney Allen Robinson, who immediately exclaimed, "well, how about that, the shark is dying." I examined the damaged fork of the motorcycle and the tool marks thereon, the wheel alleged to have caused the damage and the marks it displayed, etc. This required considerable travel and time on my part and of course I took lots of photographs.

Eventually, I was subpoenaed to a pre-trial deposition with the complaining victim attorneys. After several hours of examination and testimony, attorney Robinson broke in and said "enough is enough, show them the dying shark Charlie." I had the display in an art valise and pulled it out to show them. After a few short questions it was over. I feel sure they were satisfied they had been victimized by their alleged expert.

I was on call for the trial when Robinson advised I would not be needed to testify. Further he stated the other side had withdrawn the evidence and witness concerned with the tool marks. In his humorous style he said "The black knight and his soldiers had just left the castle when they saw the white knight on the ridge. They withdrew, fled over the moat, drew the bridge and disappeared into the castle." He was a bit flamboyant but a very sharp attorney.

Not long after, he called again to tell me it was over, the firm had settled out of court. I wondered why; no one knew what vehicle caused the injuries. He told me they settled for $900,000.00. I again asked him why – that is a lot of money. He said that the firm was thrilled to settle for that amount; imagine the jury reaction when the other side wheeled the crippled victim into court!

The mutilated .22: One simple examination in Florida helped free an innocent man. An attorney from the Gulf area called and asked me to help him with a case. He advised that two rival gangs got into a fight and shootout. One gang member died and was found to have been shot with a .22 caliber firearm. His client carried a derringer pistol and it was recovered by police with two fired cases of the same type of ammunition as the bullet from the body of the victim. Furthermore, witnesses claimed that his defendant had the only small caliber weapon in the affray. He advised that the regional crime laboratory had told the authorities that the bullet was too damaged to be of assistance. He wanted me to re-examine the bullet. I told him he was probably wasting his time; it is not unusual for a soft lead .22 caliber bullet to be too damaged for identification/elimination. He asked me to do it anyway and that he had arranged for me to make the examination in the State laboratory.

I went to the laboratory and was handed the vial with the evidence bullet. After preliminary notes I used the stereoscopic microscope to examine the obviously smashed and severely damaged bullet. No rifling marks could be seen and most of the ammunition manufacturer marks were obscured as well. I had seen others like it. It was turned nearly inside out and badly mushroomed. As I turned it around under the microscope I could barely see a portion of the base. From that point I carefully pulled some lead back and revealed a curl of metal encircling the bullet. The molten appearing lead was carefully unwound exposing part of the original bearing surface which had been deeply buried.

After cleaning the bullet gently, I placed it on the comparison scope left stage, mounted so the remaining bearing surface was exposed to reveal rifling of 16 lands and grooves. The young examiner watching me said "did you find something Charlie?" I pointed toward the microscope and gave him the seat. As he looked he said "well damn it, look at that."

The pistol of the defendant was rifled with 6 lands and grooves. The fatal bullet could not have been fired from his firearm. Both the defense attorney and State Attorney thanked me for working that simple but crucial case.

Florida offered us some fun and excitement in addition to criminal investigations. On a short trip to Cape Canaveral, while surf fishing I landed a 12 ¼ lb. bluefish. Now that was exciting. The grandsons and I went on several bass fishing trips in one of the small lakes surrounding Sanford. We never caught that trophy to mount but we did catch quite a few nice ones. On one trip we spied a dead bass in the weed bed; It had to be about 10 lbs. or so. Maybe one of the big gators in there snapped it. We thought it was fun to watch the bubbles rise in a streaming line as the gator swam under the boat. We never gave it a thought that he could upset us boat and all if he desired to. The only thing we ever worried about in those lakes was the occasional cottonmouth moccasin that would swim toward the boat in a curious way. We would give the water a smack with a paddle to keep him away.

But the one fishing trip I recall the most was my last one with Larry Ziegler. Many years before in Lansing, when we took little Kathy to her first special school for the retarded, we were met at the front entranceway by a young man, who walked in a slightly crippled shuffle, and was mopping the entrance tile as we approached. He asked us "what is the name of your little girl?" We told him it was Kathy and he replied that we should not be afraid for her as he would make sure no one hurts her in any way. We found out that his name was Larry, and he was retarded, but he was a real gentleman. Larry became a dear friend of Kathy and the family for the remainder of his life. Every summer, both in Michigan and Florida, he came to visit us for a week or two for his summer vacation, and Larry loved to fish. This time I took him in the pram on a little lake that had some huge bass. We stopped at the bait shop and purchased several big gold shiners, a real lure for big bass. After some time on the lake we were fishing near a bed of weeds when suddenly a big one struck with the line whistling off his reel. I yelled "strike him Larry," but he sat there with the rod and reel extended like he was afraid of it. The reel handles were spinning like a top but he just sat there with a big grin on his face as I yelled again "for Gods sake Larry, please strike him!" Well the bass went into the weed bed and wound his line around and around with the weed stalks jerking until it finally broke. There was no way I could get to him in time without upsetting the boat. Larry just sat there with the huge grin on his face and said "geez Charlie, he was a big one!" He never lost that grin all the way home and to the dinner table so he could tell the kids about the big one that got away.

In my spare time Nancy often found little jobs for me. One evening as I returned from an examination, she said "there is something we have to do, and you will need a crowbar or two, a hydraulic jack, and an old sheet." I wondered what she was up to this time. She took me on a little drive down a side road near town where a very old home was sitting. There was a bulldozer sitting in the driveway along with a couple trucks, etc. She told me to pull up in back of the trucks and bring the crowbar and jack. I asked what in hell is going on and she told me that she spotted this equipment coming in and stopped to talk to the job super. He told her the property had been bought by a big oil company and the old home was to be demolished

LARY ZEIGLER

to build a gas station. He already had a number of leaded windows taken out and set aside for her to take. But inside the home was a beautiful huge fireplace with oak columns and stained glass shuttered book shelves, and a wonderful bronzed iron embossed front for the fireplace. The superintendent told her she could have anything there if she wanted but it had to come out tonight. Tomorrow the dozer and crane go to work. So we made a couple of runs home with the Suburban full of antique windows and then the fireplace unit, oaken columns trussed to the top of the suburban, etc. You might wonder what the tools were for; well we had to jack up an archway and then break the fireplace out of the corner of the archway and wall with crowbars. We mounted it in a perfect spot in our family room with a fake tile surround. It was fabulous. All our neighbors admired it, and especially one who was an antiques nut and a good friend. When we finally moved to North Carolina Nancy sold it to her for half of the worth and she said she would be eternally grateful for that.

Then there was the time that Nan took the children for a hike while their dad was gone. When I returned I found them patiently awaiting and I had to take a drive with them in the station wagon, our family car at the time. They took me to a small lake where the Conservation crew was building a little park. The former owners of the property had built a fence along cedar pole supports, and now the crew was pulling the logs and tearing up the fence. The crew chief told Nancy she could have the logs so the kids and I loaded them onto the wagon and made a couple of trips back home as my beautiful wife remarked, "you know we talked about building a fence along the one side of our property, well now is your chance;" what a gal!

The prostitute murders: At about this time, I received a call from an attorney in Los Angeles asking if I could assist them in a controversial shooting case. It seemed that three prostitutes, over time, had been killed with the same firearm. A deputy sheriff had been arrested and charged with the murder. The question revolved around whether or not his spare firearm was involved.

An officer flew from LA with the evidence and stayed at a local motel while I completed the examination. There were three evidence bullets, all 9mm, one from each of three victims, and one cartridge case from one scene. The detectives on the case theorized that the killer picked up his spent cartridge cases but failed to find it at one scene. This all occurred in the city of Los Angeles.

During the investigation a deputy from the Office of the Sheriff, stopped to talk to a prostitute in LA. This was in the same area where the murders took place. City police checked him out and was told by the prostitute witness that the Deputy had two guns, one on him and a spare in the trunk. The officer also had a packet of hard narcotics in the glove compartment. It was alleged that all of the victims were into prostitution to pay for their drug habit. This is a fairly common occurrence among that trade. The firearm the Deputy carried could not be involved. The 2nd firearm in the trunk was a 9mm Smith &

Wesson pistol, and it had the right kind of class characteristics. It was claimed that the Laboratory had identified the three bullets as having been fired from the same weapon. They were also reported to have stated that the Smith and Wesson pistol of the defendant was the firearm that discharged the three bullets and one cartridge case in evidence.

The case developed a problem when an independent examiner in California stated that the pistol was wrongfully identified with the evidence. This is a rare occurrence in the discipline but it has happened on a few occasions. The evidence was then taken to the State Department of Justice where two examiners determined that there was insufficient evidence to identify the pistol with the bullets and they felt it probably was not the firearm used, and that the cartridge case was not fired in this pistol.

All the examiners agreed the three bullets from the three victims were all fired from the same firearm. So, the City asked me to make the examination to help clear it up. My opinion matched that of the State examiners; i.e., all three evidence bullets were fired through the same barrel; the evidence cartridge case was definitely not fired in the pistol of the deputy and the evidence bullets were probably not fired in the pistol. The last I heard from this case the deputy was suing the city of Los Angeles.

The Kentucky Trooper case: Perhaps one of the toughest cases I ever worked was this one. That was due to the degree of difficulty. I forwarded enlarged photomicrographs (photos taken through the comparison microscope) to the other members of a special subcommittee of AFTE, The Criteria for Identification committee. The purpose was to show a set of markings that I felt constituted identification, but was just over the threshold for such a finding.

A captain of the Kentucky State Police delivered the evidence and waited four days in a local motel waiting for the report and evidence to return. The primary evidence was a .223 or 5.56mm bullet fired from a Ruger Mini-14 rifle. But which one was the question? The bullet had characteristically broken into fragments on entrance in the victim. The victim was a K-9 police officer following the trail of an escaped killer through a corn field. When the killer came to the end of the field he started to run ignoring commands to stop. On a bluff above the field were three State Police officers armed with .223 caliber Ruger rifles. They occupied different positions in the event the killer exited in their direction. A couple of shots were fired from the bluff. One went into the corn field and by sheer fate struck the unseen K-9 officer in the face killing him. All three officers denied shooting in that direction.

I identified test bullets from one rifle with the evidence fragments. I later learned that the State Police had taken the evidence to four examiners before the investigation was concluded; one was their own State Police examiner, one was another independent examiner, one was an agent of the FBI in their Laboratory, and me. Although I worked for the State of Florida, the Commissioner granted me permission to work on the Kentucky case without charge. I learned that the Kentucky examiner and I identified the same rifle as the one involved. The independent and FBI examiners were inconclusive in their determination due to the condition of the evidence.

Interestingly, one of the oldest and best analysts in the Country, Al Biasotti asked to examine the photomicrographs. Within a short time, he stated, "I really wonder why you found this examination so difficult – the evidence is there to see!" A few hours later, he told me, "I take it back Charlie, it is a close one and I would have to look at the evidence itself."

At some later date, I was very pleased to receive a letter and certificate advising that the Gov. of Kentucky, Martha Collins, had appointed me to the Kentucky Colonels as a reward for my assistance. It is one of the rewards I cherish and hangs on my bedroom wall.

The dentist murder: Some time ago, I received a request to referee another case involving the shooting of a dentist and his dog in Ohio. The Prosecutor contacted me and asked for my assistance. They had an older case allegedly involving the shooting of a dentist and his guard dog by a subject looking for drugs. He advised that after I believe it was seven years a suspect had been arrested and his firearm compared to the evidence by a young examiner in Ohio. He further advised that the Defense attorney had an independent examiner look at the evidence and alleged he would testify in court that the identification was mistaken.

It was all sent to me for examination. I believe there were a total of three bullets involved, again it was our old friend the .22 caliber lead bullets. I was informed that the young State examiner had been able to positively identify one bullet, the least damaged. Upon examination I reported that all three were identified as having been fired from the evidence firearm. In retrospect I recall thinking that the young examiner may have been too conservative as there were sufficient matching striations to identify all three. But then, it is better to be too conservative than too quick to make a decision, especially for a young person with a minimal amount of experience.

I never heard back or was subpoenaed for trial. I have to assume the so-called independent expert bailed out.

It is very surprising to see some of the charlatans in action. One I will always remember happened back in Michigan when an expert came in from Ohio. In the old days we used to do everything but give them the answer. When this one showed up pertaining to a court order, we had the evidence bullet mounted on the left stage and a test bullet on the right stage with one of the best marked areas, the so-called phase relationship, aligned for him. He sat at the microscope, faked adjusting the focus, and began rotating the bullets without really examining the area we had in focus. As the bullets rotated quickly, all too quickly I might add, the evidence bullet lost some of the adhesion and drooped so that now it was describing large arcs instead of a circle. We knew there was no way the bullets could be in focus or even seen. He arose from the seat, said "that is a match alright," collected his money and went back to Ohio. I never thought of it before but now I wonder, despite the intervening years, could that be the same man as on the dentist case from Ohio? We will never know but one has to wonder.

These charlatans all have degrees, some even with post-graduate education, but as a rule they are taking advantage of the system, for money and without taking into account the possible influence on the State, our system of justice, or for that matter the defendant.

But now it was time to attend to pressing family matters. My daughter Kim who provided three wonderful grandsons, the first one adopted, the next two on her own, was transferred in her job with the bank to Charlotte, North Carolina. Nancy and I helped her and her husband Tim and the boys move to a temporary home. We hoped all would go well with them, but in short order we learned she was very unhappy with Charlotte. No place for raising the boys. She told us one day, Charlotte is just like Orlando, only not as pretty. She confided that they were cruising on weekends looking for a better place where the bank was situated. Then one evening she called and said I found the perfect place to raise the children and we have a branch bank there. It is Boone, NC, a small college town in the mountains, beautiful, and with little crime. It will take time to get there, not many openings you know. But about six months later she got the assignment.

The first summer after the move we came up with an RV and stayed most of the season. The second year, while driving around, found a small cottage on a unkempt lot but with a neat red metal shed for storage. The house and property needed TLC badly but the price was right. So we became six up, six down guests, or half-backs as they called us around town. That is to describe people who fled the snow and ice of up North, went to Florida, and now are half-way back.

We were fortunate to have a young son-in-law who was a builder type. He tore the old rotten porch off, replaced it with a new one and built a pretty wooden storage shed. Nancy and I cleared the lot, put in a garden, and planted some fruit trees. We had the RV parked next door in case we had company. The grand sons loved the place. There was a small woods above the garden and home, where they could pretend to bear hunt, etc. Down the road about a mile was a wonderful stretch of trout creek to take the boys fishing. We almost always caught a couple there. And just a few miles down the road was the New River, wonderful for floating, canoeing, and fishing. We spent several summers at the little place and then it was time to go back to Florida. I will never forget the last time. It was November 19th and the sun was shining, it was in the high 60s, and beautiful on the mountains. Nancy said, "What are we going back to Florida for?" I said, "It beats me." By the next summer we were living on a permanent basis in Jefferson, NC, the lovely county seat of Ashe County.

However, getting here would prove to not be easy. We had made a previous trip looking for property. We found a pretty home in Jefferson with a local realtor and placed a sizeable deposit to hold it for our return. The sellers had accepted our offer and we were to close when we got here. When we arrived with our moving van and trailer full we were advised the owners had changed their mind and withdrawn the home from the market. It was a sour grapes way to start and it did not help when we had to threaten the realtor to get our deposit back and found out from the owners in Maryland the realtor lied to us as his contract had already run out when we contacted him. Sad to say, but we wondered where is the so-called Southern hospitality? Glad to say that was the first and last time we had that kind of experience in the region. We ultimately found out the local people were as good as their word.

But our furnishings all went into storage as we began our search all over again. Then God smiled on us again, as one day a new realtor told us about a pretty older home with beautiful flowers and bushes around the yard at the foot of Mt. Jefferson. He asked us to meet him there at noon and gave us directions. It was a gorgeous day in early May, the sun was shining and a cool breeze rippled the leaves of a large silver maple in the front yard. A sloping bank on one side of the yard was in full bloom with red azaleas. The front of the yard was garnished with a solid bank of spirea in bloom. As my watch showed 12 noon beautiful music from the church below found the way to the front yard. When the realtor arrived, Nancy said, "thank you we will accept the price offer." He said, "You might want to see the interior." She replied, "Any old lady (we were informed an elderly woman had it for sale) who keeps a yard this pretty will have a pretty interior too." And of course Nancy was right. As we checked the property I had to recall a comedy movie starring Chevy Chase where he and his wife built a skating rink in the winter, had people skating on it in old style costumes, and released deer to run in front of their prospective buyers, in order to influence them to pay the price. It looked like a scene from the old Saturday Evening Post. But I need not worry; our home was just as nice as advertised. So, in the end the original raw deal was a boon to us. This home was prettier, the yard was prettier, and it cost less! Oh ye of little faith, as Nan and the good book would say.

The accidental murder: Sandwiched between our moves into North Carolina were a number of consulting cases. One was interesting from the defense standpoint and from the vantage point of the firearms identification discipline. I received a call from an attorney in Florida that I had worked with previously. I advised him that he should seek help from one of the several independent examiners in Florida. He said I want you to work this case and the distance will not change things. He made arrangements with the State Attorney to have all the firearms evidence delivered to me. It was and I spent some time conducting the examinations and doing field tests in this case.

But first the history of the case thus far; you will have to bear with me as this one is slightly complicated. From the prosecution standpoint, it seemed like a slam dunk for first degree murder and likely the death penalty. A divorced couple had a severe argument at his home, when she came there to talk about a child custody battle. According to the police investigation, the argument got violent, and ended when the husband shoved the wife out of the door at gun point, then shot her, buried her body under a fresh poured concrete slab, and run her car a mile down the road where it was found deserted. Sounds simple enough, I believe.

The story of the defendant was a little different. Of course, they usually are. His story was that his wife came to the house in a horrible raging mood, and he told her to get out several times but she refused. He went to his bedroom closet and obtained a new unloaded pistol from the original box. He turned, pointed it at her face and told her to get the hell out of his home. She backed out and down the stairs from the back porch, still giving him an earful of swear words, etc. As they got to the sidewalk, she swung at his gun arm and the pistol discharged into her head, killing her. He knew no one would believe that it was accidental, so he panicked, removed part of the cement slab, dug a hole, buried her, and poured new concrete over her. He put the pistol back in the original box and back on the shelf. Later, it was turned over to the authorities when the disappearance was solved. Sounds tough, but is relatively simple as murders go.

The parents of the defendant contacted my lawyer friend. They told him that their son had a spotless record, was a wonderful son and human being, and furthermore the dead wife was known to everyone in the community as a "bitch." Therefore they believed his story. The defense attorney checked around and found that everything the mother and father said was known to be true. Even the authorities backed up this information. They had several run-ins with the wife before and stated in effect that she was a "bitch."

With the evidence was a copy of the regional Crime Laboratory report. It stated that the pistol, an inexpensive model made in California, was identified with the fatal bullet, had a normal trigger pull and was in apparent normal condition. It mentioned one other item of evidence, an unfired cartridge found lying in the grass of the side yard. The analyst mentioned that it displayed no firing pin imprint indicating no attempt at discharge of the cartridge. There was also a fired cartridge case, of the same type as the evidence bullet from the head of the victim. The report stated the fired case had been discharged in the evidence pistol. So, in review the analyst had answered all the questions posed by the police in their request for examination form. At this point everything is very straight forward and to the point.

But now the wicket gets sticky as the defense attorney recounts the information he obtained beyond the normal script. He asked the defendant, "How in the devil did you accidentally fire this pistol. Had you used the new firearm, and was it loaded, please explain it to me." The defendant told him the following details: He had purchased the pistol a short time before the incident. A good friend was visiting and they decided to take the pistol into the side yard and test it. This was an area with no obstructions or visible danger to anyone. He had purchased new ammunition for the firearm and loaded the box magazine (clip). He racked the slide rearward placing the top cartridge from the magazine into the chamber and readying the pistol to fire. He aimed and fired one shot and the weapon jammed. He described that it did not load the next round but instead the cartridge was partly protruding from the ejection port. He went on to say that he was inexperienced with firearms but felt there was something wrong with the new pistol and he was going to take it back to the sports shop. But first, he carefully pulled the slide back and teased the jammed case from the pistol and it fell to the grass. He then carefully allowed the spring to return the slide forward and ejected the magazine, positive that the weapon was now unloaded and unable to be discharged. He returned the pistol to the box awaiting return to the seller.

He continued the story saying he was sure the pistol was unloaded and would not fire and was bluffing his ex-wife when it fired. Further, there was no way it would have fired in any event if she had not struck his arm forcefully. As to the burial and disappearance story, he stated he was shocked and frightened and felt no one would ever believe him when he claimed it was accidental, so he tried to cover it up. As they say on TV news, "The cover up is what catches them every time."

The evidence was analyzed and the identifications confirmed. However, there was an interesting sidelight. The cartridge that was removed from the side yard grass displayed a small but noticeable partially crushed area of the mouth of the cartridge case. This is one form of typical damage seen in cartridges that "jammed" on loading/chambering in a semi-automatic firearm. After the initial tests, the pistol was taken into the field and tested with the same type of ammunition for two magazine capacity loads. I had my grandson with me to track ejected casings and assist with photos of the action. Tests indicated that more than a third of the discharges were accompanied by cartridge jams of the type described. I am not sure what caused this reaction although one of the magazine lips appeared slightly damaged. However, this tended to confirm at least part of the defense story.

At trial the defense attorney had me explain in minute detail this condition, and show the Jury the damaged recovered cartridge from the yard. He further had me demonstrate directly in front of the jury box how far the slide had to be pulled rearward to allow the ejection of the damaged cartridge and how much further the slide had to be pulled rearward in so doing to allow a new cartridge from the top of the magazine to be loaded into the weapon. That distance I had measured with numerous tests to be @ 1/8 of an inch. Furthermore in doing this in typical fashion it was difficult to see the new cartridge loaded into the chamber. All of this was followed by the crucial question, "It has been established that the defendant was unfamiliar with firearms and that this was a new pistol purchased a short time before the shooting. If the defendant followed the procedure he claimed and the procedure as you have demonstrated to the Jury, in your opinion is it possible that he may not have been aware that the pistol was reloaded and cocked ready to fire." I had to say that I felt it was possible.

The defense attorney called me later to report that the defendant was found guilty of manslaughter. He further advised he thought I may have saved him from the death penalty. Was the verdict just; was the defendant let off too easily; should he have been found not guilty? Many times, only God knows the answer to the tough questions. As an analyst you must tell it like it is; right or wrong is for the Jury to decide.

About this time, as I returned to North Carolina, fate decided another chapter in my personal life. One morning, Nancy shook me awake at an early hour, saying "come on, we have got a little traveling to do." It turned out that she had reviewed the advertisements in the Sunday paper and found an ad for an old cabin on a trout creek near Mountain City, Tennessee. All her life, she dreamed of finding an old log cabin and restoring it. If it were found on a trout stream, it would be all for the better. She knew one of my real interests was in fly fishing for trout. Over the years we had stalked many such ads only to find out the cabin was destroyed, flooded out, hanging on a cliff, or too expensive. I tried to talk her out of this trip saying, "You know it will either be shot or too expensive for our pocketbook." She advised me this was a new ad and she had a good feeling about it, so away we went across the Tennessee line about 35 miles all told to the location.

The cabin was a very old timber style, close to Roaring Creek, a known trout creek just a mile from Mt. City. According to the plat the lot would include @ 280 feet of frontage on the creek, and nearly one acre all together. The cabin looked pretty bad. It was a one room cabin with no front door, a broken antique lock set on the rear door, a rotten roof, a fireplace but with the chimney broken down to about shoulder height. Much of the rock foundation was gone and the last owner had raised dogs in it. Therefore the plank flooring was covered with considerable dog mess, old tin can lids, broken glass, etc. It was apparent at one time bums had used it as a stopping over place. In addition, the entire structure leaned about 5 degrees forward in line with the sloping land. The yard consisted of chest high weeds and straw. I shook my head and said, "Okay, have you seen enough?

This place is a mess." Nancy said, "It is beautiful – call your son-in-law and tell him to get over here right away." One son-in-law was a builder and he and my wife always seemed to be on the same page. Not long after he arrived, they walked around the cabin, in and out, and then up to me. I asked him, "what do you think, it is not in very good shape and did you notice the lean?" He said, "dad, it is a mess but structurally it is quite sound. It will still be standing long after you've gone!" Of course that sealed the deal. We already knew it was within the budget primarily due to the condition and the time was right for buying property.

The wife and I rebuilt the foundation by hand with creek rocks and hand mixed mortar from a wheel barrow. Son-in-law rebuilt the chimney with new fire clay inserts and creek rock. He built a rough scaffold around the chimney and went up with mortar and rocks we handed to him when they were large or he pulled up higher in a bucket and pulley arrangement. With ideas from Nancy and his tools he built a small bath with shower and kitchen with dining nook, including the necessary cabinets. He erected a stairway and enclosed the ½ story upstairs into a sleeping loft. Nan and I stained the planks and joists of rough sawn 2 inch lumber to match the old. It turned out fantastic. All I can say is "Nan was right again." Many came to visit and walk through the cabin after she had it suitably decorated and marveled at her creation. Later we assisted in the building of a home on the other end of the property. Both the home and cabin were situated on the creek bank with rear porch stairs leading down to the creek. I astounded friends and relatives by catching trout off the steps with my trusty fly rod. For a long time it was our paradise and Nan said it was the best home she had in her entire lifetime. She loved to get in the creek on a hot day and roll rocks and small boulders into place to create runs and hiding spots for the trout.

But every paradise has a snake in the grass. Our little community was about to find ours. A very good friend first told me about the coming CAFO (the confined animal feeding operation). It was reported this would be the first operation of the type in the mountains; it would be a dairy farm with huge barns and two large lagoons to care for @ 700 dairy cows. Their waste would be automatically fed into the lagoons, chemically treated and later deposited on farm lots as fertilizer. A small group of conservation types were in opposition. I knew little about this mass production of milk or mass production of any animal type. I was aware of a legal suit in another State, I believe it was in North Carolina, where the waste from a swine CAFO had overflowed and gotten into a local river killing thousands of fish and seriously contaminating the water. I was also aware of a report in my old home State of Michigan, where an entire farm family with a dairy CAFO had been overcome by toxic fumes from the lagoon and died. Further, I was aware that my youngest grandson nearly died of a bacterium of some kind that was fed into their fish pond and swimming hole along with clear water from a "trout creek." When the cause of his near fatal illness was finally diagnosed, the physician said that this was the kind of pollution that would result from the stream being used by cattle. The creek that fed their pond ran through a large cow pasture prior to feeding the pond. Therefore, I agreed to assist in handing out literature, attending meetings, attending County Council meetings, etc. to keep the CAFO out of the district. Sad to say, but we found ourselves in conflict with many local farmers who had already agreed or contracted to have the treated waste piped onto their fields, for a price of course. Worse, we found ourselves in conflict with the Tennessee State Department charged with protecting our water sheds from contamination, etc. For example, as a group we were able after some delay to have the Department schedule a public hearing at the Mt. City High School to discuss the matter. Only to be told by their representative at that meeting that the permit for the CAFO had already been granted. Further they admitted there was no recourse from their standpoint for any pollution that might occur. This would have to be pursued by a private citizen whose property would be endangered. At this point it appeared that something was beginning to stink besides cow manure.

A legal basis to stop the operation was pursued relative to a Tenn. law regulating normal or natural farming and commerce. We attempted to follow this course only to learn that a recent Attorney General opinion recognized CAFOs as constituting natural or normal farming. It appeared that our group was opposed by many farmers, not all, and highly placed politicians. I hasten to add, these are my personal beliefs and do not represent the position of any groups or other individuals.

I desired to personally seek additional information, pro or con about such an operation. An ad or story had been posted, I can not recall where, my short term memory is not what it should be, but in detail the information was about a large CAFO in Pennsylvania, lauded as one of the more modern and well managed operations and considered a model for others. I called the area Chamber of Commerce and was given the number of several persons I could call for information.

One person contacted advised he knew the operation well. The people responsible for the CAFO were wonderful residents and well intentioned farmers. However they had some problems and were tweaking the operation to improve it. He further stated that there were times when the smell was nearly unbearable. He also stated the CAFO was brightly illuminated 24 hours a day and neighbors were prevented from seeing the sky and stars at night, they called it "light pollution," this was a new one for me. It was also stated that the community had drilled a new water well source several years before and recent water assays indicated the nitrogen levels were very high and that this could indicate ground water problems with the CAFO.

By this time I felt I had enough personal information to validate my opposition to the CAFO. But one might ask what has this to do with CSI and Forensic Ballistics. The connection is indirect and unproven but the suspicion remains. The founders of the CAFO operation consisted of a trio of persons. One, Wiley Roark is the CEO and manager of a gravel and paving company called Maymead that has the operating headquarters in Mt. City, Tenn. The other two partners were man and wife, Jerry and Emily Anderson who had a dairy cow operation near Lenoir, NC.

Rumor has it that Roark was to provide the legal and financial muscle for the operation and the land for the development, while the Andersons provided the cows and needed accessories for the dairy operation. At one point in time, a large herd of cows could be seen roaming land outside of Mt. City and it was thought that these were to be a large part of the herd to end up as milk cows.

One other related development was that Mrs. Anderson had made on offer on a residential property adjacent to the CAFO development property. The closing on this property was supposedly set for a Friday, about a week before Christmas several years ago. The only problem was that Emily disappeared about a week before that Christmas and missed the appointment. In fact she was missing for nine or ten days when her pickup truck with a new diamond design tool chest was discovered in South Carolina, about 100 miles away.

The location of the vehicle was discovered and reported to authorities in South Carolina and North Carolina. A truck and flat bed trailer combination was sent to South Carolina and brought back the missing truck. After it was returned to North Carolina, a search disclosed the body of Emily Anderson in the tool chest. She had been shot twice. Her family and friends had received no word from her during the ten day period. The realtor and acquaintances in Mt. City had received no word from her. As far as could be definitely established, no one had communicated with her for ten days.

According to various reports, it was learned the Andersons had marital problems and it was disclosed Emily had hired an attorney with intention to divorce Mr. Anderson. According to published reports, migrant workers had seen Emily drive her white pickup into a wooded area behind the dairy barns. They also reported seeing Jerry drive a back hoe into the same general location. It is alleged the defense seriously damaged the migrant worker testimony by establishing one of them lied about his name on the witness stand. In reports I have seen no information showing they lied about any material facts in the case. Two neighbors claim they heard two shots from that area the morning when Emily was last seen. It has been alleged that she had a large insurance policy; rumored to be on the order of 1 ½ million dollars and with the beneficiary to be the young son of her husband, someone she had learned to love. After a relatively short investigation, the Sheriff arrested Jerry and he was charged with murder.

For those interested in the Crime Scene Investigation, where was it? It should have started the moment her truck was discovered in South Carolina, but it never got started at all until the truck was returned @ 100 miles. It appears from what I have learned that no trained CSI personnel were present. It appears that no significant evidence was uncovered in the truck. Although the husband was suspected, a complete investigation for trace evidence material, fingerprints, blood traces, etc. should have been done. Here comparisons of evidence material may have been valuable for exclusion or in the event of an accessory.

According to reports, investigators attempted to pin point the murder location in the area identified by gun shots and migrant worker descriptions, with limited success from a dog handler and his "body" dog. Searchers did find a small amount of blood on the bucket edge of the back hoe. This was taken to the State Crime Laboratory according to reports, followed by information the blood was too contaminated to determine DNA. However the serologist could testify that it was human blood of female origin. It is alleged the Judge refused to allow this testimony on the grounds it would unduly influence the Jury!

It has also been alleged that the Judge would allow no testimony concerning the insurance policy(s) on the life of Emily on the grounds it would unduly prejudice the Jury!

Apparently no testimony was presented that would connect any firearm or other evidence of this nature even inferentially with Jerry.

It appears the most critical evidence presented was that of the Asst. Medical Examiner, who testified that the victim had been dead for four or five days, although in answer to a direct question from the Prosecutor is alleged to have agreed that she could not rule out ten days! According to reports many felt this was a crushing blow to the prosecution. I wish I could have been there in person to hear this testimony. On the face of it, the second opinion sounds like an afterthought. Based on reports, it appears that some witnesses felt that way, and the ten days idea was not considered seriously. If the evidence was presented in that manner, it would be improper in my opinion.

I would not profess to have any professional opinion of my own in the determination of time of death. But I do know forensic pathologists I have known and worked with as a group would agree to attempt a relatively precise determination of time of death is fraught with danger. To quote an old friend, Prof. Robert Hendrix MD, Prof. of Pathology, University of Michigan: "In summary, except for some rare, very fortuitous sets of circumstances, exact determinations of the postmortem interval should not be attempted. The time should be expressed as a period with lower and greater limits which will fit the scientific facts and the impressions gained from them. – The temptation to appear very capable in this field should be resisted. Capable attorneys understand the difficulties and their attempts to get precise information have some ulterior motives." In my understanding, research in recent years has demonstrated that humidity and temperature are often more important factors than time itself. I have no way of knowing, but I wonder if the fact the victim did little bleeding, was encased in a clean dry environment, fully clothed, enclosed by steel, during a time of usually low temperatures, i.e., last of December, was properly evaluated?

At any rate, the Jury in the trial of the husband was unable to reach a verdict, ending in a so-called hung jury. It has been reported that the jurors were 11 – 1 for acquittal! The defendant has been released pending any new evidence. Was he guilty or was there another? We may never know and we must remember we ordinarily only get one shot at the physical evidence, and then we must live with the results.

Daniel Webster in 1830 stated "Every unpunished murder takes away something from the security of the life of every man."

By this time, @ 2000, I was nearing the end of my case involvement. I was past caring for motel and restaurant life and the associated long trips. Besides, our family was too darned happy in our digs and with the small town life. We were also busy helping with the plans for our new church, St. Anthony of Padua. As I mentioned earlier I was raised as a Catholic. While Nan had taken instructions and made her first communion while I served on the U. S. S. Leyte, the Essex class aircraft carrier. This was another surprise she had for me when I came home on leave to get married in 1951.

When we moved to Mt. City, Tenn. we welcomed another nice surprise. We heard that a Franciscan priest was in town and holding mass in a temporary schoolroom. The priest was Fr. Tom Vos and just a few minutes in his presence and you were hooked. He could ask for any errand and all you could do was say "yes Father." He was an inspirational man who spent all his spare time working to help care for the poor in the region. I recall going along with him in his pickup truck with the topper on the back delivering Christmas presents at various locations from Mt. City to somewhere in Kentucky and back again. He was also instrumental in getting heating stoves for several poor families in the area, carrying them to the homes, and helping install them. Fr. Tom as he was affectionately known started a food pantry for the poor at the new church called St. Anthony Bread. Before he got that started, he assisted other agencies in their pantries for the poor. Nancy, my daughters Kathy and Kelly, and I helped run the pantry for some time. One of the best lessons of my life then was learned when several different people came for food and told us we love you folks cause no one ever asks us what church we go to! No one could help but get close to the good Father as he was such a kind and caring individual. Nancy asked him to come for dinner several times and served him on the rear porch of the old cabin which he loved. He called it his café on the creek.

Finally the new church was completed and consecrated. It was beautiful and I heard that Fr. Tom planned much of the design himself. His pride and joy was a beautiful stained glass circular window in the chapel, the popular vision of Jesus in the garden of Gethsemane. Early on I was placed on the financial committee for the church and then I learned more about the wonderful background of this man from God. He had been a missionary in several different areas including some tough ones when he was younger. One was in South side Chicago, where I heard his life was threatened at knife point on one occasion. But the one that gave me goose pimples was finding out that he had been used as a trouble-shooter to go to parishes with severe problems and iron them out.

One was a parish in a large city, where there were two wealthy and elderly sisters. One was a consistent church attendee while the other refused to go. Fr. Tom concentrated on the fallen-away Catholic and spent many hours with her in conversation. As a result they became very good friends, but he admits he was not able to get her back in the church. But then she passed away, and Fr. received a call from the family attorney to come and see him. He told the priest that she had left him a little gift, a large sum of money. The Fr. immediately called the Bishop and asked him what to do. As a good Franciscan, he had taken the vow of poverty, and he could not touch a dime of it. The Bishop told him to send it to his office and he would see that it was properly cared for.

Some years later, he was in Mt. City. The first mass was held in the home of an elderly Catholic lady living here, unable to go to mass. As word got around a few more Catholics showed up and mass was held in several temporary locations. Eventually, the attendance grew to a size too large for even the temporary classroom. Then the parish people started to ask about building a new church. Several offered to put up some money for parts of the interior. Fr. had tried to convince them there were not enough people or enough funding to build a church, but the push was on. So, he told the newly formed building committee he would go to the area Bishop and see if he could help.

After the initial contact the Bishop advised he would get back to him. Soon, the Bishop called him back and reminded him of the gift he had received in another parish and another State some time ago. The money had been set aside in a fund for building and renovating churches. Now, a large part of it was going to help him build his new church in Mt. City, Tennessee. The church would be named for the young student of St. Francis of Assisi, who became one of the great saints of the church, St. Anthony of Padua. At the same time, financial arrangement was made with the approval of the Bishop to provide for the pantry for the poor at the new church.

That Fr. Tom is quite a guy. I recall not longer after the church was built noting in the Sunday bulletin that a generous gift was received from a couple in Indian River, Michigan toward the new church cost. I asked, "Fr. Tom, how did you get a gift like that from northern Michigan?" He said, "Trooper let us see what kind of memory you have – what landmark do you think of when you think of Indian River, Michigan?" He knew I had been stationed in Gaylord, not far from Indian River and both on US-27. I thought hard and finally it came to me – the large lighted cross on the hill above US-27 and on the edge of the village. He asked, "What is under that cross?" I said, "I never had the opportunity to find out." He told me the cross marks a Franciscan chapel and I have spent a little time there. A couple weeks later a nice gift came in from a family in Palm Beach, Florida. When I asked him about that he told me that he goes there and gives a guest homily once in a while. I understood, many of his sermons affected me that way too.

His eyes are failing and he is unable to drive anymore. He is semi-retired and spending time at one of his favorite monasteries and chapels at Indian River, Michigan. He is one of those people in life you never forget. Before he left we had a marble stone engraved with his name and service, the name of our patron saint, St. Anthony, and the words "in his footsteps." I know he was flattered and grateful, but in his usual humble way he said something like, okay that will be my gravestone; I imagine the casket is out back.

The drunk driver shooting: By this time I have been out of touch with my former associates and friendly lawyers and the case load has dwindled, thankfully. Every now and then I would receive a call for consultation, often through AFTE who received requests from attorneys for information on independent examiners in certain areas. One that got my attention was a request from a big city lawyer who represented the family of a police shooting victim. I gave them the same answer I always give; we tell it like it is, helpful or hurtful. The firm let me know that is all they hoped for. They represented the family of a woman who was admittedly a drunk driver but who was shot to death by an officer. They were suing the city.

This required a couple visits to the city, interviews with the lawyers, visits to the Crime Laboratory, and tests at a nearby range that had been reserved for such testing. I learned the city had secured the services of Luke Haag, one of if not the foremost shooting reconstruction experts in the Country. Like me, Luke was a former President of AFTE.

The city story of the events was the officer on one man night patrol duty spotted a car driving over the centerline and weaving erratically indicating the likelihood of a drunk driver. The car, the investigation would show had side-swiped cars, struck and damaged a light pole, and the driver, a lone woman, it was disclosed had a fractured knee and other injuries. The right side of her car showed devastating sideswipe damage, both of the right windows were broken and empty, and tires flattened. The officer signaled her to stop and she did in an awkward way as the car stopped, idled and backed into the curbing.

According to the police report and testimony, the patrol officer stopped his patrol car parallel to the curb and with the front end nearly touching her vehicle. This would prevent her from climbing out the driver side. He felt she was scrambling around and might try to escape. He then went to the right side of the damaged car as she was attempting to leave by that door. He claimed she either did not understand his commands or ignored them. She now was sliding back toward the driver seat when he bent forward and placed his head and trunk inside the car so as to get a better grip on her. Originally he had apparently tried to control her by gripping her right arm or shoulder. She managed to get to the shifter and a foot on the gas pedal and started the car moving away from the curb. The officer stated at this moment he was in effect trapped inside the car and was afraid that he would be dragged and injured or killed. As the struggle ensued he drew his pistol and fired three shots; one struck her in the shoulder area, one in the neck and one in the head.

The car rolled a very short distance and stopped in the street. The driver was dead at the scene. A fired cartridge case was found on the right floorboards of the car, and two were found some distance in front of the car, on the roadway and in a nearly straight line. As I recall at least one if not two of the bullets perforated her body and struck the car interior in a line from the passenger side downward into the car on the driver side.

The Office of the Prosecuting Attorney reviewed the case and declined any charges against the officer, saying in effect the shooting was in self-defense and justified. There had been some static about the decision. The woman was black and the officer white therefore there was some racial unrest in the city.

The story from the other side was a little different. The information about the drunk driver, the various collisions, and the stop coincided with that of the officer. However, they claimed the officer was in a position where the shooting was unnecessary and therefore unlawful. Furthermore, they produced statements of two witnesses to the incident that painted a slightly different picture. One was some distance from the scene and was not entirely convincing. However, the second was a young man, in the military or just home from the military as I recall, and he insisted he was across the street and had a good view of the shooting. He said as he looked toward the cars, the officer appeared to straighten up, with his body outside the damaged vehicle, as a shot was fired. Further he stated the officer was walking swiftly or nearly running alongside the car as the remaining shot(s) was fired.

The city had promised full cooperation and the laboratory had been instructed to turn any requested evidence over to me. Upon my request to see and examine/test the blouse/shirt of the victim, I was told it was not available and that it had been "thrown away." This evidence was vital in that powder residue tests would indicate in at least one and probably two shots how far the muzzle of the pistol was from the victim at discharge. I hoped this did not indicate problems with the State side of the case and I was bitterly disappointed to say the least. However, there had been no criminal prosecution and some time had lapsed. Gladly I can say that they cooperated fully from then on.

Ejection tests with the pistol indicated the fired cases were thrown out to the right and slightly backward. This would agree with the location of the casings found on the roadway. It would also indicate the ejection port of the pistol was probably inside the window opening when the first shot was fired and outside the window opening when the last two were fired. Residues about the opening indicated discharge at a very close range. It appeared to me that the second witness may have been right, although my impressions were based on the likely weapon position at discharge. On my final interview with the attorneys I remember distinctly part of the conversation. It was agreed that I had been a police officer for many years and had about eight years road and training experience. I was asked if I was ever placed in a situation like the officer in this case. I said yes I had and they asked me to tell them about it.

While stationed in Northern Michigan, another Trooper and I were investigating a fatal highway accident. I was standing on the centerline of the road, steering oncoming traffic to one lane to avoid the crashed vehicle and body. This was late at night, the patrol car lights were blinking and rotating and I was using a fusee to get the drivers attention. I noticed an older pickup truck coming at an obvious high rate of speed for the conditions. I waved the fusee furiously to get his attention and readied myself to jump for the ditch as I thought he was going to slam into me and the accident scene. At the last second he slammed on the brakes and skidded to a stop. One look at him and I knew he had been drinking. I ordered him to put the car on the shoulder and turn off the key. He looked at me and said "f--- you Trooper!" He shoved the truck into gear and started to drive off around the scene. I jumped onto the running board, reached through the open window, got my fingers around the back of his neck and into his cheek and mouth. This was one of the most effective come along holds ever invented. I twisted his head to the right and backwards as if I were going to break his neck. He screamed "I will kill you, you s.o.b." I screamed back as the truck was gathering speed "Then you will kill us both a------." He slammed on the brakes, skidding to a stop. I pulled him out through the window and body slammed him to the pavement. Once again, if the camcorders were there I would have been in trouble. I handcuffed him, took him back to the scene and sat him on the shoulder. He had nothing more to say to me. The lead attorney then asked "but you failed to shoot him, why?" I told them he was not guilty of a felony and I had no right to shoot him. They then asked, "Were you frightened that he might hurt or kill you?" I told them, "certainly, but that is part of the life of a police officer; if you can't accept it, you should get a different job."

I was informed later that the city settled out of court.

They usually do in these cases. I have been involved in a number of cases both for the Prosecution and Defense in criminal court where this kind of decision is debated. It has always been my view that when death or serious injury for the officer seems certain, he must do what he can to avoid it. It is a life and death decision made in the fraction of a second. In that scenario, the officer should be given the benefit of the doubt. I recall one scenario where a young inexperienced patrol officer ran down a robber in a driving rain. Backup had not arrived as yet and he had the felon on his knees with his hands on top of his head. The sidearm of the officer was in his right hand and the revolver was cocked. As he attempted to handcuff the robber the revolver discharged. The bullet went through the top right side shoulder and into the chest cavity, killing the suspect.

In this case a gung-ho Prosecutor charged the officer with second degree murder. In pre-trial interview, he told me in clipped terms the police officer was gun happy and that he deliberately blew the suspect away. In an incredulous tone I said something to the effect, hell if he wanted to blow him away, he would have put the revolver muzzle against the back of his head, not near his right shoulder. It was an accident, and thank God the jury believed that it was.

In nearly every case of mine where a police officer accidentally shoots his victim, he has carried a double-action revolver. In each incident, the revolver was cocked ready for single action discharge when it fired. When a revolver is used double- action, the hammer is down in a safe position, the trigger is pulled in a long steady motion rearward, causing the double-action sear to be engaged, pulling the hammer rearward to near a cocked position from whence it falls causing the firing pin to strike the cartridge primer, or in some models the hammer to strike an intervening metal block which forces the firing pin forward to strike the cartridge primer. This type of trigger pull requires a force of on the average in excess of 6 lbs. to more than 10 lbs. pressure to fire the weapon. Whereas in single action discharge, the hammer is first cocked by pulling it all the way rearward allowing the single action sear to be engaged, then a slight pull on the trigger causes discharge. Single action force is variable with the firearm model, but is usually @ 3 lbs. to 6 lbs. pressure. In addition, certain wear or touch-up alteration of the key parts may make the pressure even lighter. To sum up; it is not too difficult to discharge most revolvers single action accidentally. The safest way to handle this type of weapon is to keep it un-cocked and the finger off the trigger unless you anticipate needing it. Many departments today concentrate on double-action only shooting.

In another case, the patrol officer was attempting to shoot out a rear tire on the speeding get-away car, when the patrol car hit a bump causing him to inadvertently jerk the revolver upwards and fire it. The bullet went through the back window of the car and into the head of the passenger.

In another police shooting an officer was chasing the suspect across a field. He had his revolver out and cocked. He slipped on a slight slope and fell to his knees discharging the revolver as he went down. The bullet struck the felon in the back of his head.

I could go on, but I think you get the idea. Years ago, it was much safer for police officers than today. Sometimes when we approached a suspicious car we had our sidearm out, down alongside our trousers where it would escape a casual glance. It was a rare occasion to have it out and pointed at the head or face of a suspect or violator. In the world today, it is common for it to happen on a near daily basis, in some areas.

I often wonder why we have a war v. drugs, a war v. Iraq, a war v. Afghanistan or the Taliban, etc. How about conducting a war v. violent crime? It is sometimes talked about and nearly always quickly forgotten. What were the statistics for last year? I believe that in excess of 20,000 citizens were murdered in one year in this Country. It is probably safer in some areas of Iraq than in some areas of Detroit, my old home town. It really hurts to hear the media discussing which major city is #1 in homicides for the year; is it Philadelphia or Detroit? Where are all the so-called mandatory tough laws on violent crimes? There are more violent criminals on the streets than in the prisons. Sad to say, but we must release dangerous criminals because there is not enough room in the prisons. Then build more prisons, damn it. Use our tax dollars for something worthwhile for a change, if you want change.

Sorry, but I had to get on the soap box for a minute.

Each time we move I would stop at the local police department and offer my services pro bono. They rarely availed themselves of the offer. However twice I have been of some assistance since we moved to the mountains. The first time involved an unsolved murder where I unwittingly became a go-between. My youngest daughter called me one day and said a neighbor of hers had a problem and wondered if I could help. I said sure, what does she need and she told me she just wanted to talk to me about something serious. She came the next day and the neighbor was one of the poor Southern whites, the kind we call hillbillies. She told me that she knew from my daughter, who lived in the boonies on a little creek at the time, not far from a small settlement of the original settlers, that I had been a Michigan State Police officer. She advised that she had heard they had a good reputation as honest cops. She asked me if she gave me some confidential information, would I do the right thing with it, but keep her name out of it. I told her I certainly would but asked why not tell your Sheriff. She said "He is dumber than a box of rocks and besides he is a blabbermouth," I had never heard the box of rocks comparison before but found out it was a very common expression hereabouts. She also said if a certain party finds out I am here and tell you what I have to tell you, my family will be murdered and my house burned to the ground. She actually shook as she passed this word.

She then asked me if I knew about the several year old unsolved murder of a 16 year old boy who was found beaten and strangled. There had been several articles over time in the local news and I was aware of the story. She then told me who the killer was and about another male who might be an accomplice. As they left, I placed a call to the office of the Sheriff and asked for a certain detective I had met once and who had been with a large department up North before relocating here. I asked for him to come to the house and he said he would be right over. I told him the information but not the name of the woman who supplied it. He stated he had been in charge of this case for some time and he had an idea who the informant might be but would not ask her name. He also said the killer she named was on their short list of suspects. A month or so later the named individual was arrested, tried, and convicted of murder. So, even here in the mountains, the reputation of my former outfit was put to good use.

By the way, I hope the use of the hillbilly slur did not upset anyone. We have had wonderful neighbors and friends from several areas here in the Appalachians, who fit the loose expression in that they were relatively low income, Southern born and bred, with that distinctive drawl, but were unusually courteous, helpful, and would never take a dime for helping a neighbor. I learned that the hard way when we worked on the log home. One neighbor who remains a dear friend volunteered to cut the weeds with his big mower, and then brought a long extension hose from his water spigot for us to use to mix mortar. He saw us going to the creek with a bucket and said around here you need water call your neighbor. Another distant neighbor I had never formally met came over one day with his tractor and plow. He told me he heard that my wife wanted a garden in and he knew this dirt had not been worked for years so it had to be plowed first. He said mark it off; I did and he plowed it twice. Later he came back with the discs and chopped it up fine for us. I offered him some money for all his work and he got a stern look on his face. He said I know you yanks may not understand but around here that is considered an insult to offer money to a neighbor for his help. He remained a very good friend until we moved. Over time, I found out he had a reputation for blunt straight forward talk.

I had dropped a copy of my book "Silent Evidence" to the Sheriff and Chief of Police. I finally got a bite one day when a uniformed deputy stopped by the house. He said that perhaps I might help him and I agreed that I would try. He produced a pill box with a damaged large bullet inside. He said we took this out of the inside wall of a house trailer that had been looted and shot up. I asked him in and did a quick check of the bullet under the stereomicroscope and checked the weight. I told him he was in luck; this one was kind of easy. It is a .45 Colt bullet fired from a revolver. If he found someone with a Colt revolver in that caliber he might have his man. He excitedly told me, the victim has a neighbor that has a .45 caliber Colt Single-action Army revolver. I told him that very well could be his culprit.

11

Back to Teaching

In the early 2000s, I embarked on one of the more pleasurable endeavors of my older life. An old friend, co-worker, and retired Michigan State Policeman, Terry LaVoy contacted me. He had just retired for the 2nd time from the Florida Department of Law Enforcement Crime Laboratory at Tampa, FL. He advised me he had been asked to set-up a training program for Firearms and Tool Mark Analysts. It was to be a 40 hour a week program, with an experienced analyst or two with the students at all times and the phase I training to be accomplished in 6 months. This in effect would replace the standard 1 year to 1 ½ year on-the-job program usually in place. The standard system worked alright but it occupied one or more analysts to conduct it part time at the expense of the case work which was backlog building in all the laboratories. The idea was that the new program, more intensive and full time would be conducted by retired analysts thereby assisting in managing the current case loads. It sounded like a great idea to me and I knew that Terry was a fantastic organizer and he and his wife were well practiced in computer operation. Terry advised he wanted me to handle the most important part of the program teaching the students the practice of comparing and identifying bullets and cartridge cases, including the theory of identification, the methods, the pitfalls, and then evaluating their performances. I was thrilled to be asked and it gave me a great deal of pleasure when he stated he wanted one of the best to do this important job. I thought, thanks Terry, I will do my very best.

This phase of the training program was divided into several segments. First, there was an introduction outlining materials and program. Secondly, students were introduced to equipment and aids available.. This was followed by an arms course conducted by one of the very best, an experienced Florida Dept. of Law Enforcement instructor with the most amazing memory of weapon systems and ammunition I had ever encountered.

Next there was a special segment on class characteristics of firearms conducted by a member of the FBI staff who specialized in the area. Then a lengthy segment on class and individual characteristics and identification of firearms conducted by myself accompanied with constant supervision by Terry and a stream of informal lectures with note taking and copies of important articles, papers, etc. by staff.

Later in the school, there was supervised mock case work with hands on training and supervision by several analysts, including Terry, myself, and Dave Townshend from guess where, of course, the Michigan State Police laboratory retired. A special session on microscopy and photomicrography was presented by an industrial expert on the Leitz comparison microscope.

Terry had arranged to have the Laboratory large meeting room converted to a mini-laboratory with modern comparison scopes and stereo microscopes for each student, along with shared photographic accessories of the latest type, mini-tool sets, and a separate office to study and store notebooks, etc. There was also a new copy machine in the office devoted to our students and their instructors. All of us provided a treasure trove of current and old time notes and papers on Firearms and Tool Marks which were dutifully copied and distributed to each student. When the students left the program, they left with countless full notebooks of information, more than I had ever seen assembled in any one place. The instructors were impressed and I believe the students were too, although this was new to them.

Altogether we conducted two such schools, with eight students in the first and nine in the second. They were limited in size to get maximum personal exposure and comparison of notes and ideas with one another. The students were all graduates with BS degrees and had already been screened and accepted for a position in the Laboratory when they finished their training. They represented Florida, Georgia, and the Bahamas.

The armorer section was devoted to modern firearm types with various forms of action such as blow-back, short recoil, gas operated, single action, double action, semi-automatic, full automatic fire, etc. The students were first acquainted with the many firearms used, taught to disassemble them for cleaning, taught concerning their operating features, and finally how to safely fire them. During this phase they also discussed ammunition, substitutes, dangers in handling, primers, gunpowder, etc. When I first saw them, they were still talking about this phase and the wonderful and enjoyable experience.

My phase of the training was the most extensive in the program, requiring several lengthy sessions and approximately a third of the entire phase I program. It included basic introduction to and practice in the comparison of striated and impressed markings and their identification. This was accompanied by continuous discussions of parts and the role they play in the process.

A few students had some exposure as technicians in various laboratories, but it was not extensive and not related to any amount of microscopic comparison work. Therefore the program was designed to start at the very beginning and meticulously review the various plus and minus attributes of evidence fired bullets.

The students were provided blank copies of laboratory work sheets in order for them to fill in the required information and note any exceptional information, drawings, photomicrographs, etc. After a brief review of microscopic good habits and use, we began.

I started with a set of two 9mm full metal cased projectiles that had been fired from a Ruger pistol. There was a set for each student. These were deliberately chosen from several handguns in my personal collection. They were chosen because the exhibits clearly displayed marked land and groove dimensions suitable for measurements, driven and trailing edges, well marked striae on the various parts, including those remaining from the initial straight forward thrust of the bullet into lead and breech bore areas and some in line with the twist of the rifling. They also demonstrated many striae that were congruous with those in the same area of the other bullet. In the parlance of today, they could be easily matched.

Each land impressed area of each bullet was marked identically so there could be no mix-ups in their relative positions under the microscope. Each area was examined in detail from low to comparatively high power or magnification. As each remarkable stria (striation) and/or groups of striae were closely examined students were asked to discuss what they were seeing. I, as instructor, went from one to another, little by little, bit by bit to insure they were seeing and describing the various same items. The students from the very beginning seemed to enjoy this tedious but absolutely necessary type of examination and learning. The bullets were later rotated in order to the non-matching positions to visualize the differences.

They all realized what we were trying to accomplish, although not at the same rate. I recall in the first class there were a couple that were trying to push forward faster than I would allow and obviously understanding immediately where we were going. My explanations of what they were supposed to see and realize were long-winded, but they grew used to that because that is one of my hallmark traits; i.e., lengthy discussions. I recall at one time discussing axial markings with them to the point they would inquire before the next session, "Charlie, do we need any more on axial ?"

What they could not know was that these pointed discussions and tedious examination of markings was not done just to acquaint them but to analyze their abilities unknown to them. It is not common, but I vividly recall, over many years of instructing would-be analysts, two individuals who for the lack of the proper phraseology were microscopically blind. At least that is what I have come to call it. It is an unnerving and difficult situation when it occurs. But picture yourself in this type of microscopic examination lesson, and as I would ask, now look at the first prominent stria next to the driven edge of the land impression, and the two finer or narrower striae next to it forming a cluster of three remarkable striations or lines. Now reviewing the image through each student scope and finding all but one are looking at the same exact area. One is looking elsewhere on the image and when asked to describe what he sees is really unable to do so. Either this guy is a little slow to comprehend or he has a problem.

With one individual it became pronounced one day when he asked me what I was working on. It was case work where at this point it was important to demonstrate that two different powder samples from dissimilar cartridges could be easily differentiated under the stereo microscope. I had drawn an approximate circle and divided it into three pie shaped sections. In one section was an entire gunpowder flake removed from the shirt of the victim near the bullet entrance hole. In another section was a flake of unburned gunpowder which had a small hole near the center, if my memory is still correct this common powder was known as Bullseye, a slightly faster burning form which ignites from the inside and outside, and in the third section was a flake of gunpowder from a separate cartridge sample of nearly the same size and shape as the other two, and with a dark dot in the center. This occurred a long time ago but I think it was called red dot. The evidence and one sample showed the dot in the center. My would be student looked at it as I asked him which two were similar and he picked the dot in the evidence section and the flake with the hole in it in the other. This was an intelligent and very conscientious individual and he was serious. I had seen less disturbing signs before but this was the finishing blow. I had to tell him the laboratory was not the place for him.

The second individual was much more difficult and although I felt he may have a problem I was unable to put my finger on it in the early stages of training. But as we began to actually compare markings it came to a head. On two different occasions, he would advise me, "okay Charlie, I have these two bullets lined up properly, take a look." So I looked; there were a number of striae on two bullets, seemingly in an array, but with some wider ones lined up with some narrower ones, spaces out of sync, etc. I would tell him, take the microscope pointer and show me which ones you are talking about. As he described the match and I asked tell me how those are the same or even very similar, he would get a blank look on his face and I knew he did not know what in hell he was talking about. Worse yet, he apparently failed to understand what I was talking about.

But, with this first school class, there were few problems and most were quick to catch on. Early on, while working on the first set of Ruger bullets, I asked the class if they had discovered anything unusual about them. Almost immediately one student, a young attractive tall lady with blonde hair, spoke up asking "Charlie are you referring to the scratch on both that starts on the ogive and continues up to the bearing surface?" She was exactly right, and quickly the class chimed in and several indicated they compared the striations within the gouge and they appeared identical. From the excited voices, I could tell the class was already hooked and would probably pose few problems. The gouge they referred to was an abnormality with this particular firearm. Not anything that would effect the operation of the firearm but a minute defect where a spur of metal persisted from the manufacture, apparently missed on inspection, that consistently marked every bullet as the chambering operation ensued.

Next each student received three .45 automatic caliber fired bullets. Two were from my .45 automatic caliber Colt model 1911-A1 pistol and one was from my .45 automatic Colt Government model 70 series pistol. Here they determined that the class characteristics compared favorably, but that the individual characteristics were similar between only two. These bullets were all pre-marked so that once more students could compare the areas in detail that were sufficiently similar to those that were not. Each land and groove area was examined individually, discussed and notes made thereon. With these larger bullets, the students were able to see certain striae slightly curve from their axial position (straight and in line with the long axis of the bullet) to a position in line with the rifling as the bullet began the rotation caused by the lands as they circumscribed the bullet. This rotational process is the action that causes the bullet to leave the barrel spiraling about its long axis as it flies to the target.

Well that will be enough of that. This is not a teaching manual for firearms examiners or analysts. I am attempting to give you a feel for the detail and minutia involved in the process. After a long session on the microscope it was time for discussion and resting the eyes. As is my habit, every once in a while I attempted to lighten the process with a little humorous story. I know the students appreciated the break from their slave driver instructor. On several occasions one would remark, "Hey Charlie, do you think this would be a good time to break, my stomach tells me it needs food and the clock tells me we were supposed to break for lunch a half hour ago!" This has always been a habit of mine, getting on a subject and attempting to finish the area no matter how long it takes. I suppose you might call it a fault, but the students rarely complained.

Having come from the old world I was amazed when each student showed for class with a personal computer. There were times when it was useful for them, but I forced them to do nearly everything during class by hand to be sure they understood the process.

I remember the first day when it was necessary to go into land and groove measurements, determination of diameter and caliber. We had a large flip chart in the room and I used it often. As an example; if you add the land and groove width measures, multiply by the number of lands and grooves, and divide by pi you end with the approximate diameter of the bullet and thence the caliber. So, with a badly damaged bullet, if you can microscopically determine the width of one land and one groove and measure the smashed remnant for the number of lands and grooves, you can determine the caliber. You also need to understand that the result will be slightly smaller than the actual diameter as microscopically you are measuring the chord, a straight line across an arc. At that point, I heard a male voice say "Now that is something, he is actually doing that by hand!" As I glanced at the class they nearly all had an incredulous look on their face and then we all laughed.

During the long tiring sessions, every now and then a student would spot something in the microscope field that was unexpected. Then the entire class would be directed to that location and discussion would follow. As time progressed, we examined every type of bullet on the market and every kind of marking one could expect; the characteristics of the various rifling processes and how one could determine the process used for most barrel bores. We made countless casts of bores, chambers, etc. using our old friend Mikrosil, a special casting material widely used in forensic science.

Eventually we pursued the same processes with fired and unfired cartridge cases; learning about their manufacture, markings from the process, including what we call sub-class markings or machining marks that can be repeated over a number of cases, etc. Then the class and individual markings created by a number of the loading, firing, extraction and ejection processes created by different firearms.

Since the students had completed their classes in firearms recognition, safe handling, and firing they were required to fire their own tests during many of the projects that followed. The Crime Lab as do other major crime laboratories has a firing range devoted to testing firearms to obtain undamaged test fired bullets by firing into a lengthy water tank, and an extended range for distance and accuracy determinations, with a suitable backstop, etc. This procedure also gave them a break from the microscope and was enjoyed by all. Of course, I used the range often to fire numerous tests to prepare for the next day at the microscope.

During the training, on two occasions, students discovered a peculiar defect or unusual mark found on tests from other firearms of the same type and manufacture. I advised them to do a literature search to determine if the defect had been previously reported. In one case it had not, so the student was advised in his/her spare time to write a technical paper for AFTE. Not as if they had much spare time. Each week they were given reading assignments to be done on their own time. If they had questions about the assignment, and they often did, bring them to the next day class for discussion.

One other item was a little different than usual in my experience. Among the total of seventeen students for the two classes, there were five females. The two in the first class looked like they should have been models, not firearm analysts. One was tall and blonde, the other of average height and with dark hair. They were both beautiful and very intelligent. I still recall about thirty years before when a lady firearms examiner was so rare that the first one to join AFTE found her face on the front cover of the Journal! At the AFTE annual meeting and training session in Miami, I was asked to provide a few remarks for the members at the banquet. I included comments about the fact that when I entered the field, there were no lady firearms analysts, but now at the meeting I would judge about a third of the membership in attendance were female; actually it was a welcome change.

About the recent AFTE meeting; this was an experience in several ways. I accepted the invitation to attend although I had not been to one for several years. At my age (83) I did not expect to see many of my old acquaintances from the discipline. The great majority of them are dead. So I left for the meeting with some trepidation. And rather than attempt the long drive by myself I elected to take the train from Deland to Miami.

I enjoyed the train ride down. However, when we got there it was late and after dark. Based on information from Amtrak I planned on taking a bus from the train platform to the hotel about 10 miles away. The train cars expelled many passengers here, at the end of the rails. Some had cars waiting for them, some took cabs, and a few waited for the buses. I had explicit directions on which bus I must get on to get to the hotel. The other buses came and went but not mine. There was one young black waiting along side me and I asked him if he knew about my bus. He talked Spanish to the waiting cab drivers and although I am not able to converse with them, from the expressions and loud voices I could tell they were giving him a hard time. He walked back to me and said something about they think I will cheat them out of a fare. I had been warned beforehand that cabbies in Miami are not cheap. Within moments my young friend vanished into a waiting car and I looked around the front of the depot and there was no one left there but me and a few cab drivers. I looked inside the depot and it was vacant. I had been waiting 40 minutes for the bus that was supposed to arrive within ten minutes of the train. Frankly, I was getting a little nervous as the first cabbie in line opened the door to his cab and said "you ready yet?" I handed him my bag and crawled inside.

He got me to the hotel and it cost $24.00 for the ride. Oh well, it was raining now and I was dry and arrived safely. The following morning I registered at the AFTE desk, and was met with "Charlie Meyers, oh that is wonderful," by a couple of young ladies working around the desk. And from that moment on, it was wonderful. It seemed like every time I turned around one of them was there asking me if I was alright, did I need anything, would you like something to drink, etc., etc., etc. My time at the meeting was wonderful.

I became re-acquainted with a number of examiners I had met some years before but had been out of touch with for some time. My old friend and confidante Al Biasotti passed away several years ago, and I missed him as we always had time for a spirited conversation about the discipline. However, one of his disciples Bruce Moran, trained by another old friend John Murdock, was there and I was delighted to see him presented with the Calvin Goddard award, a special and highly desired award named after the primary founder of modern firearms identification. I have a special warm place in my heart for Bruce for two reasons. One he has authored many fine papers for AFTE that has helped with the various problems we face. And he authored a book review of "Silent Evidence" that was honest and complimentary at the same time. I really appreciated his remarks that appeared in the Journal of Forensic Sciences.

At the banquet, I was seated next to Barbara Howe, the daughter of Walter Howe. She was the guest speaker for the evening. She is a lawyer and practicing Judge, vivacious in appearance and demeanor. I felt she was remindful of Walter alright. After the meeting, one of my students from the first training school (circa 2000), the tall beautiful blonde came over out of the crowd and sat on my lap. Trailing her was a photographer who took several photographs according to her instructions. Wow – I hope to get a copy any day now.

As soon as I returned from the meeting, I dropped a note to the Miami Crime Laboratory firearms section, thanking them for all the services and the wonderful meeting. I told them it was the first time in my life that I was treated like a rock star!

Writing this must be an omen or a magnet as I was interrupted only minutes before by a rap on the door. It was no guest. It was your friendly FedEx driver with a huge package for me. The box was about 30x36x12 inches in size. Heavy packaging tape sealed every nook and cranny. The box interior was filled with layers of wrapping paper, properly rolled to insulate the contents from jars, and finally several layers of bubble wrap. At the very center was a frame (20x28 inches) enclosing a large color photo of the Miami crew that sponsored and worked the 2009 AFTE meeting along with the former Presidents. There was also an embossed thank you card signed by all the worker bees and a patch from the Miami Dade Metropolitan Crime Laboratory. It will hang on my graffiti wall, among my large photo of me in Captain's uniform with the Michigan State Police, certificates from AAFS, SAFS (Southern Assn. of Forensic Scientists), the Kentucky

Colonels, plaques from AFTE and FDLE (Florida Dept. of Law Enforcement), my Bravery Award, my Navy discharge from WW II, and my signed photo from the "Firearms Eight," with a hand printed statement "Thank you Charlie for sharing your time, knowledge, and stories with us. It has been the experience of a lifetime." It is signed Ed Lenihan, Jeff Foggy, Terri Gleason, Alison Quereau, Andy Smith, John Ryan, Ron VanFleet, and Omar Felix. Among this class, there are a number who will become shining stars in the discipline, if they stick with this line of work.

All my adult life I have enjoyed lecturing and teaching in my field. I have had the opportunity to appear at Michigan State University, the University of Michigan, Oakland Community College, Delta Community College, Ferris Institute, the University of Indiana, The University of Florida, Northern Florida University at Jacksonville, and too many police departments and associations of prosecuting attorney to mention here.

Chasing Tail Lights to Forensic Ballistics

12

The Later Years

Being a declared retiree, I have had only a few direct contacts regarding case work in the last few years. But I have given in to entreaties a couple of times.

In one case, the chief investigator for the Prosecutor came to see me and explained they were having difficulty in determining the position of the shooter. He brought a series of photographs and notes for me to examine. The victim had started to slide out of the driver seat, so the door was partly open. One of several shots missed the victim and struck the inside windshield. In examining the photograph, looking in through the partly open door, the hole and radiating cracks were barely visible next to the left windshield cowling. I pointed out to the investigator that the open door and left side of the car formed a triangle with the impact hole in the windshield the apex of the triangle. The narrow triangle extending back from the car formed a space the shooter had to be inside of. If they could determine or limit approximately how far away he was they could position the shooter there.

The last one, I allowed myself to become involved in was for a Public Defender. It involved a rare dispute between a firearms examiner from each side, one for the Prosecution and one for the defense.

The dispute revolved around whether or not the fatal bullet was fired from the suspect firearm. It was a case from an area far distant and I told the Public Defender I did not like the long trips anymore and I hesitated to be involved. But, since a former associate was involved and had given my name, I agreed. The Defender assured me that she only wanted me to examine photomicrographs and advise her whether I felt she should pursue the issue.

As I reviewed the photographs which purported to show evidence of a bullet match, I had difficulty believing what I was seeing or rather what I was not seeing. There definitely was no evidence of an identification or match. Rather, there was evidence of non-identity. Some time later I was notified that I would be needed for trial, and I thought here we go again. But thankfully a plea was accepted and no further appearance on my part was required. Note: The investigators learned that I was correct.

Although I have not attended the AFTE meetings for several years, I have tried to stay active by reviewing all the publications and Journals. In addition I have authored several lengthy technical papers which have been published in the Journal, including "Some Basic Bullet Striae Considerations; Tool Marks – Novel Scientific Evidence (Ramirez Revisited); and Challenging Firearms and Tool Mark Identification – Part One by Adina Schwartz – A Commentary." The latter two papers are intended as at least a partial answer to court decisions and to one of our antagonists.

Court decisions and trials can be very frustrating, especially when the Courts make serious decisions based on misinformation or just poor understanding of what forensic science is all about. You may find it hard to believe but some decisions are based on pure ignorance.

The one paper concerns a famous Florida case where the defendant Ramirez was charged with rape and murder. He had already been tried and convicted of first degree murder but was released on a technicality twice. In the third trial conviction, an appeal claimed that part of the convincing evidence against him was based on tool mark evidence that was not reliable for various reasons.

The evidence consisted of striated tool marks in the cartilage of the victim as compared with test marks from the knife of Ramirez. Let me furnish part of the State Supreme Court decision overturning the conviction once again: "the procedure is a classic example of the kind of novel scientific evidence that Frye was intended to banish – i.e., a subjective, untested, unverifiable identification procedure that purports to be infallible ... in order to preserve the integrity of the criminal justice system in Florida, particularly in the face of rising nationwide criticism of forensic science in general, our state courts- both trial and appellate- must apply the Frye test in a prudent manner to cull science fiction and junk science from fact." Frye is a precedent setting case regarding forensic science and expert testimony.

My response began "anyone claiming even book knowledge of criminalistics would immediately realize that the words novel, science fiction, and junk science do not apply to Tool Mark Identification in general or this procedure specifically." Either the Judges failed to read and digest scientific literature provided or disregarded it.

Tool markings as an identification technique have been known and recognized since the 1800s at least. A famous medical legal scholar in Liege published a series of papers (1900-1903) regarding tool markings made with a knife. It has long been recognized that any object can be identified by the striated markings the business edge of the object causes if that surface is tool finished or damaged in such a way that the markings are unique. These papers were published in the German Journal Kriminalistik.

It sometimes seems that some trial or appellate court judges relish dumping on the police or agency witnesses. I recall one of our older Circuit Court trial judges was known for one of his oft quoted remarks, "if I learned one thing on the bench it is to never believe a police officer!"

After discussing issues in detail for over 5 pages, I concluded by summing up two homicide cases featured back-to-back on a forensic science show. I recognized the analysts and cases in both instances. One involved the solution of a child murder by comparison of plastic garbage bags by tool marks and micro/trace evidence comparison at the Orlando FDLE laboratory and the identification of knife tool marks in cartilage in the rape/murder of a woman in Alaska, involving the Alaskan State Crime Laboratory. In both cases the Prosecutors raved about the physical evidence as "the most convincing evidence I have ever encountered."

Another paper was to take issue with the remarks and testimony of a professional expert witness testifying for the defense in shooting cases. She has degrees in Philosophy and Law and is a University Professor. So she is properly addressed as Doctor, and as is usual receives a rousing welcome from the bench due to her status and learning. She is extremely well read and apparently devours every item she can obtain concerning firearms and tool marks. However, she has no standing or training or experience in the discipline she attacks so skillfully. It is difficult to understand why the courts can allow someone to testify as an expert on an issue they only know by reading. I guess we have to assume that because she understands what she reads, she also understands the significance of the procedures. Ah, but she is a PhD!

Perhaps I have become a bit bitter over the years. But one thing I can truthfully state is that despite the fact that the laboratory analysts are paid much less, and undergo more criticism, and only have a BS or possibly an MS degree, there is a smaller percentage of error or deception in their work and testimony than in the ranks of the more famous MDs and PhDs who are known for their scientific knowledge and prowess and who blather misinformation on TV and in court for big bucks!

But once more I must climb down off the soap box and quiet down.

As I sat here typing away I started to laugh a bit to myself. I wonder sometime if the children think I am losing it. Actually, I could see the mother doe bringing down her two fawns to nibble on the horde of downed apples off the old orchard trees. The deer love them. But, it brought back sudden recall of an incident on police patrol at night in Northern Michigan. Bob Johnston and I were cutting across country on a gravel road. It was during bow season for deer.

We spotted a car, driving very slowly and playing a spotlight into the adjoining woods. We drove further down the road, killed our lights, and crept onto the trail road finally coming up close behind the car. They were so intent on trying to violate the law they never knew we were there. One of them was sitting on the front fender with his bow half drawn waiting for a shot and the other drove and played the spotlight into the fields. Then Bob put on the headlights, the rotating flasher and the siren all at once. The archer dropped his bow, lunged off the fender and ploughed into an adjoining swamp. The driver stalled the car engine, then sat and waited for his arrest. Bob and I approached the car as he asked the driver, "What in hell do you think your doing?" The driver stated something like we have hunted for three days and never got a shot and in fact hardly saw a deer. This country must be hunted out but we were told this is prime hunting territory. Bob laughed at him and said you were told right. He asked him where they were staying and the driver identified a nearby lodge. Bob told him to go there and we would follow. The poor guy asked what about his partner and Bob told him the lodge is only a couple miles he will find his way there. When we got there Bob told him to make a pot of coffee. We were all sitting with a hot cup of java in our hand when the partner showed. He was sopping wet and his hunting pants were half ripped off.

Bob said you want to see some deer? They replied that would be great so we put them in the back seat and took off. We spotted several in twos or threes and then we came to a huge field of wild oats. There was a light misty rain falling now but it was quite warm. The spotlight reflected eyes all over the field. They were deer lying down and there were more than twenty of them! Bob asked them if they had seen enough. He told them to get out early tomorrow and take a stand on the edge of the woods and watch for them. They should be able to get a shot or two off. He asked them if they could hunt legally and they assured us they could. We then let them go. Yes, those were the days my friend.

Another pleasant occurrence happened in recent years. Terry LaVoy, the former associate and school organizer forwarded me a pleasant surprise regarding one of our second class participants. We had two black students from the Bahamas. They were both lots of fun and pleasant to work with. I became good friends with both of them. Apparently a difficult trial came up and their regular examiner was gone and could not testify. They were told to provide someone to testify in place of their primary analyst. So the responsibility went to Constable Dino Deveaux. Dino was a graduate of our second training class. He reviewed the case work and was called to testify in a complex multiple shooting. The following reports and citations were received by Terry and I from the authorities in the Bahamas:

To: Mr. Paul Farquharson, Actg. Commissioner of Police
Re: 2232 Dino Deveaux

"The captioned officer testified in a trial I just recently completed, namely the Quarry Mission murders. I was successful in having him accepted by the court as an expert witness so he should not have any difficulties in that regard in the future.

However, my main purpose for writing is to commend Constable Deveaux for the excellent way in which he testified. The knowledge he has of his field is comprehensive … It was indeed a pleasure working with and leading this officer in evidence in chief and the way he stood up under cross examination. Even the defense counsel (all 5 of them) commended him on the grasp of his field, firearms. "

Albertha L. Bartlett, Chief Counsel
ROYAL BAHAMAS POLICE FORCE
Certificate of Appreciation
Presented to
Charles Meyers

In appreciation of your invaluable assistance, guidance, knowledge and instruction imparted at the Firearms and Toolmark Identification School, 2000-2001 held at Florida Department of Law Enforcement Tampa Bay Regional Operation Center.

James Carey, Ch/Supt.
Director Forensic Services
Paul H. Farquharson
Commissioner of Police (actg.)

Now that is what I call a first class letter and certificate of appreciation. It is printed here for two reasons. One is to brag about our student and his "knowledge of firearms." The second is to brag about our training endeavor. You have to hand it to the British, they do things up right.

Dino is not the only student of our program to be commended for his knowledge and ability. Andy Smith from the first school was the primary target of a defense appeal in an important case in San

Francisco, with the appeal based on the Daubert v. Dow Supreme Court decision. Andy is an analyst with the San Francisco Crime Laboratory. Andy and Alison Quereau of "The Firearms Eight," are both active in AFTE and reputed to be top quality analysts. I am sure there are others from the two programs that are doing well, but I just have not been made aware of details.

As time progressed changes had to be made in life style and home surroundings. After Nancy passed away, the Mountain City home became too much to care for and too filled with memories of her. It was placed on the market and eventually sold. Now I decided I must make the hard decision to get rid of most of my stuff that was devoted to consulting and case work. After all I was supposed to really be retired now.

After advertising a bit, I received a request from a young examiner in Connecticut who was interested in the comparison microscope. At this time, although it is still useful and in good condition, it might be considered an antique or curio of some sort. Eventually, I sold it to the young examiner for @ half its value so that it would remain with someone active in the discipline.

Next to go was the library. A few personal items were removed, but nearly all the books and Journals were placed on the market; @ 200 hard bounds and paper backs and all the AAFS Journals of Forensic Science, and all the AFTE Journals from the first Newsletter to the present were included. I had already decided if at all possible they should be sold as a lot to someone in the field who would value them and use them. I received a call from a student in the first class at Tampa, "the Firearms Eight," Andy Smith who wanted the collection. Again I sold them for less than half their value, but I knew they would be in good hands and useful to him.

A local Sport shop and gun dealer had admired the old shoot tank, so I had him bring a truck and take it away. The gunsmith tools were given to my youngest grandson, currently serving in the Navy on board the aircraft carrier, U.S.S. George Washington (CV-73). He likes to do things with his hands and work on automobiles, so I felt he would use them in some way.

All that remains are copies of papers, certain documents and some memorabilia. One item I have a special fondness for is an antique stereo-opticon viewer. In place of the special cards (dual photographs or drawings) that are brought together in the angled lens of the viewer to create the three dimension stereo effect, there are two .45 automatic caliber fired bullets. They are mounted on the picture crossbar at the right places so that the viewer will see them superimposed as one image. There is a legend (I am not sure whether or not there is truth to it) about a cowboy named Hec Ramsey who carried such a viewer in his saddlebags and claimed to be a "ballistics expert." There was a short-lived TV series some years ago, loosely fashioned after his life. Obviously the images are not enlarged to any degree, and I am sure Hec Ramsey knew nothing about striae and matching striae, etc., if he existed at all. But it is true, that certain opinions could be given in court about similarities in bullet formation, calibers, mold markings, etc. in the days of yore. Like all that old stuff, these viewers when found in good condition cost more than ten times the original cost.

I sold or gave away most of my personal firearms, including a .45 auto. caliber Colt Government model pistol engraved in the Colt shop, a 9mm Luger caliber Ruger pistol, a very old German .25 auto. (6.35 mm) pistol, etc. My long guns such as a 12 gauge double shotgun about 60 years old, .22 cal. Remington rifle about 70 years old, Mauser rifle of WW II vintage, etc. were given to the grandsons. A .38 S&W caliber, Smith and Wesson hammerless (the lemon squeezer) about 100 years old went to one daughter. I retained an Army model cap and ball revolver, a black powder rifle, and my all-time favorite a .45 Auto. caliber Colt model 1911-A1 pistol, with target slide and adjustable sights, bone grips, etc. This particular firearm I worked on when I was in training in the Crime Laboratory about 53 years ago. The action is smooth as silk, and the trigger pull is very clean at about 4 lbs. pressure. It is good looking and shoots extremely well.

I also retained my graffiti wall with the various photos, certificates, plaques, etc. accompanied by a clock fashioned to look like an old target on a board fence full of bullet holes and with a superimposed model of a cap and ball revolver, and a genuine Army model cap and ball revolver encased in a leather holster.

The other wall contains framed photographs of family, children, and grandchildren, along with several of the most cherished of Nancy. In one she is standing on a diving board at Susterka Lake, near Detroit, and she looks like a model. In another she is standing alongside our first new car a 1955 Buick Century hard top and she is dressed for an occasion; again she looks like a model. A third one is of the two of us dressed for a wedding ceremony of her youngest sister. She looks just like Elizabeth Taylor, only better, and after 15 years of marriage. Wow – she was some gal!

Now I had more time for family and hobbies. Some was spent fly-fishing for trout. Some was spent in the garden and in the establishment of a bed of red raspberries. But I had to do something to try and keep the cobwebs away from my brain. So I tried to do a little writing. All my writing up to this time had been technical papers and/or reports. The only recent exemption was a rough unedited and rambling version of life and major events done at the urging of my children. I called it "Turn right raw ass" in honor of my probationary period as a Trooper under my fantastic senior officer, Bob Johnston.

But I knew I could use some help, so for a period I attended the meetings of the High Country Writers held in Boone. The group of mostly women, consisted of known authors, recently established new authors, and a sprinkling of would-be authors like me. I was amazed to sit next to a woman who was@ 95 years old, still writing and traveling to advertise her books. Needless to say but the group gave me some valuable tips and encouraged me to finish my first book and led me to a local publisher, Rao Aluri.

I called the book "Silent Evidence" based on a famous in forensic circles 1947 court decision where the Judge who wrote the opinion pretty much spelled out what forensic science is all about. The entirety of that part of the opinion can be found just ahead of the Foreword. The cover of the book shows a yellow sign with the words "ROAD ENDS. The sign appears to be suspended in mid-air with a trace of a gravel roadway below. I am not sure that this choice was the best I might have made. But it meant a lot to me as it was from a crime scene down the road where there was only one house. In that house was the body of a baby sitter, 14 years old and already her life gone because some mad man attacked and killed her. Sometimes I feel a bit ashamed about my sex as it seems there are so many males who are complete idiots and cruel besides. But, I am not going to get on the soap box again. As part of the CSI team, I was playing photographer this night. The "Road Ends" photograph was an early one to mark the location for posterity as it was at the junction of a main secondary road with the short side road. It was very late and no outside lighting available. The sign is illuminated by the camera flash. I always felt it gave an eerie sense to the scene and case.

It was even more important for one simple reason. It marked the best preserved crime scene of my career. When we arrived from Headquarters, the corner was manned by a State Police detective from the closest Post. I knew him well as did everyone in the State Police. There was no one at the crime scene with the exception of one uniformed Trooper who had been posted there by the Detective to guard the scene. I soon learned that the Post Commander and Assistant District Commander, a much older Lieutenant, had already been refused entrance to inspect the scene and were turned away at the road sign corner. We were assured that the only persons that had been inside of the home were the lady of the house who discovered the crime and a brief inspection by Detective Steve Cloonan.

Steve was infamous in the Department as the gun fancier who carried two at all times and practiced quick draw. Now he was in plain clothes, but it was claimed that he still always packed two handguns. At this point in time there was a popular TV series where the hero carried his pistol hidden behind his back and held in place by his belt. It is claimed that Steve actually dislocated his shoulder practicing quick draw from that hidden position. It is probably only a nasty rumor, the kind police officers love. Knowing Steve it might have been true.

Some years before, Steve was a uniformed Trooper and a story about him was one of the most popular going around the Department. It seemed that Steve and another Trooper, working night patrol near the Ohio border, stopped at a roadhouse to eat and were joined by Troopers from the Ohio Highway Patrol. Michigan officers used an issue holster which was mounted on the opposite side from their strong hand and faced backwards requiring a cross draw. In addition the revolver in use then a .38 Special caliber Colt Official Police model was covered by a snapped flap. Whereas the Ohio Troopers used a front facing holster on the same side as their gun hand, which had just a tiny strap over the butt of their revolver. While eating the officers started a discussion about the respective holsters and one Ohio Trooper stated something to the effect that kind of holster used by Michigan was stupid and he could get his revolver out and shoot someone with that kind of holster before their gun cleared the leather. The discussion turned into a rather loud argument as Steve told the Ohio officer that he was dead wrong. The restaurant was full. It was a popular truck stop and many truckers were there listening to the loud talk. The Troopers challenged each other to a duel, unloaded their respective firearms and double checked them to insure they were empty of any ammunition.

Everyone in the place filed outside as the Troopers faced each other like a Western movie. A pretty young waitress held a handkerchief with the instruction that the officers should draw when it dropped out of her hand. So it dropped and they drew. What the Ohio Trooper could not know was that Steve was very ambidextrous and had practiced drawing his firearm from the left hand holster by flicking the flap up with his left thumb and drawing the weapon with one quick twisting motion. He also had a two barrel derringer pistol under his Sam Browne uniform belt right front.

As the hankie dropped Steve snaked the revolver out of his holster with his left hand, immediately followed by drawing his derringer pistol with the right hand and saying "there is one and now two!" before the Ohio Trooper could align his drawn weapon. All this was done to the amusement of the crowd. The Ohio Trooper bought lunch. As the famous commentator always said; "and that is the rest of the story."

My little book Silent Evidence contains 14 case histories covering the forensic evidence aspect, written like short stories. In addition there is an appendix which deals with the history, drama, and theory of "Firearms and Tool Mark Identification," for any interested student of forensic science. I soon found out that the known publishing houses were not interested in this type of material from an unknown author. But the High Country Writers put me next to one of their members, a small local publisher, Rao Aluri, who published under the Parkway Publishing name. He published the book and the writers group awarded it their non-fiction of the year award for 2005.

Rao quit publishing for a time and the book is currently being published by Catawba Publishing out of Charlotte, North Carolina. As of this time, more than 700 have been sold or given away. That is not a lot of books, but this is without any publicity of note, etc. Several in my old discipline who teach forensic science on the side have purchased copies to use in their course work. But, I wrote the book as a hobby not as an intended source of revenue. It was a way to keep the brain ticking, occupy some vacant time, and still enjoy what I was doing. This book is being written in the same vein. I have also written a second book on the order of Silent Evidence. It is called Wherever He Steps, Whatever He Touches. I have no way of knowing if I will ever get it published. After all, I am now older than dirt and I am sure I will not be around forever. It could be of value for students of forensic science. The cases are chosen from among thousands I have worked for their varied uses and applications of physical evidence in my discipline. I also positioned several appendices at the end to offer more insight into Firearms and Tool Mark Identification.

When we lived in Mountain City, Tennessee, we thought that it was a small town. It is the furthest East town in the State, sitting up in that Northeast corner, just a few miles from Virginia and North Carolina. But now my daughters, Kathy the Miracle Child and Kelly Miss Green Thumb, and I live a few miles North of Lansing, North Carolina, close to the Virginia border and the Tennessee State line. I sometimes wonder if I am jinxed, after all I spent much of my adult life in and around Lansing, Michigan, the State capitol and former home of Oldsmobile. Well, Lansing, NC is a little different. It is about three blocks long and the same wide. It is positioned next to Big Horse Creek a local trout stream and surrounded by small mountains and deep valleys or hollows as they are called in the area. When we first moved here I thought the locals were saying hollers and I could not associate that with hollows. But, we soon found out hollows marked the location of families, clans, etc. in this country in the fertile pastures between the mountains. We live several miles beyond the village, out in the boondocks. We have a little home on a small bluff on 1.3 acres which is on the edge of an old apple orchard and looks toward a mountain on the other side of the blacktop highway.

There is a small rushing creek running near the highway which is said to contain some small native brook trout. Deer and wild turkey abound and often use our driveway to go from the woods down to the creek for water. They are difficult to spot but we hear Ruffed Grouse booming every now and then. The wind whistles as it comes down the slope and over the house. It is beautiful and serene. We have just completed a covered porch out front, and this summer I will be able to sit in the proverbial rocking chair and contemplate whatever.

Last winter we started something new; that is for us. Some of the money obtained from sale of the Mt. City property was used to purchase a duplex in a retirement type community called Fairgreen in New Smyrna Beach, Florida. The community is very quiet and kind of secluded for Florida anyway. It sports a very busy golf course and a swimming pool with hot tub and a community meeting place. We are less than 10 minutes from the inter-coastal waterway and about 20 minutes from the ocean. It is a very well kept area and we soon found out loaded with lots of nice people. The duplex is fairly large with two big bedrooms, many closets, two nice baths, a huge living room, a nice size kitchen, and a large sun room porch. The only thing it needed was some exterior paint. My grandson Joey helped me greatly in getting that taken care of. In addition he and Kelly did a real number on plants and mulch, improving the entire neighborhood. I think I am going to really like it. There is a lot going on, and much of the action is free... well okay. Some sun bathing, hot tubing and surf fishing ought to get my attention. One other thing, there is a great pizza place and a couple of terrific restaurants within a couple miles of the home! Now those are important items, as you well know.

So, in a few months we will pack it in and head for the Sunshine State. It is a great place to visit and okay for living part-time, but for me, after nearly 20 years there, part time is better. I have made a solid vow to go crappie fishing; the best tasting fresh water fish and fun to catch those big ones in Florida. Now if the weather will cooperate; no hurricanes and good fishing.

Chasing Tail Lights to Forensic Ballistics

NANCY – SWEET & PRETTY, AGE 19

NANCY – HOW BEAUTIFUL- AGE 41

NANCY'S CABIN NR. MOUNTAIN CITY, TN

13

Finis

The sum total of my life and any value it may have is wrapped up in my wife and children. It is often said that family is the vital force of this life. That is not to say I don't have a certain amount of ego, too much some times, and that the role I played in the military, police profession, crime laboratory, CSI and forensic science were without value. But, as many of the profound books say, as you get older and reflect on your life you are a bit smarter. There is an old German saying "Too soon old, und too late smart," that says it well.

At this stage I would like to say a little bit about my wife, Nancy Smith Meyers. Throughout I have referred to her as beautiful, and she was. But there was a lot more to her than good looks. Not that she was perfect, no human is, but her greatest personal trait was she was completely unselfish. Throughout our years together, I can never recall her asking for anything for herself. It was always about me, her children, her grandchildren, our friends, our neighbors, ad infinitum. I have mentioned her sacrifices for our special child, Kathy. How do you keep score on that?

When we were young and daring and foolish and having fun, she was into everything legal. She was often the life of the party; when she was not available I was. She was always a good sport and when we went to the occasional dinner party and dance she was dressed to the nines as they say. But, she bought simple outfits, and then spiced them up herself with a dash of ribbon, costume jewelry, etc. She stood out every where she went.

I remember one of my favorite outfits she wore to my 20th high school anniversary. It was a black pants suit with a silver slave belt drooping about her waist. I damn near got into a couple of fights that night, trying to keep the other guys from wanting to dance with her or converse with her at the expense of their own wives. You want to talk sexy – she was it. But at the same time she never really flirted with other men. I am sorry I can not say the same for myself with other women. It is a man thing I guess. The good thing is we always came and went together.

But, she had a temper. Not that it was uncontrollable; it was more aimed than that. I recall when we went to get the marriage license. I had learned from her mother that she had been working lots of overtime trying to save money for our marriage and she had developed several bladder or kidney infections. Her mother felt she was working too hard and that brought on her problems. So going to be the big protector husband I said something to her about what I had learned and "I am telling you now you must stop that." She gave me a hard look and said something to the effect look big boy, you are not going to tell me what to do and you can forget the wedding. With that she crumpled up the wedding license and threw it out the car window. I immediately told her I was not trying to be bossy but only concerned about her welfare, as I stopped the car and started to back up to look for the license. At that she laughed and said "you must think that I'm a real dope," as she opened her clenched fist to show the crumpled license in it. She straightened it out and we were on our way.

But this was no joke to her and it became very clear to me that if you wanted Nancy to do something, just ask, but never order her no matter what. We had our arguments at times; a few were quite hard on both of us. But we finally reached that plateau that comes when you comfortably settle into a partnership and learn to live with each others personalities. The spring of our lives was exciting, the summer frustrating, the fall romantic and the winter peaceful and beautiful.

Our homes everywhere we lived were always neat and clean and appropriately decorated for the season. She had a knack with flowers and loved plants in lieu of cut flowers unless the cut flowers came from the garden; flowers like zinnias, marigolds, poppies, daisies, and her personal favorite, cosmos.

She could outwork anyone in the family, man, woman, or child. She as a girl had always been a tomboy I found out. I have to laugh when I think of some of her escapades I learned about from her grandfather. He was a little wiry Canadian farmer who lived into his late eighties. One summer when she stayed with grandma and him she decided to tease his bull. He had warned her and her little brother not to mess with the bull as he was mean. There was a haystack near the barn and in the corral where the bull was kept at this time. She and her brother Monty were in the corral on top of the haystack taunting the bull. He paid no attention to them, so Nancy climbed down, picked up a piece of board and hit him on the rear. The bull whirled so fast he cut off her escape route to the haystack. In desperation she shinnied up a small tree on the edge of the corral area. The bull started banging his head into the trunk of the tree trying to shake her down. By this time she was screaming so loud grandpa came to her rescue. He said she never told him about the board until a few years later.

In another of her escapades, she and the neighborhood gang went to the nearby park where there was a huge slide for winter sports. It consisted of wooden slats supported by timbers and with a rail to keep the toboggans on the track. But this was summer and they were pulling a wagon. She talked one of the neighborhood boys, a lifelong friend with an undying crush, into trying something new, going down the slide in the wagon. So he did and the wagon went so fast it crashed and nearly flew off the slide leaving her friend Bill sliding on his butt for the last 50 feet or so. They had to have her dad take him to the hospital to remove a dozen or so huge splinters from his butt. But, he still loved her.

It was said that every boy in her neighborhood was afraid of her as she had proved she could fist fight with the best of them. She was an incessant walker and pacer; one of the things that attracted me to her when she was working as a waitress. She was that way nearly all her life until the last couple years or so. I used to kid her about her butt and thigh muscles. Pinch an inch – no way, you could not pinch anything even when she was 70 years old. I used to call her iron butt to kid her.

In her last years, there came a time when two rival factions formed in the church parish and there was little or no cooperation between them. Nancy was the one who took it upon herself to work to get them together. Our closest friends were all in one faction. Nancy overheard one from the other faction discussing the fact that a number of family members were coming for the upcoming holiday, they did not have enough room for them and really were not in a position to pay for a hotel for them. So, she barged into the conversation and told the lady they would be welcome to stay in her beautiful cabin. That began the thawing period that is still going on today. The younger sister of the family who stayed there is an artist. She drew a beautiful painting of the cabin, framed it, and sent it to Nancy to thank her.

Nancy, Kelly, and Kathy volunteered to work on every charitable endeavor of the church. And as usual, nobody worked harder than Nan or stayed longer. It is no wonder that our favorite Priest Father Tom Vos liked her so much and had dinner with us on several occasions. I recall one holiday period when on the previous Sunday Fr. Tom asked, "Nancy I imagine you are going to fix a special dinner for Chuck for Fathers day." She told him that she certainly would and he asked her if she decided on the menu yet. When she said no, that devilish Priest said something like would that not be an ideal time for prime rib? And I imagine you are inviting me? It was like a game the two of them played. I feel sure the old Priest was one more man that loved her, in a different way but nonetheless loved and admired her.

In 2005 and 2006 she complained about pain for the first time in her life. She always bragged the only time she was in a hospital was to have babies. But now she was having back pains and pain shooting down her one leg. When she complained I knew it had to be bad. She went to a neurosurgeon and was told she had a spinal problem that may require an operation. She decided she had to consider it and was scheduled for pre-operation exams to determine her suitability for a difficult operation. She went to several different physicians for tests. The heart doctor told her the tests indicated she may have a heart problem.

She was scheduled for a heart catheterization with a heart surgeon with a terrific reputation. He told us that he had reviewed her tests and while doing the catheter examination if he discovered something that needed immediate fixing he would do so while she was on the table. Obviously he suspected a real problem and he was right. She almost died on the table as he placed five stents in her main artery/veins. He told us later that her main blood vessel was over 90% blocked. He told me if she had not come for the catheter test she would have dropped dead just walking across the yard and probably within several weeks. She had complained of fatigue and pain walking but felt it was due to her spinal problem.

As soon as she was barely able she was out in the garden, rolling rocks in the creek, doing housework, cooking dinners, etc. like nothing happened. She seemed stronger and better than she had in a couple of years. Obviously her spine was not her main problem. It was her heart.

For nearly a year she seemed better than ever in her older years. But there were apparent warning signs I failed to see until it was too late. I am not sure we could have done anything about it, but now I feel certain that she knew in her heart and mind that her time was limited.

One day, several months before she died she suddenly said to me "Chuck you know where I keep my stash I hope." She pulled open a drawer of her good antique cherry cupboard and showed me a hidden space where a small tea canister was lying. She told me that just in case anything happened to her she wanted to make sure it was accounted for. I knew that she usually rat-holed a bit of cash from her household expenditures. Several months after she was gone something reminded me of that conversation. I pulled out the canister and discovered a roll of $100 bills. There were 25 of them; i.e., $2,500.00. Wow – what a gal.

Then there were the greeting cards. All our married life we never forgot a birthday or wedding anniversary, but the cards were usually the normal, not gushy, the see I did not forget you kind. But my last fathers' day before she passed, she gave me a different kind of card that read as follows:

"You are the man I love; today as we celebrate your role as a father, I wonder if you know how truly special you are to me, how much I cherish you as the one who bring so much happiness and joy to my life. I wonder if you know what a difference it makes to have your strength to lean on, your honesty to trust in and your passion to share. I wonder if you know the intensity of my feeling for you, and how very precious you are to me. Have a happy fathers' day and know that I am looking forward to all the beautiful tomorrows still ahead of us." The card was signed "Love you so much, Nan"

I am eternally grateful that on her last Mothers day (2006) I sent a card that was carefully selected and read as follows:

"For my wife – I know that sometimes I let too much time go by between I love you and when I get busy or pre-occupied. I let too many uh-huhs pass for conversation. But not many men are half as lucky as I am, having a wife like you… It is not that I do not realize or think about how many good things you bring to my life, and how much I really love you—It is just that I am not always good at expressing myself. And, I am sorry if I have slacked off on the romantic touches you deserve so much… Please know I plan to take the time to get back to the things that matter most… like just being with you, because that is what makes me happy. Have a happy Mothers day. The card is signed "I will always love you, Chuck" If you have read this memoir you may have guessed by now that I have always been an incredible romantic. Since I was a small boy and sang in the choir, I have been a music lover. The music I love the most by far would fall in the pop music category of romantic ballads and the big band sound of the forties. Nan and I found each other in the early fifties and our favorite pop singer has always been Nat King Cole. Our favorite songs were made popular again by him in the early sixties. Her favorite was "Unforgettable," and she would remind me of the part that goes "Darling it's incredible that anyone so unforgettable thinks that I am unforgettable too." My favorite is "I remember you," and I always reminded her of the last stanza that goes "When my life is through, and the angels ask me to recall, the thrill of them all, then I shall tell them I remember you."

The light of my life was extinguished on Easter Sunday morning 2007. There is an old legend that claims anyone dying on Easter Sunday goes straight to heaven.

Since her passing, I am tormented by another old ballad, Memories of You, and the final verse which goes "Your face beams - In my dreams – In spite of all I do. Everything – Seems to bring – Memories of you."

AFTER 55 YEARS – STILL IN LOVE

Acknowledgements

There was a wonderful family, mother and father, sisters and brother, who set a path to follow; my beloved wife Nancy, who not only stood beside me but worked so many extra hours to support and assist me; our children who inspired me; the devoted sisters and priests from St. Leo in Detroit, who helped me learn self-discipline as well as reading, writing and arithmetic; my sailor friends from NAB (Naval Air Base) 824 KwaJalein (NDJ) and the USS Leyte (CV-32); the highly motivated Troopers, Officers, and civilian co-workers of the Michigan State Police (48 - 73); the fellow teachers and associates from Delta College Michigan (73 - 76); the Crime Laboratory associates from the Florida Department of Law Enforcement (76 - 89); and the many fine police officers and lawyers from many areas of the Country with whom I had the pleasure of working for more than sixty years.

I would like to offer my appreciation to all those who contributed to the various anecdotes, some unwittingly.

A special thank you goes to Richard A. (Rick) Wiles, MA/Ed.S, Petoskey, Michigan, researcher, writer, and teacher who took time from his busy schedule to help edit and correct the manuscript.

About the Author

The author has served the Criminal Justice Community for more than sixty years and has practiced in the discipline of Crime Scene Investigation and Firearms (Forensic Ballistics) and Tool Mark Identification for more than fifty years. His career included twenty-five years with the Michigan State Police, three years teaching at Delta College, Michigan, and more than twelve years with the Florida Department of Law Enforcement. Since 1989 he has been an independent consultant.

His education includes a Bachelor of Science degree from Michigan State University, with a year of Police Science (Criminalistics) and a minor in Natural Science. Over the years he has been active in professional groups, is an Emeritus Member and Past-President of the Association of Firearm and Tool Mark Examiners, a Retired Fellow of the American Academy of Forensic Sciences, a member of the Southern Association of Forensic Sciences, and a Kentucky Colonel.

He has testified in more than a thousand judicial hearings, mostly regarding homicide cases. He has also published and lectured extensively regarding Forensic Science and his discipline.

In 2004 he published a unique book entitled "Silent Evidence - Cases from Forensic Science," which received the High Country Writer's award for Non-Fiction Book of the Year. He is in progress of writing a follow-up book with additional case histories and anecdotes from the world of Crime Scene Investigation and Crime Laboratory Analysis entitled "Wherever He Steps - Whatever He Touches," and finalizing the memoir entitled "Chasing Tail Lights & Forensic Ballistics."